Leon Trotsky

In Defence of Marxism

(Against the Petty Bourgeois Opposition)

NEW PARK PUBLICATIONS LTD., LONDON

In Defence of Marxism — credits

Published by New Park Publications Ltd.,
21b Old Town, Clapham, London SW4 0JT

First published in 1942
from articles and letters written
between September 1939 and August 1940

Foreword
Copyright © New Park Publications Ltd
1971

Fourth impression 1982

Set up, Printed and Bound
by Trade Union Labour

Distributed in the United States by:
Labor Publications Inc.,
GPO 1876 NY
New York 10001

ISBN 0 902030 18 3

Printed in Great Britain by
Astmoor Litho Ltd (TU)
21-22 Arkwright Road, Runcorn, Cheshire

Contents

v

vi

APPENDIX

Introduction

BETWEEN the founding of the Fourth International in 1938 and his death in 1940, Trotsky made a number of invaluable contributions to Marxist theory. Writing on the coming world war, on the defence of the conquests of the October Revolution against imperialism and against the Stalinist bureaucracy, on the integration of the trade unions into the capitalist state, Trotsky deepened the characterisation of the epoch which he had made in the founding programme of the Fourth International, 'The Death Agony of Capitalism and the Tasks of the Fourth International'. Lenin had called imperialism 'the highest stage of capitalism', an era of wars and revolutions. Trotsky based himself on this historical view of the tasks of the proletariat. Mankind's productive forces had begun to stagnate, and society was consequently threatened with the destruction of civilisation itself; this crisis of humanity could be resolved only by proletarian revolution. However, for the proletariat to successfully conquer power, the crisis of leadership within the working class must be resolved: the Fourth International would be built only in the course of implacable struggle against the established social-democratic and Stalinist leaderships, both now gone over to the camp of counter-revolution.

The construction of this alternative leadership, and all the problems involved in it, constitute the essence of Trotsky's struggle. It was a task undertaken, necessarily, in a period initiated and characterised by defeats for the proletariat and victories for the blackest reaction, particularly in Germany and Spain. The same crisis which produced Fascism in Italy, Germany and Spain, and strengthened the parasitic bureaucracy within the degenerated workers' state in the USSR, produced many varieties of the politics of disorientation among the petty-bourgeois of the 'democratic' countries. Tossed between the fascist ruthlessness of finance capital on the one hand and the potential power of the proletariat on the other, they were prey to the superficial attractions of 'popular fronts' which embraced all lovers of democracy, regardless of class interest. Insofar as the working-class parties were included in such fronts, it was through the middle-class apparatus which controlled them. The spate of so-called 'proletarian culture' in the thirties was an attempt by the left middle class intelligentsia to tailor the working class and its strength to the demands of this 'democratic' alliance. It was permissible to extol the strength and vitality of the working class, but it was a sin to mobilise it independently for revolution.

The Fourth International of Trotsky was naturally anathema to the vast majority of these petty-bourgeois intellectuals and their bureaucratic allies. Lawyers, historians, scientists and literary men alike found no difficulty in accepting the falsifications of the Moscow trials, in which Trotsky and the whole Bolshevik 'old guard' were 'proved' to be imperialist and fascist agents of long standing. But in the course of Trotsky's battle against the Stalinist bureaucracy, a number of intellectuals of the left were attracted to his ideas, and participated in the work of the early groups which eventually were to form the Fourth International. The Trotskyist criticism of the abuses of Stalinist bureaucracy in the USSR and in the Communist International enabled many of these individuals to square their socialist convictions with the degeneration of the workers' state and the betrayals of the international communist movement. At the same time, the brilliant contributions of Trotsky in many fields impressed them, in contrast with the leaden orthodoxy which had overtaken all spheres of Marxist scholarship at the hands of the Stalinist bureaucracy.

For the most part, those won on this sort of basis turned out to be accidental figures who made only fleeting contributions to the work of the Left Opposition and the Fourth International. The essence of Trotsky's fight evaded them. To learn how to criticise the abuses of Stalinism was one thing, but to do this consistently in the context of defending the gains of the October Revolution was another. Such defence was possible, and is still, only by the method of proletarian revolution. The construction of

new, revolutionary parties for the social revolution in the capitalist
countries, and for the political revolution against the bureaucracy
in the degenerated workers' state—this task was to prove the
dividing line for the professed supporters of Trotsky. The first
year of the Second World War posed the question more decisively
than ever before. Stalin had signed his pact with Hitler; Soviet
troops were in Poland and Finland; the Communist parties of the
world were making propaganda against the French and British
imperialists but less against the German imperialists. Consequently
there was a hysterical reaction from the 'democratic' middle-class
intelligentsia which had until now accepted the line of 'unity' of
Communists, peace-lovers and democrats against Hitlerism. In
this 'democratic' milieu, many who had previously had to stand
forth with criticisms of Stalinism had the duty to *defend* the USSR,
despite the policies of Stalin. But they found the pressure of their
professional surroundings stronger than the necessities of the
historic struggle for the political independence of the working class.
Like the erstwhile 'allies' of the working class in the 'popular
fronts' they found it necessary to condemn unconditionally the
actions of the Kremlin, and eventually to support the war of the
'Western democracies' against Fascist Germany and Italy, who
were sustained by the Stalin-Hitler pact. For a brief interim
period they talked, like Burnham and Shachtman, about a 'third
camp'—what Trotsky called 'the camp of the stampeding petty-
bourgeois'!

In Defence of Marxism is the record of Trotsky's writings
against a group of these capitulators who raised the flag of opposition in the Socialist Workers' Party (USA) in 1939. The leading
exponent of the views of this opposition was James Burnham, later
to achieve fame as the author of *The Managerial Revolution,* and
notoriety as an open advocate of atomic war against the USSR. In
fact, *The Managerial Revolution* was based upon the theories ex-
pounded already in 1933 by Bruno Rizzi. His book, *La Bureaucratisation du Monde* (The Bureaucratisation of the World) is referred
to by Trotsky in the discussion contained in the present volume.
Burnham added nothing but a hastily gathered series of impressions
in the intervening years. Recently, scholarly investigators in
Europe have been painstakingly rediscovering the resemblance between the two books, after two decades during which sociologists
and political 'scientists' had come to treat *The Managerial Revolution*
as some sort of gospel. Lenin was not wrong when he insisted,
sixty years ago, that the weakness and near-disintegration of bour-

geois ideology necessitated the existence of *revisionism* within the Marxist movement. Only this would be able to provide the rationalisations necessary to capitalism in the epoch of wars and revolutions.

It is his struggle against this revisionism and for the continuity of revolutionary Marxism which constitutes the essence of this book by Trotsky. For the building of the Fourth International, and particularly of a section inside the USA, this fight against revisionism necessitated a return to the fundamental basis of Marxism, dialectical materialism. Burnham and Shachtman protested violently that Trotsky's exposition of materialist dialectics was a diversion, that the 'concrete questions' must be the deciding questions. They asserted that agreement on political perspectives did not in any way depend upon agreement on the Marxist method. But the very discussion in which they were engaged had a character which could not be understood except through this method. Marxists insist that the so-called concrete questions of current politics must be approached from the class criterion, i.e., by a method which contains the premise of the actual content of the forces whose struggle makes up these 'concrete questions'. If a tendency within our movement rejects this approach, they accept, one way or another, the categories of bourgeois thought, categories for the various fields of thought which abstract the latter from the class struggle which is their material base.

In other words, the struggle against the petty-bourgeois opposition in the SWP in 1939-40 was not not just an argument about immediate political questions, nor about the 'philosophical' questions which Trotsky introduced. It was a struggle of living forces, of the proletarian revolutionaries fighting for Bolshevism in the Fourth International against the revisionist representatives of bourgeois class interests. Trotsky explained this in his 'Open Letter to Burnham' :

> 'The nub of the matter however consists in this, that discussion has its own objective logic, which does not coincide at all with the subjective logic of individuals and groupings. The *dialectic* character of the discussion proceeds from the fact that its objective course is determined by the living conflict of opposing tendencies and not by a preconceived logical plan. The *materialist* basis of the discussion consists in its reflecting the pressure of different classes. Thus, the present discussion in the SWP, like the historic process as a whole, develops—with or without your permission, comrade Burnham—according to the laws of dialectical materialism. There is no escape from these laws.'

All the theoretical positions taken up by the Burnham-Shachtman opposition derived from its class character, and Trotsky pointed out at the beginning that the Party had necessarily to embark on a long and exhaustive struggle :

> 'Like any petty-bourgeois group inside the socialist movement, the present opposition is characterised by the following features: a disdainful attitude toward theory and an inclination toward eclecticism; disrespect for the tradition of their own organisation; anxiety for personal "independence" at the expense of anxiety for objective truth; nervousness instead of consistency; readiness to jump from one position to another; lack of understanding of revolutionary centralism and hostility toward it; and finally, inclination to substitute clique ties and personal relationships for party discipline.'

The fight against the petty-bourgeois opposition to centralism, against their rejection of the traditions of the movement, was the *same* as the struggle to defend dialectical materialism against the dominant pragmatism of the American radical intelligentsia, which the opposition carried into the SWP. Cannon and the SWP majority leadership fought tenaciously to defend and build the Party and to drive out the opposition, once they had proved intractable to every attempt to win them to revolutionary positions. But the principal lesson of the 1939-40 controversy was lost on this leadership, with tragic results. The philosophical outlook carried into the SWP by the petty-bourgeois opposition was not just a set of arguments picked up by Burnham and the others to justify their capitulation to the pressure of 'democratic' opinion. It expressed the dominant mode of thought in American bourgeois ideology. This same pragmatism permeates every sphere of capitalist ideology in the USA, including of course the labour movement. Trotsky gave a serious warning to the SWP that unless a systematic struggle for materialistic dialectics was constantly waged against pragmatism, then a revolutionary vanguard would not be built in America. A scientific understanding of American imperialism and its whole social and political superstructure, necessary for the elaboration of correct strategy and tactics, cannot be gained except through a thoroughgoing critique of the pragmatist heritage. This is not an academic pursuit to be allotted only to philosophical 'specialists' in the party (though it includes specialist work, of course), but a constant fight inside the revolutionary party for the dialectical materialist outlook and method. Dialectical materialism is the unity of theory and practice. It is in the practical struggle to lead the proletariat and build the party that the essential problems of the fight against pragmatism are brought to the surface and hammered out. This was the importance of the 1939-40 discussion. It was the first step, and a prodigious one, in this whole process of a fight for Marxism in the SWP.

The subsequent years revealed ever more clearly that this unity of theory and practice, the need to *develop* theory, had not been absorbed by the SWP leadership. Marxism was seen by them as a programme and a set of ideas which conformed to the interests of the working class, a sort of natural conclusion for any class-conscious worker to accept. They did not grasp the Marxist theory of knowledge, the social, class basis of all ideology in society. They never worked through the historical roots of their own political and ideological background in the American labour movement. Besides understanding, as Cannon so well did, that Marxism was the necessary successor to the best traditions of the IWW and the early militant struggles of the American working class, it was necessary also to understand the limitations of these early movements, the opportunist and sectarian traits, of a special 'American' and pragmatic character, which they necessarily brought into the Communist movement.

For years this basic weakness in the SWP was not obvious. Inevitably, the ripening of the crisis of American capitalism brought it to the surface. So responsive to the international contradictions of imperialism is the United States, that the preliminary battles of the American revolution already contain an enormous explosive charge. Far from the wealthy imperialist countries providing examples of 'peaceful roads to socialism', their social structures are characterised by the most extreme contradictions. Generations of 'adjustment', 'compromise', and pragmatic patching-up have only allowed the more concentrated accumulation of all the basic problems. The superstructure of politics has been dominated by the representatives of the middle classes and the better-off workers. Their ideological nostrums have served for a long time to create an image of permanent adjustment and re-adjustment. But this very exclusion of the larger layers of the working class from the bureaucratic and political forms of 'official' society and of the labour movement, has prepared the violent and elemental outbreaks which now characterise American society. The 'recognised' protest movements, themselves only the left arm of the whole conservative superstructure, rather than the expression of organised revolt, are utterly unable to consciously respond to this situation. For that a

Marxist leadership is required. It could only have been prepared along precisely the lines indicated above, by the use of the dialectical method to probe beneath the surface of every development within the US and internationally. Without a struggle against revisionism, constantly renewing and developing the materialist and dialectical foundations of Marxism and the party's programme, any movement is in danger of falling victim to the responses of the left petty bourgeoisie instead of developing an independent programme for the masses who are impelled into struggle with the deepening crisis of capitalism, joined in our day with the mortal crisis of the Stalinist bureaucracy.

Within the Fourth International, a new revisionism matured in the years after the Second World War. It took the form, expressed most consistently in the ideas and methods of Michel Pablo, at that time the Secretary of the International, of a capitulation to the Kremlin bureaucracy. Reaching its peak in 1952-53, this liquidationist tendency threatened the very existence of the International and its sections. The post-war 'relation of forces' on a world scale was interpreted by Pablo in a way quite foreign to Marxism. According to this interpretation, not only was the bureaucracy able to survive the war, but its control over the international communist movement continued even when capitalist power was destroyed in whole new areas, from Jugoslavia to China. Pablo concluded that the crisis of imperialism would lead inevitably to a Third World War, which he called the war-revolution, because in it the workers' states controlled by the Stalinists would have to fight for their existence against the imperialists, and this would lead to revolutionary struggles for power in the capitalist countries, under the leadership of the Stalinist parties. The consequences would be 'centuries of degenerated workers' states'. Since this process was already afoot, and did not await the building of Trotskyist parties, said Pablo, it was the obvious responsibility of Marxists to recognise the objective forces at work and act accordingly. The evident result was liquidationism.

It was only when Pablo's line threatened to disturb the SWP's internal life that Cannon was jolted into recognising the liquidationist and revisionist character of Pabloism. At the end of 1953, Cannon published the 'Open Letter' of the SWP to the Trotskyist parties of the world, denouncing Pabloism as a non-Trotskyist tendency and making a definite break from it. He characterised the break with Pabloism as equally decisive as the breach between Bolshevism and Social Democracy in 1914. Yet the SWP failed to carry through this split in the manner taught by Trotsky in 1939-40. After only a few months the theoretical discussion died. Instead of driving to the methodological and philosophic roots of this international revisionism, Cannon and the SWP leaders very soon found themselves negotiating for 'reunification' with the Pabloite forces and drawing away from the International Committee which they had supported since 1953. Their convention resolutions and policy statements began to be characterised by equivocal and then by clearly revisionist formulations on questions of international perspectives. Eventually the 'reunification' they sought was achieved, not on the principled basis of carrying through the struggle begun in 1953, but precisely on the so-called 'concrete questions' of the type so beloved of Burnham-Shachtman in 1940. What Burnham and Shachtman were unable to do to the SWP in 1940 was achieved by Cannon in 1961-63. Avoiding a discussion of the theoretical basis of the 1953 split, he returned to the Pabloite camp on the grounds that these concrete questions found the SWP and the Pabloites in identical positions.

In fact the SWP had accepted the liquidationism of Pablo. They found their way to this position primarily through subordinating themselves to Castroism and its middle-class following in the US, rather than by the direct subordination to the Stalinist apparatus which Pablo carried out. The end-result was identical, and Cannon praised the actions of Khrushchev in withdrawing missiles during the Cuban crisis of 1962 with the rhetorical question: 'what else could he have done in the given circumstances?' Via Castro and Pabloism, Cannon arrived at exactly the point in methodology where stood Burnham and Shachtman in 1939-40. Instrumental in achieving this remarkable transformation was the same 'radical milieu' in the United States which had provided the steam for Burnham-Shachtman. To insist on the independent mobilisation of the working class behind a conscious Trotskyist vanguard would draw the accusation from these middle-class radicals of 'sectarianism', as they pointed to the successes of the new type of leader, Fidel Castro. This cheap impressionism was raised to the level of a 'theory'. The cadres of the Fourth International were asked to accept the idea that revolutionary leadership would be thrown up 'in the process of the revolution itself'. Not only that, but petty-bourgeois nationalist leaders would be forced by the objective logic of the struggle in some cases to become Marxists. Fidel Castro, for example, was a 'natural' or 'unconscious' Marxist. As always, empiricism showed itself only a short step away from the wildest idealism.

Inevitably, this abandonment of Marxism had its consequences in the politics of the SWP within the United States. We have already indicated that only a party trained in Marxist theory along the lines insisted on by Trotsky would be able to meet the especially virulent and explosive problems of the capitalist social crisis in the USA. The assassination of President J. F. Kennedy (November 22, 1963) drew from the National Committee of the SWP a letter of condolence to the widow! In the ever-mounting, raging torrent of the Negro movement, the SWP has tailed behind first the 'democratic' and then the black nationalist leaders, providing them with a left cover. This even went so far as demanding the intervention of the armed forces of the US government to implement de-segregation against the reactionary administrations of the Southern States! In the movement against the Vietnam war, SWP members have fought against those Marxists who raise the banner of the class war against their own bourgeoisie, siding with the Vietnamese workers and peasants, and calling for the military defeat of the US forces.

This degeneration calls to mind the various statements in this book by Trotsky concerning the extreme dangers as well as potentialities of the period of imperialist decay. All the more reason for the primary stress on the independent revolutionary party and its programme. Trotsky writes in his 'Open Letter to Burnham' : 'The disintegration of capitalism, which engenders sharp dissatisfaction among the petty bourgeoisie and drives its bottom layers to the left, opens up broad possibilities but it also contains grave dangers.' Cannon fell victim to these dangers. In the course of the 1940 discussion he wrote a small book, *The Struggle for a Proletarian Party,* which Trotsky praised highly as the work of a genuine workers' leader. In that book, Cannon made a thoroughgoing characterisation and critique of the petty bourgeois opposition. But the 'turn to the working class', which Trotsky had indicated and Cannon executed, would eventually be frustrated if the struggle for theory was not accepted as the life-blood of the revolutionary party. Trotsky warned : 'It is precisely the Party's penetration into the trade unions and into the workers' milieu in general that demands heightening the theoretical qualification of our cadres.

The SWP could not develop as the leadership of the American working class except by the most scrupulous attention to its

international responsibilities. Just as it was the revolutionary experience
of Trotsky and his mastery of Marxist theory, developed over
generations of international struggle and particularly through the
Russian Revolution, so the problems of building a leadership for
the working class in the great struggles now facing the American
workers will be resolved from the starting point of the experience
and riches of the *International* Trotskyist movement in combatting
revisionism. Cannon and his friends prefer the type of 'International' which permits the SWP to continue with its own brand
of opportunist adaptation. In such a movement it is not possible
to learn the real lessons of the fight with Burnham and Shachtman
in 1939-40. But for the cadres of the International Committee
of the Fourth International and its sections, in the USA as everywhere else, this book will be an indispensable guide and educator.
Many thousands of young workers and intellectuals, drawn into
politics by the crisis of imperialism and of the Stalinist bureaucracy, now developing at a frenzied pace, will learn from this
book, which is already one of the classics of Marxism.

                                                              C.S.

NOTE

The development of revisionism in the SWP in recent years
was the subject of a lengthy discussion in the International Committee, in which the problems of dialectical materialism, pragmatism, and the class criterion in social and political analysis, raised
in this book by Trotsky, are once again thrashed out in detail.

In their failure to carry forward the struggle for Marxism
against pragmatism, the SWP leadership contributed not only to
the degeneration of their own party but also to the very grave
crisis suffered by the Fourth International at the hands of the petty
bourgeois revisionists led by Pablo. Readers of *In Defence of
Marxism* can read the written discussion on these questions in the
Journal 'Fourth International' (incorporating 'Labour Review'),
Vol. 1, No. 1 (Spring 1964) and Vol. 2, No. 1 (Summer 1965).

A letter to James P. Cannon†

Dear Jim:

I am writing now a study on the social character of the USSR in connection with the war question. The writing, with its translation, will take at least one week more. The fundamental ideas are as follows:

1. Our definition of the USSR can be right or wrong, but I do not see any reason to make this definition dependent on the German-Soviet pact.

2. The social character of the USSR is not determined by her friendship with democracy or fascism. Who adopts such a point of view becomes a prisoner of the Stalinist conception of the People's Front epoch.

3. Who says that the USSR is no more a degenerate workers' state, but a new social formation, should clearly say what he adds to our *political conclusions.*

4. The USSR question cannot be isolated as unique from the whole historic process of our times. Either the Stalin state is a transitory formation, it is a deformation of a worker state in a backward and isolated country, or 'bureaucratic collectivism' (Bruno R., *La Bureaucratisation du Monde;* Paris 1939) is a new social formation which is replacing capitalism throughout the world (Stalinism, Fascism, New Deals, etc.). The terminological experiments (workers' state, not workers' state; class, not class; etc.) receive a sense only under this historic aspect. Who chooses the second alternative admits, openly or silently, that all the revolutionary potentialities of the world proletariat are exhausted, that the socialist movement is bankrupt, and that the old capitalism is transforming itself into 'bureaucratic collectivism' with a new exploiting class.

Documents in this volume marked with † were written by Leon Trotsky in English: the others are English translations of the original Russian text.—Ed.

The tremendous importance of such a conclusion is self-explanatory. It concerns the whole fate of the world proletariat and mankind. Have we the slightest right to induce ourselves by purely terminological experiments in a new historic conception which occurs to be in an absolute contradiction with our programme, strategy and tactics? Such an adventuristic jump would be doubly criminal now in view of the world war when the perspective of the socialist revolution becomes an imminent reality and when the case of the USSR will appear to everybody as a transitorial episode in the process of world socialist revolution.

I write these lines in haste, which explains their insufficiency, but in a week I hope to send you my more complete thesis.

Comradely greetings,
V. T. O. [*Leon Trotsky*]*

---

* Because of the conditions of his residence in the various countries in which he lived after his exile, Trotsky often used pseudonyms in his letters. His letters were frequently signed with the name of his English secretary. —Ed.

The USSR in War

The German-Soviet Pact and the Character of the USSR

Is it possible after the conclusion of the German-Soviet pact to consider the USSR a workers' state? The future of the Soviet state has again and again aroused discussion in our midst. Small wonder; we have before us the first experiment in the workers' state in history. Never before and nowhere else has this phenomenon been available for analysis. In the question of the social character of the USSR, mistakes commonly flow, as we have previously stated, from replacing the historical fact with the programmatic norm. Concrete fact departs from the norm. This does not signify, however, that it has overthrown the norm; on the contrary, it has reaffirmed it, from the negative side. The degeneration of the first workers' state, ascertained and explained by us, has only the more graphically shown what the workers' state should be, what it could and would be under certain historical conditions. The contradiction between the concrete fact and the norm constrains us not to reject the norm but, on the contrary, to fight for it by means of the revolutionary road. The programme of the approaching revolution in the USSR is determined on the one hand by our appraisal of the USSR as an objective historical *fact,* and on the other hand, by a *norm* of the workers' state. We do not say: 'Everything is lost, we must begin all over again.' We clearly indicate those elements of the workers' state which at the given stage can be salvaged, preserved, and further developed.

Those who seek nowadays to prove that the Soviet-German pact changes our appraisal of the Soviet state take their stand, in essence, on the position of the Comintern—to put it more correctly, on yesterday's position of the Comintern. According to this logic, the historical mission of the workers' state is the struggle for imperialist democracy. The 'betrayal' of the democracies in favour of fascism divests the USSR of its being considered a workers' state. In point of fact, the signing of the treaty with Hitler supplies only an extra gauge with which to measure the degree of degeneration of the Soviet bureaucracy, and its contempt for the international working class, including the Comintern, but it does not provide any basis whatsoever for a re-evaluation of the sociological appraisal of the USSR.

Are the Differences Political or Terminological?

Let us begin by posing the question of the nature of the Soviet state not on the abstract-sociological plane but on the plane of concrete-political tasks. Let us concede for the moment that the bureaucracy is a new 'class' and that the present regime in the USSR is a special system of class exploitation. What new political conclusions follow for us from these definitions? The Fourth International long ago recognized the necessity of over-throwing the bureaucracy by means of a revolutionary uprising of the toilers. Nothing else is proposed or can be proposed by those who proclaim the bureaucracy to be an exploiting 'class'. The goal to be attained by the overthrow of the bureaucracy is the re-establishment of the rule of the soviets, expelling from them the present bureaucracy. Nothing different can be proposed or is proposed by the leftist critics.* It is the task of the re-generated soviets to collaborate with the world revolution and the building of a socialist society. The overthrow of the bureaucracy therefore presupposes the preservation of state property and of planned economy. Herein is the nub of the whole problem.

Needless to say, the distribution of productive forces among the various branches of economy and generally the entire content of the plan will be drastically changed when this plan is determined by the interests not of the bureaucracy but of the producers themselves. But inasmuch as the question of over-throwing the parasitic oligarchy still remains linked with that of preserving the nationalized (state) property, we called the future

---

* We recollect that some of these comrades who are inclined to consider the bureaucracy a new class, at the same time objected strenuously to the exclusion of the bureaucracy from the soviets.

revolution *political*. Certain of our critics (Ciliga, Bruno and others) want, come what may, to call the future revolution *social*. Let us grant this definition. What does it alter in essence? To those tasks of the revolution which we have enumerated it adds nothing whatsoever.

Our critics as a rule take the facts as we long ago established them. They add absolutely nothing essential to the appraisal either of the position of the bureaucracy and the toilers, or of the role of the Kremlin on the international arena. In all these spheres, not only do they fail to challenge our analysis, but on the contrary they base themselves completely upon it and even restrict themselves entirely to it. The sole accusation they bring against us is that we do not draw the necessary 'conclusions'. Upon analysis it turns out, however, that these conclusions are of a purely terminological character. Our critics refuse to call the degenerated workers' state—a workers' state. They demand that the totalitarian bureaucracy be called a ruling class. The revolution against this bureaucracy they propose to consider not political but social. Were we to make them these terminological concessions, we would place our critics in a very difficult position, inasmuch as they themselves would not know what to do with their purely verbal victory.

Let Us Check Ourselves Once Again

It would therefore be a piece of monstrous nonsense to split with comrades who on the question of the sociological nature of the USSR have an opinion different from ours, insofar as they solidarize with us in regard to the political tasks. But on the other hand, it would be blindness on our part to ignore purely theoretical and even terminological differences, because in the course of further development they may acquire flesh and blood and lead to diametrically opposite political conclusions. Just as a tidy housewife never permits an accumulation of cobwebs and garbage, just so a revolutionary party cannot tolerate lack of clarity, confusion and equivocation. Our house must be kept clean!

Let me recall for the sake of illustration, the question of Thermidor. For a long time we asserted that Thermidor in the USSR was only being prepared but had not yet been consummated. Later, investing the analogy to Thermidor with a more precise and well-deliberated character, we came to the conclusion that Thermidor had already taken place long ago. This open rectification of our own mistake did not introduce the slightest consternation in our ranks. Why? Because the *essence* of the processes in the Soviet Union was appraised identically by all of us, as we jointly studied day by day the growth of reaction. For us it was only a question of rendering more precise a historical analogy, nothing more. I hope that still today despite the attempt of some comrades to uncover differences on the question of the 'defence of the USSR'—with which we shall deal presently —we shall succeed by means of simply rendering our own ideas more precise to preserve unanimity on the basis of the programme of the Fourth International.

Is It a Cancerous Growth or a New Organ?

Our critics have more than once argued that the present Soviet bureaucracy bears very little resemblance to either the bourgeois or labour bureaucracy in capitalist society; that to a far greater degree than fascist bureaucracy it represents a new and much more powerful social formation. This is quite correct and we have never closed our eyes to it. But if we consider the Soviet bureaucracy a 'class', then we are compelled to state immediately that this class does not at all resemble any of those propertied classes known to us in the past; our gain consequently is not great. We frequently call the Soviet bureaucracy a caste, underscoring thereby its shut-in character, its arbitrary rule, and the haughtiness of the ruling stratum which considers that its progenitors issued from the divine lips of Brahma whereas the popular masses originated from the grosser portions of his anatomy. But even this definition does not of course possess a strictly scientific character. Its relative superiority lies in this, that the make-shift character of the term is clear to everybody, since it would enter nobody's mind to identify the Moscow oligarchy with the Hindu caste of Brahmins. The old sociological terminology did not and could not prepare a name for a new social event which is in process of evolution (degeneration) and which has not assumed stable forms. All of us, however, continue to call the Soviet bureaucracy a bureaucracy, not being unmindful of its historical peculiarities. In our opinion this should suffice for the time being.

Scientifically and politically—and not purely terminologically—the question poses itself as follows: Does the bureaucracy represent a temporary growth on a social organism or has this growth already become transformed into a historically indispensable organ? Social excrescences can be the product of an 'accidental' (i.e., temporary and extraordinary) enmeshing of historical circumstances. A social organ (and such is every class, including an exploiting class) can take shape only as a result of the deeply rooted inner needs of production itself. If we do not answer this question, then the entire controversy will degenerate into sterile toying with words.

The Early Degeneration of the Bureaucracy

The historical justification for every ruling class consisted in this—that the system of exploitation it headed raised the development of the productive forces to a new level. Beyond the shadow of a doubt, the Soviet regime gave a mighty impulse to economy. But the source of this impulse was the nationalization of the means of production and the planned beginnings and by no means the fact that the bureaucracy usurped command over the economy. On the contrary, bureaucratism, as a system, became the worst brake on the technical and cultural development of the country. This was veiled for a certain time by the fact that Soviet economy was occupied for two decades with transplanting and assimilating the technology and organization of production in advanced capitalist countries. The period of borrowing and imitation still could, for better or for worse, be accommodated to bureaucratic automatism, i.e., the suffocation of all initiative and all creative urge. But the higher the economy rose, the more complex its requirements became, all the more unbearable became the obstacle of the bureaucratic regime. The constantly sharpening contradiction between them leads to un-interrupted political convulsions, to systematic annihilation of the most outstanding creative elements in all spheres of activity. Thus, before the bureaucracy could succeed in exuding from itself a 'ruling class', it came into irreconcilable contradiction with the demands of development. The explanation for this is to to be found precisely in the fact that the bureaucracy is not the bearer of a new system of economy peculiar to itself and imposs-ible without itself, but is a parasitic growth on a workers' state.

The Conditions of the Omnipotence and Fall of the Bureaucracy

The Soviet oligarchy possesses all the vices of the old ruling classes but lacks their historical mission. In the bureaucratic degeneration of the Soviet state it is not the general laws of modern society from capitalism to socialism which find expres-sion but a special, exceptional and temporary refraction of these laws under the conditions of a backward revolutionary country in a capitalist environment. The scarcity in consumer goods and the universal struggle to obtain them generate a policeman who arrogates to himself the function of distribution. Hostile pressure from without imposes on the policeman the role of 'defender' of the country, endows him with national authority, and permits him doubly to plunder the country.

Both conditions for the omnipotence of the bureaucracy—the backwardness of the country and the imperialist environment—bear, however, a temporary and transitional character and must disappear with the victory of the world revolution. Even bourgeois economists have calculated that with a planned economy it would be possible to raise the national income of the United States rapidly to 200 billion dollars a year and thus assure the entire population not only the satisfaction of its primary needs but real comforts. On the other hand, the world revolution would do away with the danger from without as a supplementary cause of bureaucratization. The elimination of the need to expend an enormous share of the national income on armaments would raise even higher the living and cultural level of the masses. In these conditions the need for a policeman-distributor would fall away by itself. Administration as a gigantic co-operative would very quickly supplant state power. There would be no room for a new ruling class or for a new exploiting regime, located between capitalism and socialism.

And What If the Socialist Revolution Is Not Accomplished?

The disintegration of capitalism has reached extreme limits, likewise the disintegration of the old ruling class. The further existence of this system is impossible. The productive forces must be organized in accordance with a plan. But who will accomplish this task—the proletariat or a new ruling class of 'commissars'—politicians, administrators and technicians? Historical experience bears witness, in the opinion of certain rationalizers, that one cannot entertain hope in the proletariat. The proletariat proved 'incapable' of averting the last imperialist war although the material prerequisites for a socialist revolution already existed at that time. The successes of fascism after the war were once again the consequence of the 'incapacity' of the proletariat to lead capitalist society out of the blind alley. The bureaucratization of the Soviet state was in its turn the consequence of the 'incapacity' of the proletariat itself to regulate society through the democratic mechanism. The Spanish Revolution was strangled by the fascist and Stalinist bureaucracies before the very eyes of the world proletariat. Finally, the last link in this chain is the new imperialist war, the preparation of which took place quite openly, with complete impotence on the part of the world proletariat. If this conception is adopted, that is, if it is acknowledged that the proletariat does not have the forces to accomplish the socialist revolution, then the urgent task of the statification of the productive forces will obviously be accomplished by somebody else. By whom? By a new bureaucracy, which will replace the decayed bourgeoisie as a new ruling class on a world scale. That is how the question is beginning to be posed by those 'leftists' who do not rest content with debating over words.

The Present War and the Fate of Modern Society

By the very march of events this question is now posed very concretely. The Second World War has begun. It attests incontrovertibly to the fact that society can no longer live on the basis of capitalism. Thereby it subjects the proletariat to a new and perhaps decisive test.

If this war provokes, as we firmly believe, a proletarian revolution, it must inevitably lead to the overthrow of the bureaucracy in the USSR and regeneration of Soviet democracy on a far higher economic and cultural basis than in 1918. In that case the question as to whether the Stalinist bureaucracy was a 'class' or a growth on the workers' state will be automatically solved. To every single person it will become clear that in the process of the development of the world revolution the Soviet bureaucracy was only an *episodic* relapse.

If, however, it is conceded that the present war will provoke not revolution but a decline of the proletariat, then there remains another alternative: the further decay of monopoly capitalism, its further fusion with the state and the replacement of democracy wherever it still remained by a totalitarian regime. The inability of the proletariat to take into its hands the leadership of society could actually lead under these conditions to the growth of a new exploiting class from the Bonapartist fascist bureaucracy. This would be, according to all indications, a regime of decline, signalizing the eclipse of civilization.

An analogous result might occur in the event that the proletariat of advanced capitalist countries, having conquered power, should prove incapable of holding it and surrender it, as in the USSR, to a privileged bureaucracy. Then we would be compelled to acknowledge that the reason for the bureaucratic relapse is rooted not in the backwardness of the country and not in the imperialist environment but in the congenital incapacity of the proletariat to become a ruling class. Then it would be necessary in retrospect to establish that in its fundamental traits the present USSR was the precursor of a new exploiting regime on an international scale.

We have diverged very far from the terminological controversy over the nomenclature of the Soviet state. But let our critics not protest; only by taking the necessary historical perspective can one provide himself with a correct judgment upon such a question as the replacement of one social regime by another. The historic alternative, carried to the end, is as follows: either the Stalin regime is an abhorrent relapse in the process of transforming bourgeois society into a socialist society, or the Stalin regime is the first stage of a new exploiting society. If the second prognosis proves to be correct, then, of course, the bureaucracy will become a new exploiting class. However onerous the second perspective may be, if the world proletariat should actually prove incapable of fulfilling the mission placed upon it by the course of development, nothing else would remain except only to recognize that the socialist programme, based on the internal contradictions of capitalist society, ended as a Utopia. It is self-evident that a new 'minimum' programme would be required—for the defence of the interests of the slaves of the totalitarian bureaucratic society.

But are there such incontrovertible or even impressive objective data as would compel us today to renounce the prospect of the socialist revolution? That is the whole question.

The Theory of 'Bureaucratic Collectivism'

Shortly after the assumption of power by Hitler, a German 'left-communist', Hugo Urbahns, came to the conclusion that in place of capitalism a new historical era of 'state capitalism' was impending. The first examples of this regime he named as Italy, the USSR, Germany. Urbahns, however, did not draw the political conclusions of his theory. Recently, an Italian 'left-communist', Bruno R., who formerly adhered to the Fourth International, came to the conclusion that 'bureaucratic collectivism' was about to replace capitalism. (Bruno R.—*La Bureaucratisation du Monde,* Paris 1939, 350 pp.) The new bureaucracy is a class, its relation to the toilers is collective exploitation, the proletarians are transformed into the slaves of totalitarian exploiters.

Bruno R. brackets together planned economy in the USSR, fascism, National Socialism and Roosevelt's 'New Deal'. All these regimes undoubtedly possess common traits, which in the last analysis are determined by the collectivist tendencies of modern economy. Lenin even prior to the October Revolution formulated the main peculiarities of imperialist capitalism as follows: gigantic concentration of productive forces, the heightening fusion of monopoly capitalism with the state, an organic tendency toward naked dictatorship as a result of this fusion. The traits of centralization and collectivization determine both the politics of revolution and the politics of counter-revolution; but this by no means signifies that it is possible to equate revolution, Thermidor, fascism and American 'reformism'. Bruno has caught on to the fact that the tendencies of collectivization assume, as a result of the political prostration of the working class, the form of 'bureaucratic collectivism'. The phenomenon in itself is incontestable. But where are its limits, and what is its historical weight? What we accept as the deformity of a transitional period, the result of the unequal development of multiple factors in the social process, is taken by Bruno R. for an independent social formation in which the bureaucracy is the ruling class. Bruno R. in any case has the merit of seeking to transfer the question from the charmed circle of terminological copybook exercises to the plane of major historical generalizations. This makes it all the easier to disclose his mistake.

Like many ultra-lefts, Bruno R. identifies in essence Stalinism with fascism. On the one side the Soviet bureaucracy has adopted the political methods of fascism; on the other side the fascist bureaucracy, which still confines itself to 'partial' measures of state intervention, is heading toward and will soon reach complete statification of economy. The first assertion is absolutely correct. But Bruno's assertion that fascist 'anti-capitalism' is capable of arriving at the expropriation of the bourgeoisie is completely erroneous. 'Partial' measures of state intervention and of nationalization in reality differ from planned state economy just as reforms differ from revolution. Mussolini and Hitler are only 'co-ordinating' the interests of the property owners and 'regulating' capitalist economy, and, moreover, primarily for war purposes. The Kremlin oligarchy is something else again: it has the opportunity of directing economy as a body only owing to the fact that the working class of Russia accomplished the greatest overturn of property relations in history. This difference must not be lost sight of.

But even if we grant that Stalinism and fascism from opposite poles will some day arrive at one and the same type of exploitive society ('bureaucratic collectivism' according to Bruno R.'s terminology) this still will not lead humanity out of the blind alley. The crisis of the capitalist system is produced not only by the reactionary role of private property but also by the no less reactionary role of the national state. Even if the various fascist governments did succeed in establishing a system of planned economy at home then, aside from the, in the long run, inevitable revolutionary movements of the proletariat unforeseen by any plan, the struggle between the totalitarian states for world domination would be continued and even intensified. Wars would devour the fruits of planned economy and destroy the bases of civilization. Bertrand Russell thinks, it is true, that some victorious state may, as a result of the war, unify the entire world

in a totalitarian vice. But even if such a hypothesis should be
realized, which is highly doubtful, military 'unification' would
have no greater stability than the ·Versailles treaty. National
uprisings and pacifications would culminate in a new world war,
which would be the grave of civilization. Not our subjective
wishes but the objective reality speaks for it, that the only way
out for humanity is the world socialist revolution. The alternative to it is the relapse into barbarism.

The Proletariat and Its Leadership

We shall very soon devote a separate article to the question
of the relation between the class and its leadership. We shall
confine ourselves here to the most indispensable. Only vulgar
'Marxists' who take it that politics is a mere and direct
'reflection' of economics, are capable of thinking that leadership
reflects the class directly and simply. In reality leadership,
having risen above the oppressed class, inevitably succumbs to
the pressure of the ruling class. The leadership of the American
trade unions, for instance, 'reflects' not so much the proletariat
as the bourgeoisie. The selection and education of a truly
revolutionary leadership, capable of withstanding the pressure of
the bourgeoisie, is an extraordinarily difficult task. The dialectic
of the historic process expressed itself most brilliantly in the
fact that the proletariat of the most backward country, Russia,
under certain historic conditions, has put forward the most
far-sighted and courageous leadership. On the contrary, the
proletariat in the country of the oldest capitalist culture, Great
Britain, has even today the most dull-witted and servile leadership.

The crisis of capitalist society which assumed an open
character in July 1914, from the very first day of the war produced a sharp crisis in the proletarian leadership. During the
25 years that have elapsed since that time, the proletariat of the
advanced capitalist countries has not yet created a leadership
that could rise to the level of the tasks of our epoch. The

experience of Russia testifies, however, that such a leadership can be created. (This does not mean, of course, that it will be immune to degeneration.) The question consequently stands as follows: Will objective historical necessity in the long run cut a path for itself in the consciousness of the vanguard of the working class; that is, in the process of this war and those profound shocks which it must engender, will a genuine revolutionary leadership be formed capable of leading the proletariat to the conquest of power?

The Fourth International has replied in the affirmative to this question, not only through the text of its programme, but also through the very fact of its existence. All the various types of disillusioned and frightened representatives of pseudo-Marxism proceed *on the contrary* from the assumption that the bankruptcy of the leadership only 'reflects' the incapacity of the proletariat to fulfill its revolutionary mission. Not all our opponents express this thought clearly, but all of them—ultra-lefts, centrists, anarchists, not to mention Stalinists and social-democrats—shift the responsibility for the defeats from themselves to the shoulders of the proletariat. None of them indicate under precisely what conditions the proletariat will be capable of accomplishing the socialist overturn.

If we grant as true that the cause of the defeats is rooted in the social qualities of the proletariat itself then the position of modern society will have to be acknowledged as hopeless. Under conditions of decaying capitalism the proletariat grows neither numerically nor culturally. There are no grounds, therefore, for expecting that it will sometime rise to the level of the revolutionary tasks. Altogether differently does the case present itself to him who has clarified in his mind the profound antagonism between the organic, deep-going, insurmountable urge of the toiling masses to tear themselves free from the bloody capitalist chaos, and the conservative, patriotic, utterly bourgeois character of the outlived labour leadership. We must choose one of these two irreconcilable conceptions.

Totalitarian Dictatorship—A Condition of Acute Crisis and Not a Stable Regime

The October Revolution was not an accident. It was forecast long in advance. Events confirmed this forecast. The degeneration does not refute the forecast, because Marxists never believed that an isolated workers' state in Russia could maintain itself indefinitely. True enough, we expected the wrecking of the Soviet state, rather than its degeneration; to put it more correctly, we did not sharply differentiate between those two possibilities. But they do not at all contradict each other. Degeneration must inescapably end at a certain stage in downfall.

A totalitarian regime, whether of Stalinist or fascist type, by its very essence can be only a temporary transitional regime. Naked dictatorship in history has generally been the product and the symptom of an especially severe social crisis, and not at all of a stable regime. Severe crisis cannot be a permanent condition of society. A totalitarian state is capable of suppressing social contradictions during a certain period, but it is incapable of perpetuating itself. The monstrous purges in the USSR are most convincing testimony of the fact that Soviet society organically tends towards ejection of the bureaucracy.

It is an astonishing thing that Bruno R. sees precisely in the Stalinist purges proof of the fact that the bureaucracy has become a ruling class, for in his opinion only a ruling class is capable of measures on so large a scale.* He forgets however

---

* True enough, in the last section of his book, which consists of fantastic contradictions, Bruno R. quite consciously and articulately refutes his own theory of 'bureaucratic collectivism' unfolded in the first section of the book and declares that Stalinism, fascism and nazism are transitory and parasitic formations, historic penalties for the impotence of the proletariat. In other words, after having subjected the views of the Fourth International to the sharpest kind of criticism, Bruno R. unexpectedly returns to those views, but only in order to launch a new series of blind fumblings. We see no grounds for following in the footsteps of a writer who has obviously lost his balance. We are interested in those of his arguments by means of which he seeks to substantiate his views that the bureaucracy is a class.

that Czarism, which was not a 'class', also permitted itself rather large-scale measures in purges and moreover precisely in the period when it was nearing its doom. Symptomatic of his oncoming death agony, by the sweep and monstrous fraudulence of his purge, Stalin testifies to nothing else but the incapacity of the bureaucracy to transform itself into a stable ruling class. Might we not place ourselves in a ludicrous position if we affixed to the Bonapartist oligarchy the nomenclature of a new ruling class just a few years or even a few months prior to its inglorious downfall? Posing this question clearly should alone in our opinion restrain the comrades from terminological experimentation and overhasty generalizations.

The Orientation Toward World Revolution and the Regeneration of the USSR

A quarter of a century proved too brief a span for the revolutionary re-arming of the world proletarian vanguard, and too long a period for preserving the soviet system intact in an isolated backward country. Mankind is now paying for this with a new imperialist war; but the basic task of our epoch has not changed, for the simple reason that it has not been solved. A colossal asset in the last quarter of a century and a priceless pledge for the future is constituted by the fact that one of the detachments of the world proletariat was able to demonstrate in action *how* the task must be solved.

The second imperialist war poses the unsolved task on a higher historical stage. It tests anew not only the stability of the existing regimes but also the ability of the proletariat to replace them. The results of this test will undoubtedly have a decisive significance for our appraisal of the modern epoch as the epoch of proletarian revolution. If contrary to all probabilities the October Revolution fails during the course of the present war, or immediately thereafter, to find its continuation in any of the advanced countries; and if, on the contrary, the proletariat is thrown back everywhere and on all fronts—then we should doubtless have to pose the question of revising our conception of the present epoch and its driving forces. In that case it would be a question not of slapping a copybook label on the USSR or the Stalinist gang but of re-evaluating the world historical perspective for the next decades if not centuries: Have we entered the epoch of social revolution and socialist society, or on the contrary the epoch of the declining society of totalitarian bureaucracy?

The twofold error of schematists like Hugo Urbahns and Bruno R. consists, first, in that they proclaim this latter regime as having been already finally installed; secondly, in that they declare it a prolonged transitional state of society between capitalism and socialism. Yet it is absolutely self-evident that if the international proletariat, as a result of the experience of our entire epoch and the current new war, proves incapable of becoming the master of society, this would signify the foundering of all hope for a socialist revolution, for it is impossible to expect any other more favourable conditions for it; in any case no one foresees them now, or is able to characterize them. Marxists do not have the slightest right (if disillusionment and fatigue are not considered 'rights') to draw the conclusion that the proletariat has forfeited its revolutionary possibilities and must renounce all aspirations to hegemony in an era immediately ahead. Twenty-five years in the scales of history, when it is a question of profoundest changes in economic and cultural systems, weigh less than an hour in the life of man. What good is the individual who, because of empirical failures in the course of an hour or a day, renounces a goal that he set for himself on the basis of the experience and analysis of his entire previous lifetime? In the years of darkest Russian reaction (1907 to 1917) we took as our starting point those revolutionary possibilities which were revealed by the Russian proletariat in 1905. In the years of world reaction we must proceed from those possibilities which the Russian proletariat revealed in 1917. The Fourth International did not by accident call itself the world party of the socialist revolution. Our road is not to be changed. We steer our course toward the world revolution and by virtue of this very fact toward the regeneration of the USSR as a workers' state.

Foreign Policy Is the Continuation of Domestic Policy

What do we defend in the USSR? Not that in which it resembles the capitalist countries but precisely that in which it differs from them. In Germany also we advocate an uprising against the ruling bureaucracy, but only in order immediately to overthrow capitalist property. In the USSR the overthrow of the bureaucracy is indispensable for the preservation of state property. Only in this sense do we stand for the defence of the USSR.

There is not one among us who doubts that the Soviet workers should defend the state property, not only against the parasitism of the bureaucracy, but also against the tendencies toward private ownership, for example, on the part of the kolkhoz aristocracy. But after all, foreign policy is the continuation of policy at home. If in domestic policy we correlate defence of the conquests of the October Revolution with irreconcilable struggle against the bureaucracy, then we must do the same thing in foreign policy as well. To be sure, Bruno R., proceeding from the fact that 'bureaucratic collectivism' has already been victorious all along the line, assures us that no one threatens state property, because Hitler (and Chamberlain?) is as much interested, you see, in preserving it as Stalin. Sad to say, Bruno R.'s assurances are frivolous. In event of victory Hitler will in all probability begin by demanding the return to German capitalists of all the property expropriated from them; then he will secure a similar restoration of property for the English, the French and the Belgians so as to reach an agreement with them at the expense of the USSR; finally, he will make Germany the contractor of the most important state enterprises in the USSR in the interests of the German military machine. Right now Hitler is the ally and friend of Stalin; but should Hitler, with the aid of Stalin, come out victorious on the Western Front, he would on the morrow turn his guns against the USSR. Finally, Chamberlain, too, in similar circumstances would act no differently from Hitler.

The Defence of the USSR and the Class Struggle

Mistakes on the question of defence of the USSR most frequently flow from an incorrect understanding of the methods of 'defence'. Defence of the USSR does not at all mean rapprochement with the Kremlin bureaucracy, the acceptance of its politics, or a conciliation with the politics of her allies. In this question, as in all others, we remain completely on the ground of the international class struggle.

In the tiny French periodical, *Que Faire*, it was recently stated that inasmuch as the 'Trotskyites' are defeatists in relation to France and England they are therefore defeatists also in relation to the USSR. In other words: If you want to defend the USSR you must stop being defeatists in relation to her imperialist allies. *Que Faire* calculated that the 'democracies' would be the allies of the USSR. What these sages will say now we don't know. But that is hardly important, for their very method is rotten. To renounce defeatism in relation to that imperialist camp to which the USSR adheres today or might adhere tomorrow is to push the workers of the enemy camp to the side of their government; it means to renounce defeatism in general. The renunciation of defeatism under the conditions of imperialist war which is tantamount to the rejection of the socialist revolution—rejection of revolution in the name of 'defence of the USSR'—would sentence the USSR to final decomposition and doom.

'Defence of the USSR', as interpreted by the Comintern, like yesterday's 'struggle against fascism', is based on renunciation of independent class politics. The proletariat is transformed—for various reasons in varying circumstances, but always and invariably—into an auxiliary force of one bourgeois camp against another. In contradistinction to this, some of our comrades say:

Since we do not want to become tools of Stalin and his allies we therefore renounce the defence of the USSR. But by this they only demonstrate that their understanding of 'defence' coincides essentially with the understanding of the opportunists; they do not think in terms of the independent politics of the proletariat. As a matter of fact, we defend the USSR as we defend the colonies, as we solve all our problems, not by supporting some imperialist governments against others, but by the method of international class struggle in the colonies as well as in the metropolitan centres.

We are not a government party; we are the party of irreconcilable opposition, not only in capitalist countries but also in the USSR. Our tasks, among them the 'defence of the USSR', we realize not through the medium of bourgeois governments and not even through the government of the USSR, but exclusively through the education of the masses through agitation, through explaining to the workers what they should defend and what they should overthrow. Such a 'defence' cannot give immediate miraculous results. But we do not even pretend to be miracle workers. As things stand, we are a revolutionary minority. Our work must be directed so that the workers on whom we have influence should correctly appraise events, not permit themselves to be caught unawares, and prepare the general sentiment of their own class for the revolutionary solution of the tasks confronting us.

The defence of the USSR coincides for us with the preparation of world revolution. Only those methods are permissible which do not conflict with the interests of the revolution. The defence of the USSR is related to the world socialist revolution as a tactical task is related to a strategic one. A tactic is subordinated to a strategic goal and in no case can be in contradiction to the latter.

The Question of Occupied Territories

As I am writing these lines the question of the territories occupied by the Red Army still remains obscure. The cable dispatches contradict each other, since both sides lie a great deal; but the actual relationships on the scene are no doubt still extremely unsettled. Most of the occupied territories will doubtless become part of the USSR. In what form?

Let us for a moment conceive that in accordance with the treaty with Hitler, the Moscow government leaves untouched the rights of private property in the occupied areas and limits itself to 'control' after the fascist pattern. Such a concession would have a deep-going principled character and might become a starting point for a new chapter in the history of the Soviet regime; and consequently a starting point for a new appraisal on our part of the nature of the Soviet state.

It is more likely, however, that in the territories scheduled to become a part of the USSR, the Moscow government will carry through the expropriation of the large land-owners and statification of the means of production. This variant is most probable not because the bureaucracy remains true to the socialist programme but because it is neither desirous nor capable of sharing the power, and the privileges the latter entails, with the old ruling classes in the occupied territories. Here an analogy literally offers itself. The first Bonaparte halted the revolution by means of a military dictatorship. However, when the French troops invaded Poland, Napoleon signed a decree: 'Serfdom is abolished.' This measure was dictated not by Napoleon's sympathies for the peasants, nor by democratic principles, but rather by the fact that the Bonapartist dictatorship based itself not on feudal, but on bourgeois property relations. Inasmuch as Stalin's Bonapartist dictatorship bases itself not on private but on state property, the invasion of Poland by the Red Army should, in the nature of the case, result in the abolition of private capitalist property, so as thus to bring the regime of the occupied territories into accord with the regime of the USSR.

This measure, revolutionary in character—'the expropriation of the expropriators'—is in this case achieved in a military-bureaucratic fashion. The appeal to independent activity on the part of the masses in the new territories—and without such an appeal, even if worded with extreme caution, it is impossible to constitute a new regime—will on the morrow undoubtedly be suppressed by ruthless police measures in order to assure the preponderance of the bureaucracy over the awakened revolutionary masses. This is one side of the matter. But there is another. In order to gain the possibility of occupying Poland through a military alliance with Hitler, the Kremlin for a long time deceived and continues to deceive the masses in the USSR and in the whole world, and has thereby brought about the complete disorganization of the ranks of its own Communist International. The primary political criterion for us is not the transformation of property relations in this or another area, however important these may be in themselves, but rather the change in the consciousness and organization of the world proletariat, the raising of their capacity for defending former conquests and accomplishing new ones. From this one, and the only decisive standpoint, the politics of Moscow, taken as a whole, completely retains its reactionary character and remains the chief obstacle on the road to the world revolution.

Our *general* appraisal of the Kremlin and the Comintern does not, however, alter the *particular* fact that the statification of property in the occupied territories is in itself a progressive measure. We must recognize this openly. Were Hitler on the morrow to throw his armies against the east to restore 'law and order' in eastern Poland, the advanced workers would defend against Hitler these new property forms established by the Bonapartist Soviet bureaucracy.

We Do Not Change Our Course!

The statification of the means of production is, as we said, a progressive measure. But its progressiveness is relative; its specific weight depends on the sum-total of all the other factors. Thus, we must first and foremost establish that the extension of the territory dominated by bureaucratic autocracy and parasitism, cloaked by 'socialist' measures, can augment the prestige of the Kremlin, engender illusions concerning the possibility of replacing the proletarian revolution by bureaucratic manoeuvres, and so on. This evil by far outweighs the progressive content of Stalinist reforms in Poland. In order that nationalized property in the occupied areas, as well as in the USSR, become a basis for genuinely progressive, that is to say socialist development, it is necessary to overthrow the Moscow bureaucracy. Our programme retains, consequently, all its validity. The events did not catch us unawares. It is necessary only to interpret them correctly. It is necessary to understand clearly that sharp contradictions are contained in the character of the USSR and in her international position. It is impossible to free oneself from those contradictions with the help of terminological sleight-of-hand ('workers' state'—'not workers' state'). We must take the facts as they are. We must build our policy by taking as our starting point the real relations and contradictions.

We do not entrust the Kremlin with any historic mission. We were and remain against seizures of new territories by the Kremlin. We are for the independence of Soviet Ukraine, and if the Byelo Russians themselves wish—of Soviet Byelo Russia. At the same time in the sections of Poland occupied by the Red Army, partisans of the Fourth International must play the most decisive part in expropriating the landlords and capitalists, in dividing the land among the peasants, in creating soviets and workers' committees, etc. While so doing, they must preserve their political independence, they must fight during elections to the soviets and factory committees for the complete independence of the latter from the bureaucracy, and they must conduct revolutionary propaganda in the spirit of distrust toward the Kremlin and its local agencies.

But let us suppose that Hitler turns his weapons against the east and invades territories occupied by the Red Army. Under these conditions, partisans of the Fourth International, without changing in any way their attitude toward the Kremlin oligarchy, will advance to the forefront, as the most urgent task of the hour, the military resistance against Hitler. The workers will say: 'We cannot cede to Hitler the overthrowing of Stalin; that is *our own task.*' During the military struggle against Hitler, the revolutionary workers will strive to enter into the closest possible comradely relations with the rank-and-file fighters of the Red Army. While arms in hand they deal blows to Hitler, the Bolshevik-Leninists will at the same time conduct revolutionary propaganda against Stalin preparing his overthrow at the next and perhaps very near stage.

This kind of 'defence of the USSR' will naturally differ, as heaven does from earth, from the official defence which is now being conducted under the slogan: 'For the Fatherland! For Stalin!' *Our* defence of the USSR is carried on under the slogan: 'For Socialism! For the World Revolution! Against Stalin!' In order that these two varieties of 'defence of the USSR' do not become confused in the consciousness of the masses it is necessary to know clearly and precisely how to formulate slogans which correspond to the concrete situation. But above all it is necessary to establish clearly just *what* we are defending, just *how* we are defending it, against *whom* we are defending it. Our slogans will create confusion among the masses only if we ourselves do not have a clear conception of our tasks.

Conclusions

We have no reasons whatsoever at the present time for changing our principled position in relation to the USSR.

War accelerates the various political processes. It may accelerate the process of the revolutionary regeneration of the USSR. But it may also accelerate the process of its final degeneration. For this reason it is indispensable that we follow painstakingly and without prejudice these modifications which war introduces into the internal life of the USSR so that we may give ourselves a timely accounting of them.

Our tasks in the occupied territories remain basically the

same as in the USSR itself; but inasmuch as they are posed by events in an extremely sharp form, they enable us all the better to clarify our general tasks in relation to the USSR.

We must formulate our slogans in such a way that the workers see clearly just what we are defending in the USSR (state property and planned economy), and against whom we are conducting a ruthless struggle (the parasitic bureaucracy and its Comintern). We must not lose sight for a single moment of the fact that the question of overthrowing the Soviet bureaucracy is for us subordinate to the question of preserving state property in the means of production in the USSR; that the question of preserving state property in the means of production in the USSR is subordinate for us to the question of the world proletarian revolution.

September 25, 1939.

A letter to Sherman Stanley†

October 8, 1939.

Dear Comrade Stanley,

I received your letter to O'Brien in view of his departure. The letter produced upon me a strange impression, because in opposition to your very good articles, it is full of contradictions.

I didn't receive as yet any material about the plenum and don't know either the text of the majority resolution or that of M. S.,* but you affirm that there is not an irreconcilable opposition between the two texts. At the same time you affirm that a 'disaster' approaches the party. Why? Even if there have been two *irreconcilable* positions, it would signify not a 'disaster' but a necessity to fight out the political struggle to the end. But if both motions represent only nuances of the same point of view expressed in the programme of the Fourth International, how can arise from this unprincipled (in your opinion) divergence, a catastrophe? That the majority preferred their own nuance (if it is only a nuance) is natural. But what is absolutely unnatural is that the minority proclaims: 'because you, the majority, accept your own nuance and not ours we foretell catastrophe'. From the side of whom ? ? ? ... And you affirm that you 'look objectively upon the different groupings'. It is not my impression at all.

You write for example that from my article 'one page *for some reason or other* was missing'. You express in this way a very venomous suspicion towards responsible comrades. The page was missing by a regrettable nonchalance in our office here, and we sent already a new, complete text for translation.†

---

* The reference is to Max Shachtman.—Ed.

† The document, 'The USSR in War', arrived while the plenum of the National Committee of the Socialist Workers Party was in session. One page was missing. The political line of this document was endorsed by the majority of the plenum. The minority raised a hue and cry about the missing page, charging, among other things, that it was being deliberately suppressed.—Ed.

Your argument about the degenerated 'workers *empire*' seems to me not a very happy invention. 'Czarist expansion programme' was objected to‡ the Bolsheviks almost from the first day of the October Revolution. Even a sound workers state would tend toward expansion, and the geographical lines would inevitably coincide with the general lines of the Czarist expansion because revolutions don't ordinarily change geographical conditions. What we object to about the Kremlin gang is not the expansion and not the geographical direction of the expansion but the bureaucratic, counter-revolutionary methods of the expansion. But at the same time because we as Marxists 'look objectively' upon historic happenings we recognize that neither the Czar, nor Hitler, nor Chamberlain had or have the custom of abolishing, in the occupied countries, capitalist property, and this fact, a very progressive one, depends upon another fact; namely, that the October Revolution is not definitely assassinated by the bureaucracy, and that the last is forced by its position to take measures which we must defend in a given situation against imperialist enemies. These progressive measures are, of course, incomparably less important than the general counter-revolutionary activity of the bureaucracy: it is why we find it necessary to overthrow the bureaucracy . . .

The comrades are very indignant about the Stalin-Hitler pact. It is comprehensible. They wish to get revenge on Stalin. Very good. But today we are weak, and we cannot immediately overthrow the Kremlin. Some comrades try then to find a purely verbalistic satisfaction: they strike out from the USSR the title, workers' state, as Stalin deprives a disgraced functionary of the order of Lenin. I find it, my dear friend, a bit childish. Marxist sociology and hysteria are absolutely irreconcilable.

With best comradely greetings,

CRUX [*Leon Trotsky*]

‡ i.e., charged against.—Ed.

Again and Once More Again on the Nature of the USSR

Psychoanalysis and Marxism

Certain comrades, or former comrades, such as Bruno R., having forgotten the past discussions and decisions of the Fourth International, attempt to explain my personal estimate of the Soviet state psychoanalytically. 'Since Trotsky participated in the Russian Revolution, it is difficult for him to lay aside the idea of the workers' state inasmuch as he would have to renounce his whole life's cause', etc. I think that the old Freud, who was very perspicacious, would have cuffed the ears of psychoanalysts of this ilk a little. Naturally I would never risk taking such action myself. Nevertheless I dare assure my critics that subjectively and sentimentality are not on my side but on theirs.

Moscow's conduct, which has passed all bounds of abjectness and cynicism, calls forth an easy revolt within every proletarian revolutionary. Revolt engenders need for rejection. When the forces for immediate action are absent, impatient revolutionaries are inclined to resort to artificial methods. Thus arises, for example, the tactic of individual terror. More frequently resort is taken to strong expressions, to insults, and to imprecation. In the case which concerns us certain comrades are manifestly inclined to seek compensation through 'terminological' terror. However, even from this point of view the mere fact of qualifying the bureaucracy as a class is worthless. If the Bonapartist riffraff is a class this means that it is not an abortion but a viable child of history. If its marauding parasitism is 'exploitation' in the scientific sense of the term, this means that the bureaucracy possesses a historical future as the ruling class indispensable to the given system of economy. Here we have the end to which impatient revolt leads when it cuts itself loose from Marxist discipline!

When an emotional mechanic considers an automobile in which, let us say, gangsters have escaped from police pursuit over

a bad road, and finds the frame bent, the wheels out of line, and
the motor partially damaged, he might quite justifiably say: 'It
is not an automobile—devil knows what it is!' Such an estimate
would lack any technical and scientific value, but it would
express the legitimate reaction of the mechanic at the work of
the gangsters. Let us suppose, however, that this same mechanic
must recondition the object which he named 'devil-knows-what-
it-is'. In this case he will start with the recognition that it is a
damaged automobile before him. He will determine which parts
are still good and which are beyond repair in order to decide
how to begin work. The class-conscious worker will have a
similar attitude toward the USSR. He has full right to say that
the gangsters of the bureaucracy have transformed the workers'
state into 'devil-knows-what-it-is'. But when he passes from this
explosive reaction to the solution of the political problem, he is
forced to recognize that it is a damaged workers' state before
him, in which the motor of economy is damaged, but which still
continues to run and which can be completely reconditioned with
the replacement of some parts. Of course this is only an analogy.
Nevertheless it is worth reflecting over.

'A Counter-Revolutionary Workers' State'

Some voices cry out: 'If we continue to recognize the USSR
as a workers' state, we will have to establish a new category: the
counter-revolutionary workers' state.' This argument attempts
to shock our imagination by opposing a good programmatic norm
to a miserable, mean, even repugnant reality. But haven't we
observed from day to day since 1923 how the Soviet state has
played a more and more counter-revolutionary role on the international arena? Have we forgotten the experience of the
Chinese Revolution, of the 1926 general strike in England and
finally the very fresh experience of the Spanish Revolution?
There are two completely counter-revolutionary workers' internationals. These critics have apparently forgotten this 'category'.
The trade unions of France, Great Britain, the United States and

other countries support completely the counter-revolutionary politics of their bourgeoisie. This does not prevent us from labelling them trade unions, from supporting their progressive steps and from defending them against the bourgeoisie. Why is it impossible to employ the same method with the counter-revolutionary workers' state? In the last analysis a workers' state is a trade union which has conquered power. The difference in attitude in these two cases is explainable by the simple fact that the trade unions have a long history and we have become accustomed to consider them as realities and not simply as 'categories' in our programme. But, as regards the workers' state there is being evinced an inability to learn to approach it as a real historical fact which has not subordinated itself to our programme.

'Imperialism'?

Can the present expansion of the Kremlin be termed imperialism? First of all we must establish what social content is included in this term. History has known the 'imperialism' of the Roman state based on slave labour, the imperialism of feudal land-ownership, the imperialism of commercial and industrial capital, the imperialism of the Czarist monarchy, etc. The driving force behind the Moscow bureaucracy is indubitably the tendency to expand its power, its prestige, its revenues. This is the element of 'imperialism' in the widest sense of the word which was a property in the past of all monarchies, oligarchies, ruling castes, medieval estates and classes. However, in contemporary literature, at least Marxist literature, imperialism is understood to mean the *expansionist policy of finance capital* which has a very sharply defined economic content. To employ the term 'imperialism' for the foreign policy of the Kremlin— without elucidating exactly what this signifies—means simply to identify the policy of the Bonapartist bureaucracy with the policy of monopolistic capitalism on the basis that both one and the other utilize military force for expansion. Such an identification, capable of sowing only confusion, is much more proper to petty-bourgeois democrats than to Marxists.

Continuation of the Policy of Czarist Imperialism

The Kremlin participates in a new division of Poland, the Kremlin lays hands upon the Baltic states, the Kremlin orients toward the Balkans, Persia and Afghanistan; in other words, the Kremlin continues the policy of Czarist imperialism. Do we not have the right in this case to label the policy of the Kremlin itself imperialist? This historical-geographical argument is no more convincing than any of the others. The proletarian revolution, which occurred on the territory of the Czarist empire, attempted from the very beginning to conquer and for a time conquered the Baltic countries; attempted to penetrate Rumania and Persia and at one time led its armies up to Warsaw (1920). The lines of revolutionary expansion were the same as those of Czarism, since revolution does not change geographical conditions. That is precisely why the Mensheviks at that time already spoke of Bolshevik imperialism as borrowed from the traditions of Czarist diplomacy. The petty-bourgeois democracy willingly resorts to this argument even now. We have no reason, I repeat, for imitating them in this.

Agency of Imperialism?

However, aside from the manner in which to appraise the expansionist policy of the USSR itself, there remains the question of the help which Moscow provides the imperialist policy of Berlin. Here first of all, it is necessary to establish that under certain conditions—up to a certain degree and in a certain form —the support of this or that imperialism would be inevitable even for a completely healthy workers' state—in virtue of the impossibility of breaking away from the chains of world imperialist relations. The Brest-Litovsk peace without the least doubt temporarily reinforced German imperialism against France and England. An isolated workers' state cannot fail to manoeuvre between the hostile imperialist camps. Manoeuvring means temporarily supporting one of them against the other. To know exactly which one of the two camps it is more advantageous or less dangerous to support at a certain moment is not a question of principle but of practical calculation and foresight. The inevitable disadvantage which is engendered as a consequence of this constrained support for one bourgeois state against another is more than covered by the fact that the isolated workers' state is thus given the possibility of continuing its existence.

But there is manoeuvring and manoeuvring. At Brest-Litovsk the Soviet government sacrificed the national independence of the Ukraine in order to salvage the workers' state. Nobody could speak of treason toward the Ukraine, since all the class-conscious workers understood the forced character of this sacrifice. It is completely different with Poland. The Kremlin has never and at no place represented the question as if it had been *constrained* to sacrifice Poland. On the contrary, it boasts cynically of its combination, which affronts, rightfully, the most elementary democratic feelings of the oppressed classes and peoples throughout the world and thus weakens extremely the international situation of the Soviet Union. The economic transformations in the occupied provinces do not compensate for this by even a tenth part!

The entire foreign policy of the Kremlin in general is based upon a scoundrelly embellishment of the 'friendly' imperialism and thus leads to the sacrifice of the fundamental interests of the world workers' movement for secondary and unstable advantages. After five years of duping the workers with slogans for the 'defence of the democracies' Moscow is now occupied with covering up Hitler's policy of pillage. This in itself still does not change the USSR into an imperialist state. But Stalin and his Comintern are now indubitably the most valuable agency of imperialism.

If we want to define the foreign policy of the Kremlin exactly,

we must say that it is the policy of the *Bonapartist bureaucracy
of a degenerated workers' state in imperialist encirclement.*
This definition is not as short or as sonorous as 'imperialist
policy', but in return it is more precise.

'The Lesser Evil'

The occupation of eastern Poland by the Red Army is to be
sure a 'lesser evil' in comparison with the occupation of the same
territory by Nazi troops.   But this lesser evil was obtained
because Hitler was assured of achieving a greater evil.   If somebody sets, or helps to set a house on fire and afterward saves
five out of ten of the occupants of the house in order to convert
them into his own semi-slaves, that is to be sure a lesser evil
than to have burned the entire ten.   But it is dubious that this
firebug merits a medal for the rescue.   If nevertheless a medal
were given to him he should be shot immediately after as in the
case of the hero in one of Victor Hugo's novels.

'Armed Missionaries'

Robespierre once said that people do not like missionaries
with bayonets.   By this he wished to say that it is impossible to
impose revolutionary ideas and institutions on other people
through military violence.   This correct thought does not signify
of course the inadmissibility of military intervention in other
countries in order to co-operate in a revolution.   But such an
intervention, as part of a revolutionary international policy, must
be understood by the international proletariat, must correspond
to the desires of the toiling masses of the country on whose
territory the revolutionary troops enter.   The theory of socialism
in one country is not capable, naturally, of creating this active
international solidarity which alone can prepare and justify
armed intervention.   The Kremlin poses and resolves the
question of military intervention, like all other questions of its
policy, absolutely independently of the ideas and feelings of the
international working class.   Because of this, the latest diplomatic
'successes' of the Kremlin monstrously compromise the USSR

and introduce extreme confusion into the ranks of the world proletariat.

Insurrection on Two Fronts

But if the question thus shapes itself—some comrades say—is it proper to speak of the defence of the USSR and the occupied provinces? Is it not more correct to call upon the workers and peasants in both parts of former Poland to arise against Hitler as well as against Stalin? Naturally, this is very attractive. If revolution surges up simultaneously in Germany and in the USSR, including the newly occupied provinces, this would resolve many questions at one blow. But our policy cannot be based upon only the most favourable, the most happy combination of circumstances. The question is posed thus: What to do if Hitler, before he is crushed by revolution, attacks the Ukraine before revolution has smashed Stalin? Will the partisans of the Fourth International in this case fight against the troops of Hitler as they fought in Spain in the ranks of the Republican troops against Franco? We are completely and whole-heartedly for an independent (of Hitler as well as of Stalin) Soviet Ukraine. But what to do if, before having obtained this independence, Hitler attempts to seize the Ukraine which is under the domination of the Stalinist bureaucracy? The Fourth International answers: Against Hitler we will defend this Ukraine enslaved by Stalin.

'Unconditional Defence of the USSR'

What does 'unconditional' defence of the USSR mean? It means that we do not lay any conditions upon the bureaucracy. It means that independently of the motive and causes of the war we defend the social basis of the USSR, if it is menaced by danger on the part of imperialism.

Some comrades say: 'And if the Red Army tomorrow invades India and begins to put down a revolutionary movement there shall we in this case support it?' Such a way of posing a question is not at all consistent. It is not clear above all why India is implicated. Is it not simpler to ask: If the Red Army

menaces workers' strikes or peasant protests against the bureaucracy in the USSR shall we support it or not? Foreign policy is
the continuation of the internal. We have never promised to
support *all* the actions of the Red Army which is an instrument
in the hands of the Bonapartist bureaucracy. We have promised
to defend only the USSR as a workers' state and solely those
things within it which belong to a workers' state.

An adroit casuist can say: If the Red Army, independently of
the character of the 'work' fulfilled by it, is beaten by the insur-
gent masses in India, this will weaken the USSR. To this we
will answer: The crushing of a revolutionary movement in India,
with the co-operation of the Red Army, would signify an incomparably greater danger to the social basis of the USSR than
an episodical defeat of counter-revolutionary detachments of the
Red Army in India. In every case the Fourth International will
know how to distinguish where and when the Red Army is
acting solely as an intrument of the Bonapartist reaction and
where it defends the social basis of the USSR.

A trade union led by reactionary fakers organizes a strike
against the admission of Negro workers into a certain branch of
industry. Shall we support such a shameful strike? Of course
not. But let us imagine that the bosses, utilizing the given
strike, make an attempt to crush the trade union and to make
impossible in general the organized self-defence of the workers.
In this case we will defend the trade union as a matter of course
in spite of its reactionary leadership. Why is not this same
policy applicable to the USSR?

The Fundamental Rule

The Fourth International has established firmly that in all
imperialist countries, independent of the fact as to whether they
are in alliance with the USSR or in a camp hostile to it, the
proletarian parties during the war must develop the class struggle
with the purpose of seizing power. At the same time the
pro!etariat of the imperialist countries must not lose sight of the

interests of the USSR's defence (or of that of colonial revolutions) and in case of real necessity must resort to the most
decisive action, for instance, strikes, acts of sabotage, etc. The
groupings of the powers since the time the Fourth International
formulated this rule have changed radically. But the rule itself
retains all its validity. If England and France tomorrow menace
Leningrad or Moscow, the British and French workers should
take the most decisive measures in order to hinder the sending
of soldiers and military supplies. If Hitler finds himself constrained by the logic of the situation to send Stalin military
supplies, the German workers, on the contrary, would have no
reason for resorting in this concrete case to strikes or sabotage.
Nobody, I hope, will propose any other solution.

'Revision of Marxism'?

Some comrades evidently were surprised that I spoke in my
article ('The USSR in the War') of the system of 'bureaucratic
collectivism' as a theoretical possibility. They discovered in this
even a complete revision of Marxism. This is an apparent
misunderstanding. The Marxist comprehension of historical
necessity has nothing in common with fatalism. Socialism is not
realizable 'by itself', but as a result of the struggle of living
forces, classes and their parties. The proletariat's decisive
advantage in this struggle resides in the fact that it represents
historical progress, while the bourgeoisie incarnates reaction and
decline. Precisely in this is the source of our conviction in
victory. But we have full right to ask ourselves: What character
will society take if the forces of reaction conquer?

Marxists have formulated an incalculable number of times the
alternative: either socialism or return to barbarism. After the
Italian 'experience' we repeated thousands of times: either
communism or fascism. The real passage to socialism cannot
fail to appear incomparably more complicated, more heterogeneous, more contradictory than was foreseen in the general
historical scheme. Marx spoke about the dictatorship of the

proletariat and its future withering away but said nothing about bureaucratic degeneration of the dictatorship. We have observed and analysed for the first time in experience such a degeneration. Is this revision of Marxism?

The march of events has succeeded in demonstrating that the delay of the socialist revolution engenders the indubitable phenomena of barbarism—chronic unemployment, pauperization of the petty-bourgeoisie, fascism, finally wars of extermination which do not open up any new road. What social and political forms can the new 'barbarism' take, if we admit theoretically that mankind should not be able to elevate itself to socialism? We have the possibility of expressing ourselves on this subject more concretely than Marx. Fascism on one hand, degeneration of the Soviet state on the other outline the social and political forms of a neo-barbarism. An alternative of this kind—socialism or totalitarian servitude—has not only theoretical interest, but also enormous importance in agitation, because in its light the necessity for socialist revolution appears most graphically.

If we are to speak of a revision of Marx, it is in reality the revision of those comrades who project a new type of state, 'non-bourgeois' and 'non-worker'. Because the alternative developed by me leads them to draw their own thoughts up to their logical conclusion, some of these critics, frightened by the conclusions of their own theory, accuse me . . . of revising Marxism. I prefer to think that it is simply a friendly jest.

The Right of Revolutionary Optimism

I endeavoured to demonstrate in my article 'The USSR in the War' that the perspective of a non-worker and non-bourgeois society of exploitation, or 'bureaucratic collectivism', is the perspective of complete defeat and the decline of the international proletariat, the perspective of the most profound historical pessimism. Are there any genuine reasons for such a perspective? It is not superfluous to inquire about this among our class enemies.

In the weekly of the well-known newspaper *Paris-Soir* of August 31, 1939, an extremely instructive conversation is reported between the French ambassador Coulondre and Hitler on August 25, at the time of their last interview. (The source of the information is undoubtedly Coulondre himself.) Hitler sputters, boasts of the pact which he concluded with Stalin ('a realistic pact') and 'regrets' that German and French blood will be spilled.

'But,' Coulondre objects, 'Stalin displayed great double-dealing. The real victor (in case of war) will be Trotsky. Have you thought this over?'

'I know,'—der Fuehrer responds, 'but why did France and Britain give Poland complete freedom of action?', etc.

These gentlemen like to give a personal name to the spectre of revolution. But this of course is not the essence of this dramatic conversation at the very moment when diplomatic relations were ruptured. 'War will inevitably provoke revolution', the representative of imperialist democracy, himself chilled to the marrow, frightens his adversary.

'I know', Hitler responds, as if it were a question decided long ago. 'I know'. Astonishing dialogue!

Both of them, Coulondre and Hitler, represent the barbarism which advances over Europe. At the same time neither of them doubts that their barbarism will be conquered by socialist revolution. Such is now the awareness of the ruling classes of all the capitalist countries of the world. Their complete demoralization is one of the most important elements in the relation of class forces. The proletariat has a young and still weak revolutionary leadership. But the leadership of the bourgeoisie rots on its feet. At the very outset of the war which they could not avert, these gentlemen are convinced in advance of the collapse of their regime. This fact alone must be for us the source of invincible revolutionary optimism!

October 18, 1939.

The Referendum and Democratic Centralism*

We demand a referendum on the war question because we want to paralyse or weaken the centralism of the imperialist state. But can we recognize the referendum as a normal method for deciding issues in our own party? It is not possible to answer this question except in the negative.

Whoever is in favour of a referendum recognizes by this that a party decision is simply an arithmetical total of branch decisions, every one of the branches being inevitably restricted by its own forces and by its limited experience. Whoever is in favour of a referendum must be in favour of imperative mandates; that is, in favour of such a procedure that every local has the right to *compel* its representative at a party convention to vote in a definite manner. Whoever recognizes imperative mandates automatically denies the significance of conventions as the highest organ of the party. Instead of a convention it is sufficient to introduce a counting of local votes. The party as a centralized whole disappears. By accepting a referendum the influence of the most advanced branches and most experienced and far-sighted comrades of the capital or industrial centres is substituted for the influence of the least experienced, backward sections, etc.

Naturally we are in favour of an all-sided examination and of voting upon every question by each party branch, by each party cell. But at the same time every delegate chosen by a branch must have the right to weigh all the arguments relating to the question in the convention and to vote as his political judgement demands of him. If he votes in the convention against the majority which delegated him, and if he is not able to convince his organization of his correctness after the convention, then the organization can subsequently deprive him of its political confidence. Such cases

---

* In the course of its factional struggle, the minority put forward the demand for a referendum on the issue in dispute concerning the USSR. The majority opposed this. Trotsky came out in support of the majority's rejection of a referendum.—Ed.

are inevitable. But they are incomparably a lesser evil than the system of referendums or imperative mandates which completely kill the party as a whole.

Coyoacan, D. F., October 21, 1939.

A letter to Sherman Stanley†

October 22, 1939.

Dear Comrade Stanley:

It is with some delay that I answer your letter of October 11.

(1) You say that 'there can be no serious differences or disagreements' on the Russian question. If this is so, why the terrible alarm in the party against the National Committee, i.e., its majority? You should not substitute your own conceptions for that of the minority members of the National Committee who considered the question serious and burning enough to provoke a discussion just at the threshold of the war.

(2) I cannot agree with you that my statement does not contradict that of Comrade M. S. The contradiction concerns two fundamental points:

(a) the class nature of the U.S.S.R.
(b) the defence of the U.S.S.R.

On the first question, Comrade M. S. places a question mark, which signifies that he denies the old decision and postpones making a new decision. A revolutionary party cannot live between two decisions, one annihilated, the other not presented. In the question of the defence of the U.S.S.R. or the new occupied territories against Hitler's (or Great Britain's) attack, Comrade M.S. proposes a revolution against Stalin and Hitler. This abstract formula signifies negating the defence in a concrete situation. I attempted to analyse this question in a new article sent yesterday by airmail to the National Committee.

(3) I agree with you completely that only a serious discussion can clarify the matter, but I don't believe that voting simultaneously for the statement of the majority and that of Comrade M. S. could contribute to the necessary clarification.

(4) You state in your letter that the main issue is not the Russian question but the 'internal regime'. I have heard this accusation often since almost the very beginning of the existence of our movement in the United States. The formulations varied

a bit, the groupings too, but a number of comrades always remained in opposition to the 'regime'. They were, for example, against the entrance into the Socialist Party (not to go further into the past). However it immediately occurred that not the entrance was the 'main issue' but the regime. Now the same formula is repeated in connection with the Russian question.

(5) I for my part believe that the passage through the Socialist Party was a salutary action for the whole development of our party and that the 'regime' (or the leadership) which assured this passage was correct against the opposition which at that time represented the tendency of stagnation.

(6) Now at the beginning of the war a new sharp opposition arises on the Russian question. It concerns the correctness of our programme elaborated through innumerable disputes, polemics, and discussions during at least ten years. Our decisions are of course not eternal. If somebody in a leading position has doubts and only doubts, it is his duty toward the party to clarify himself by fresh studies or by discussions inside the leading party bodies before throwing the question into the party—not in the form of elaborated new decisions, but in the form of doubts. Of course from the point of view of the statutes of the party, everybody, even a member of the Political Committee, has the right to do so, but I don't believe that this right was used in a sound manner which could contribute to the amelioration of the party regime.

(7) Often in the past I have heard accusations from comrades against the National Committee as a whole—its lack of initiative, and so on. I am not the attorney of the National Committee and I am sure that many things have been omitted which should have been done. But whenever I insisted upon concretization of the accusations, I learned often that the dissatisfaction with their own local activity, with their own lack of initiative, was transformed into an accusation against the National Committee which was supposed to be Omniscient, Omnipresent, Omnibenevolent.

(8) In the present case the National Committee is accused of

conservatism'. I believe that to defend the old programmatic decision until it is replaced by a new one is the elementary duty of the National Committee. I believe that such 'conservatism' is dictated by the self-preservation of the party itself.

(9) Thus in two most important issues of the last period comrades dissatisfied with the 'regime' have had in my opinion a false political attitude. The regime must be an instrument for correct policy and not for false. When the incorrectness of their policy becomes clear, then its protagonists are often tempted to say that not this special issue is decisive but the general regime. During the development of the Left Opposition and the Fourth International we opposed such substitutions hundreds of times. When Vereecken or Sneevliet or even Molinier were beaten on all their points of difference, they declared that the genuine trouble with the Fourth International is not this or that decision but the bad regime.

(10) I don't wish to make the slightest analogy between the leaders of the present opposition in our American party and the Vereeckens, Sneevliets and so on; I know very well that the leaders of the opposition are highly qualified comrades and I hope sincerely that we will continue to work together in the most friendly manner. But I cannot help being disquieted by the fact that some of them repeat the same error at every new stage of the development of the party with the support of a group of personal adherents. I believe that in the present discussion this kind of procedure must be analysed and severely condemned by the general opinion of the party which now has tremendous tasks to fulfil.

With best comradely greetings,
CRUX [*Leon Trotsky*]

P.S.—In view of the fact that I speak in this letter about the majority and the minority of the National Committee, especially of the comrades of the M.S. resolution, I am sending a copy of this letter to Comrades Cannon and Shachtman.

A letter to James P. Cannon*

October 28, 1939

Dear Jim,

Two things are clear to me from your letter of October 24: (1) that a very serious ideological fight has become inevitable and politically necessary; (2) that it would be extremely prejudicial if not fatal to connect this ideological fight with the perspective of a split, of a purge, or expulsions, and so on and so forth.

I heard for example that Comrade Gould proclaimed in a membership meeting: 'You wish to expel us.' But I don't know what reaction came from the other side to this. I for my part would immediately protest with the greatest vehemence such suspicions. I would propose the creation of a special control commission in order to check such affirmations and rumours. If it happens that someone of the majority launches such threats I for my part would vote for a censure or severe warning.

You have many new members and uneducated youth. They need a serious educational discussion in the light of the great events. If their thoughts at the beginning are obsessed by the perspective of personal *degradation,* i.e., demotions, loss of prestige, disqualifications, eliminations from Central Committee, etc., and so on, the whole discussion would become envenomed and the authority of the leadership would be compromised.

If the leadership on the contrary opens a ruthless fight against petty-bourgeois idealistic conceptions and organizational prejudices but at the same time assures all the necessary guarantees for the discussion itself and for the minority, the result would be not only an ideological victory but an important growth in the authority of the leadership.

---

* This letter was inadvertently omitted from the volume *In Defense of Marxism* and was printed for the first time in James P. Cannon's *The Struggle for a Proletarian Party,* pp. 98-99, footnote **.

'A conciliation and compromise at the top' on the questions
which form the matter of divergences would of course be a
crime. But I for my part would propose to the minority at the
top an agreement, if you wish, a compromise on the methods of
discussion and parallely on the political collaboration. For
example (a) both sides eliminate from the discussion any threats,
personal denigration, and so on; (b) both sides take the obligation
of loyal collaboration during the discussion; (c) every false move
(threats, or rumours of threats, or a rumour of alleged threats,
resignations, and so on) should be investigated by the National
Committee or a special commission as a particular fact and not
thrown into the discussion and so on.

If the minority accepts such an agreement you will have the
possibility of disciplining the discussion and also the advantage
of having taken a good initiative. If they reject it you can at
every party membership meeting present your written proposition
to the minority as the best refutation of their complaints and as
a good example of 'our regime'.

It seems to me that the last convention failed at a very bad
moment (the time was not ripe) and became a kind of abortion.
The genuine discussion comes some time after the convention.
This signifies that you can't avoid a new convention at Christmas
or so. The idea of a referendum is absurd. It could only
facilitate a split on local lines. But I believe that the majority
in the above-mentioned agreement can propose to the minority
a new convention on the basis of two platforms with all the
organizational guarantees for the minority.

The convention is expensive but I don't see any other means
of concluding the present discussion and the party crisis it
produces.

J. HANSEN [*Leon Trotsky*]

P.S.—Every serious and sharp discussion can of course lead to
some desertions, departures, or even expulsions, but the whole
party should be convinced from the logic of the facts that they

are inevitable results occurred in spite of the best will of the leadership, and not an objective or aim of the leadership, and not the point of departure of the whole discussion. This is in my mind the decisive point of the whole matter.

A letter to Max Shachtman†

November 6, 1939.

Dear Comrade Shachtman:

I received the transcript of your speech of October 15* which you sent me, and I read it, of course, with all the attention it deserves. I found a lot of excellent ideas and formulations which seemed to me in full accordance with our common position as it is expressed in the fundamental documents of the Fourth International. But what I could not find was an explanation for your attack upon our previous position as 'insufficient, inadequate and outdated'.

You say that 'It is the concreteness of the events which differ from our theoretical hypothesis and predictions that changes the situation.' (Page 17.) But unfortunately you speak about the 'concreteness' of the events very abstractly so that I cannot see in what respect they change the situation and what are the consequences of these changes for our politics. You mention some examples from the past. Hence, according to you, we 'saw and foresaw' the degeneration of the Third International (page 18); but only after the Hitler victory did we find it necessary to proclaim the Fourth International. This example is not formulated exactly. We foresaw not only the degeneration of the Third International but also the possibility of its regeneration. Only the German experience of 1929-1933 convinced us that the Comintern was doomed and nothing could regenerate it. But then we changed our policy fundamentally: to the Third International we opposed the Fourth International.

But we did not draw the same conclusions concerning the Soviet state. Why? The Third International was a party, a selection of people on the basis of ideas and methods. This selection became so fundamentally opposed to Marxism that we

---

* This speech was delivered to a membership meeting of the New York organization of the Socialist Workers Party. It is reproduced in the Internal Bulletin, Vol. II, No. 3, issued on November 14, 1939.—Ed.

were obliged to abandon all hope of regenerating it. But the Soviet state is not only an ideological selection, it is a complex of social institutions which continues to persist in spite of the fact that the ideas of the bureaucracy are now almost the opposite of the ideas of the October Revolution. That is why we did not renounce the possibility of regenerating the Soviet state by political revolution. Do you believe now that we must change this attitude? If not, and I am sure that you don't propose it, where is the fundamental change produced by the 'concreteness' of events?

In this connection you quote the slogan of the *independent Soviet Ukraine* which, as I see with satisfaction, you accept. But you add: 'As I understand our basic position it always was to oppose separatist tendencies in the Federated Soviet Republic.' (Page 19.) In respect to this you see a fundamental 'change in policy'. But: (1) The slogan of an independent Soviet Ukraine was proposed before the Hitler-Stalin pact. (2) This slogan is only an application in the field of the national question of our general slogan for the revolutionary overthrow of the bureaucracy. You could with the same right say: 'As I understand our basic position it was always to oppose any rebellious acts against the Soviet government.' Of course, but we changed this basic position several years ago. I don't really see what new change you propose in this connection now.

You quote the march of the Red Army in 1920 into Poland and into Georgia and you continue: 'Now, if there is nothing new in the situation, why does not the majority propose to hail the advance of the Red Army into Poland, into the Baltic countries, into Finland. . . .' (Page 20.) In this decisive part of your speech you establish that something is 'new in the situation' between 1920 and 1939. Of course! This newness in the situation is the bankruptcy of the Third International, the degeneracy of the Soviet state, the development of the Left Opposition, and the creation of the Fourth International. This 'concreteness of events' occurred precisely between 1920 and

1939. And these events explain sufficiently why we have radically changed our position toward the politics of the Kremlin, including its military politics.

It seems that you forget somewhat that in 1920 we supported not only the deeds of the Red Army but also the deeds of the GPU. From the point of view of our appreciation of the state there is no principled difference between the Red Army and the GPU. In their activities they are not only closely connected but intermeshed. We can say that in 1918 and the following years we hailed the Cheka in their fight against Russian counter-revolutionaries and imperialist spies but in 1927 when the GPU began to arrest, to exile and to shoot the genuine Bolsheviks we changed our appreciation of this institution. This concrete change occurred at least 11 years before the Soviet-German pact. That is why I am rather astonished when you speak sarcastically about 'the refusal even (!) of the majority to take the same position today that we all took in 1920. . . .' (Page 20.) We began to change this position in 1923. We proceeded by stages more or less in accordance with the objective developments. The decisive point of this evolution was for us 1933-34. If we fail to see just what the new fundamental changes are which you propose in our policy, it doesn't signify that we go back to 1920!

You insist especially on the necessity of abandoning the slogan for the unconditional defence of the USSR, whereupon you interpret this slogan in the past as our unconditional support of every diplomatic and military action of the Kremlin; i.e., of Stalin's policy. No, my dear Shachtman, this presentation doesn't correspond to the 'concreteness of events'. Already in 1927 we proclaimed in the Central Committee: 'for the socialist fatherland? Yes! For the Stalinist course? No!' (*The Stalin School of Falsification*, p. 177.) Then you seem to forget the so-called 'thesis on Clemenceau' which signified that in the interests of the genuine defence of the USSR, the proletarian vanguard can be obliged to eliminate the Stalin government and replace it with its own. This was proclaimed in 1927! Five years later we explained to the workers that this change of government can be effectuated only by political revolution. Thus we separated fundamentally our defence of the USSR as a *workers' state* from the bureaucracy's defence of the USSR. Whereupon you interpret our past policy as unconditional support of the diplomatic and military activities of Stalin! Permit me to say that this is a horrible deformation of our whole position not only since the creation of the Fourth International but since the very beginning of the Left Opposition.

Unconditional defence of the USSR signifies, namely, that our policy is not determined by the deeds, manoeuvres or crimes of the Kremlin bureaucracy but only by our conception of the interests of the Soviet state and world revolution.

At the end of your speech you quote Trotsky's formula concerning the necessity of subordinating the defence of the nationalized property in the USSR to the interests of the world revolution, and you continue: 'Now my understanding of our position in the past was that we vehemently deny any possible conflict between the two. . . . I never understood our position in the past to mean that we *subordinate* the one to the other. If I understand English, the term implies either that there is a conflict between the two or the possibility of such a conflict.' (page 37.) And from this you draw the impossibility of maintaining the slogan of unconditional defence of the Soviet Union.

This argument is based upon at least two misunderstandings. How and why could the interests of maintaining the nationalized property be in 'conflict' with the interests of the world revolution? Tacitly you infer that the *Kremlin's* (not our) policy of defence can come into conflict with the interests of the world revolution. Of course! At every step! In every respect! However our policy of defence is not conditioned by the Kremlin's policy. This is the first misunderstanding. But, you ask, if there is not a conflict why the necessity of subordination? Here is the second misunderstanding. We must subordinate the defence of the USSR to the world revolution insofar as we subordinate a *part* to a *whole*. In

1918 in the polemics with Bukharin, who insisted upon a revolutionary war against Germany, Lenin answered approximately: 'If there should be a revolution in Germany now, then it would be our duty to go to war even at the risk of losing. Germany's revolution is more important than ours and we should if necessary sacrifice the Soviet power in Russia (for a while) in order to help establish it in Germany.' A strike in Chicago at this time could be unreasonable in and of itself, but if it is a matter of helping a general strike on the national scale, the Chicago workers should subordinate their interests to the interests of their class and call a strike. If the USSR is involved in the war on the side of Germany, the German revolution could certainly menace the immediate interests of the defence of the USSR. Would we advise the German workers not to act? The Comintern would surely give them such advice, but not we. We will say: 'We must subordinate the interests of the defence of the Soviet Union to the interests of the world revolution.'

Some of your arguments are, it seems to me, answered in Trotsky's last article, 'Again and Once More Again on the Nature of the USSR', which was written before I received the transcript of your speech.

You have hundreds and hundreds of new members who have not passed through our common experience. I am fearful that your presentation can lead them into the error of believing that we were unconditionally for the support of the Kremlin, at least on the international field, that we didn't foresee such a possibility as the Stalin-Hitler collaboration, that we were taken unawares by the events, and that we must fundamentally change our position. That is not true! And independently from all the other questions which are discussed or only touched upon in your speech (leadership, conservatism, party regime and so on) we must, in my opinion, again check our position on the Russian question with all the necessary carefulness in the interests of the American section as well as of the Fourth International as a whole.

The real danger now is not the 'unconditional' defence of that which is worthy of defence, but direct or indirect help to the political current which tries to identify the USSR with the fascist states for the benefit of the democracies, or to the related current which tries to put all tendencies in the same pot in order to compromise Bolshevism or Marxism with Stalinism. We are the only party which really foresaw the events, not in their empirical concreteness, of course, but in their general tendency. Our strength consists in the fact that we do not need to change our orientation as the war begins. And I find it very false that some of our comrades, moved by the factional fight for a 'good regime' (which they, so far as I know, have never defined), persist in shouting: 'We were taken unawares! Our orientation turned out to be false! We must improvise a new line! And so on.' This seems to me completely incorrect and dangerous.

With warmest comradely greetings,

LUND [*Leon Trotsky*]

CC to J. P. Cannon.

P.S.—The formulations in this letter are far from perfect since it is not an elaborated article, but only a letter dictated by me in English and corrected by my collaborator during the dictation.

L.

A Letter to James P. Cannon†

December 15, 1939.

Dear Comrade Cannon,

The leaders of the opposition have not accepted the struggle upon a principled plane up to now and will undoubtedly attempt to avoid it even in the future. It is not difficult consequently to guess what the leaders of the opposition will say in regard to the enclosed article. 'There are many correct elementary truths in the article', they will say; 'we don't deny them at all, but the article fails to answer the burning "concrete" questions. Trotsky is too far from the party to be able to judge correctly. Not all petty-bourgeois elements are with the opposition, not all workers with the Majority.' Some of them will surely add that the article 'ascribes' ideas to them which they have never entertained, etc.

For answers to 'concrete' questions, the oppositionists want recipes from a cookbook for the epoch of imperialist wars. I don't intend to write such a cookbook. But from our principled approach to the fundamental questions we shall always be able to arrive at a correct solution for any concrete problem, complicated though it might be. Precisely in the Finnish problem the opposition demonstrated its incapacity to answer concrete questions.

There are never factions which are chemically pure in their composition. Petty-bourgeois elements find themselves necessarily in every workers' party and faction. The question is only who sets the tone. With the opposition the tone is set by the petty-bourgeois elements.

The inevitable accusation that the article ascribes to the opposition ideas which they never entertained is explained by the formlessness and contradictory character of the opposition's ideas which cannot bear the touch of critical analysis. The article 'ascribes' nothing to the leaders of the opposition, it only develops their ideas to the end. Naturally I can see the development of the struggle only from the side-lines. But the general traits of the struggle can often be better observed from the sidelines.

I clasp your hand warmly.

L. TROTSKY

Coyoacan, D. F.

A Petty-Bourgeois Opposition in the Socialist Workers Party

It is necessary to call things by their right names. Now that the positions of both factions in the struggle have become determined with complete clearness, it must be said that the minority of the National Committee is leading a typical petty-bourgeois tendency. Like any petty-bourgeois group inside the socialist movement, the present opposition is characterised by the following features: a disdainful attitude toward theory and an inclination toward eclecticism; disrespect for the tradition of their own organisation; anxiety for personal 'independence' at the expense of anxiety for objective truth; nervousness instead of consistency; readiness to jump from one position to another; lack of understanding of revolutionary centralism and hostility towards it; and finally, inclination to substitute clique ties and personal relationships for party discipline. Not all the members of the opposition of course manifest these features with identical strength. Nevertheless, as always in a variegated bloc the tinge is given by those who are most distant from Marxism and proletarian policy. A prolonged and serious struggle is obviously before us. I make no attempt to exhaust the problem in this article, but I will endeavour to outline its general features.

Theoretical Scepticism and Eclecticism

In the January 1939 issue of the *New International* a long article was published by comrades Burnham and Shachtman, 'Intellectuals in Retreat'. The article, while containing many correct ideas and apt political characterisations, was marred by a fundamental defect if not flaw. While polemicising against opponents who consider themselves—without sufficient reason—above all as proponents of 'theory', the article deliberately did not elevate the problem to a theoretical height. It was absolutely necessary to explain why the American 'radical' intellectuals accept Marxism without the dialectic (a clock without a spring).

The secret is simple. In no other country has there been such rejection of the class struggle as in the land of 'unlimited opportunity'. The denial of social contradictions as the moving force of development led to the denial of the dialectic as the logic of contradictions in the domain of theoretical thought. Just as in the sphere of politics it was thought possible everybody could be convinced of the correctness of a 'just' programme by means of clever syllogisms and society could be reconstructed through 'rational' measures, so in the sphere of theory it was accepted as proved that Aristotelian logic, lowered to the level of 'common sense', was sufficient for the solution of all questions.

Pragmatism, a mixture of rationalism and empiricism, became the national philosophy of the United States. The theoretical methodology of Max Eastman is not fundamentally different from the methodology of Henry Ford—both regard living society from the point of view of an 'engineer' (Eastman—platonically). Historically the present disdainful attitude toward the dialectic is explained simply by the fact that the grandfathers and great-grandmothers of Max Eastman and others did not need the dialectic in order to conquer territory and enrich themselves. But times have changed and the philosophy of pragmatism has entered a period of bankruptcy just as has American capitalism.

The authors of the article did not show, could not and did not care to show, this internal connection between philosophy and the material development of society, and they frankly explained why.

'The two authors of the present article,' they wrote of themselves, 'differ thoroughly on their estimate of the general theory of dialectical materialism, one of them accepting it and the other rejecting it. . . . There is nothing anomalous in such a situation. Though theory is doubtless always in one way or another related to practice, the relation is not invariably direct or immediate; and as we have before had occasion to remark, human beings often act inconsistently. From the point of view of each of the authors there is in the other a certain such inconsistency between "philo-sophical theory" and political practice, which might on some occasion lead to decisive concrete political disagreement. But it does not now, nor has anyone yet demonstrated that agreement or disagreement on the more abstract doctrines of dialectical materialism necessarily affects today's and tomorrow's concrete political issues—and political parties, programmes and struggles are based on such concrete issues. We all may hope that as we go along or when there is more leisure, agreement may also be reached on the more abstract questions. Meanwhile there is fascism and war and unemployment.'

What is the meaning of this thoroughly astonishing reasoning? Inasmuch as *some* people through a bad method *sometimes* reach correct conclusions, and inasmuch as some people through a correct method *not infrequently* reach incorrect conclusions, therefore . . . the method is not of great importance. We shall meditate upon methods sometime when we have more leisure, but now we have other things to do. Imagine how a worker would react upon complaining to his foreman that his tools were bad and receiving the reply: With bad tools it is possible to turn out a good job, and with good tools many people only waste material. I am afraid that such a worker, particularly if he is on piece-work, would respond to the foreman with an unacademic phrase. A worker is faced with refractory materials which show resistance and which because of that compel him to appreciate fine tools, whereas a petty-bourgeois intellectual—alas!—utilises as his 'tools' fugitive observations and superficial generalisations —until major events club him on the head.

To demand that every party member occupy himself with the philosophy of dialectics naturally would be lifeless pedantry. But a worker who has gone through the school of the class struggle gains from his own experience an inclination to-ward dialectical thinking. Even if unaware of this term, he readily accepts the method itself and its conclusions. With a petty bourgeois it is worse. There are of course petty-bourgeois elements organically linked with the workers, who go over to the proletarian point of view without an internal revolution. But these constitute an insignificant minority. The matter is quite different with the academically trained petty bourgeoisie. Their theoretical prejudices have already been given finished form at the school bench. Inasmuch as they succeeded in gaining a great deal of knowledge both useful and useless without the aid of the dialectic, they believe that they can continue excellently through life without it. In reality they dispense with the dialectic only to the extent they fail to check, to polish, and to sharpen theoretically their tools of thought, and to the extent that they fail to break practically from the narrow circle of their daily relationships. When thrown against great events they are easily lost and relapse again into petty-bourgeois ways of thinking.

Appealing to 'inconsistency' as justification for an unprincipled theoretical bloc, signifies giving oneself bad credentials as a Marxist. Inconsistency is not accidental, and in politics it does not appear solely as an individual symptom. Inconsistency usually serves a social function. There are social groupings which cannot be consistent. Petty-bourgeois elements who have not rid themselves of hoary petty-bourgeois tendencies are systematically compelled within a workers' party to make theoretical compromises with their own conscience.

Comrade Shachtman's attitude toward the dialectic method, as manifested in the above-quoted argumentation, cannot be called anything but eclectical scepticism. It is clear that Shachtman became infected with this attitude not in the school of Marx but among the petty-bourgeois intellectuals to whom all forms of scepticism are proper.

Warning and Verification

The article astonished me to such an extent that I immediately wrote to comrade Shachtman: 'I have just read the article you and Burnham wrote on the intellectuals. Many parts are excellent. However, the section on the dialectic is the greatest blow that you, personally, as the editor of the *New International*, could have delivered to Marxist theory. Comrade Burnham says:

"I don't recognise the dialectic." It is clear and everybody has
to acknowledge it. But you say: "I recognise the dialectic, but no
matter; it does not have the slightest importance." Re-read
what you wrote. This section is terribly misleading for the readers
of the *New International* and the best of gifts to the Eastmans
of all kinds. Good! We will speak about it publicly.'

My letter was written January 20, some months before the
present discussion. Shachtman did not reply until March 5,
when he answered in effect that he couldn't understand why
I was making such a stir about the matter. On March 9, I
answered Shachtman in the following words: 'I did not reject
in the slightest degree the possibility of collaboration with the
anti-dialecticians, but only the advisability of writing an article
together where the question of the dialectic plays, or should
play, a very important role. The polemic develops on two planes:
political and theoretical. Your political criticism is OK. Your
theoretical criticism is insufficient; it stops at the point at which
it should just become aggressive. Namely, the task consists of
showing that their mistakes (insofar as they are *theoretical*
mistakes) are products of their incapacity and unwillingness to
think the things through dialectically. This task could be accomplished with a very serious pedagogical success. Instead of this
you declare that dialectics is a private matter and that one
can be a very good fellow without dialectic thinking.' By allying
himself in *this* question with the anti-dialectician Burnham,
Shachtman deprived himself of the possibility of showing why
Eastman, Hook and many others began with a philosophical
struggle against the dialectic but finished with a political struggle
against the socialist revolution. That is, however, the essence of
the question.

The present political discussion in the party has confirmed
my apprehensions and warning in an incomparably sharper form
than I could have expected, or, more correctly, feared. Shachtman's methodological scepticism bore its deplorable fruits in
the question of the   nature of the Soviet state. Burnham

began some time ago by constructing purely empirically, on the basis of his immediate impressions, a non-proletarian and non-bourgeois state, liquidating in passing the Marxist theory of the state as the organ of class rule. Shachtman unexpectedly took an evasive position: 'The question, you see, is subject to further consideration'; moreover, the sociological definition of the USSR does not possess any direct and immediate significance for our 'political tasks' in which Shachtman agrees completely with Burnham. Let the reader again refer to what these comrades wrote concerning the dialectic. Burnham rejects the dialectic. Shachtman seems to accept, but . . . the divine gift of 'inconsistency' permits them to meet on common political conclusions. *The attitude of each of them toward the nature of the Soviet state reproduces point for point their attitude toward the dialectic.*

In both cases Burnham takes the leading role. This is not surprising: he *possesses* a method—pragmatism. Shachtman has no method. He adapts himself to Burnham. Without assuming complete responsibility for the anti-Marxian conceptions of Burnham, he defends his bloc of aggression against the Marxian conceptions with Burnham in the sphere of philosophy as well as in the sphere of sociology. In both cases Burnham appears as a pragmatist and Shachtman as an eclectic. This example has this invaluable advantage that the complete parallelism between Burnham's and Shachtman's positions upon two different planes of thought and upon two questions of primary importance, will strike the eyes even of comrades who have had no experience in purely theoretical thinking. The method of thought can be dialectic or vulgar, conscious or unconscious, but it exists and makes itself known.

Last January we heard from our authors 'But it does not now, nor has anyone yet demonstrated that agreement or disagreement on the more abstract doctrines of dialectical materialism necessarily affects today's and tomorrow's concrete

political issues. . . .' Nor has anyone yet demonstrated! Not more
than a few months passed before Burnham and Shachtman themselves demonstrated that their attitude toward such an 'abstraction' as dialectical materialism found its precise manifestation in
their attitude toward the Soviet state.

To be sure it is necessary to mention that the difference
between the two instances is rather important, but it is of a
political and not a theoretical character. In both cases Burnham
and Shachtman formed a bloc on the basis of rejection and semi-
rejection of the dialectic. But in the first instance that bloc was
directed against the opponents of the proletarian party. In the
second instance the bloc was concluded against the Marxist wing
of their own party. The front of military operations, so to
speak, has changed but the weapon remains the same.

True enough, people are often inconsistent. Human consciousness nevertheless tends toward a certain homogeneity.
Philosophy and logic are compelled to rely upon this homogeneity
of human consciousness and not upon what this homogeneity
lacks, that is, inconsistency. Burnham does not recognise the
dialectic, but the dialectic recognises Burnham, that is, extends
its sway over him. Shachtman thinks that the dialectic has no
importance in political conclusions, but in the political conclusions of Shachtman himself we see the deplorable fruits of his
disdainful attitude toward the dialectic. We should include this
example in the textbooks on dialectical materialism.

Last year I was visited by a young British professor of political
economy, a sympathiser of the Fourth International. During our
conversation on the ways and means of realising socialism, he
suddenly expressed the tendencies of British utilitarianism in
the spirit of Keynes and others: 'It is necessary to determine a
clear economic end, to choose the most reasonable means for
its realisation,' etc. I remarked: 'I see that you are an adversary
of dialectics.' He replied, somewhat astonished: 'Yes, I don't
see any use in it.' 'However,' I replied to him, 'the dialectic
enabled me on the basis of a few of your observations upon

economic problems to determine what category of philosophical thought you belong to—this alone shows that there is an appreciable value in the dialectic.' Although I have received no word about my visitor since then, I have no doubt that this anti-dialectic professor maintains the opinion that the USSR is not a workers' state, that unconditional defence of the USSR is an 'out-moded' opinion, that our organisational methods are bad, etc. If it is possible to place a given person's general type of thought on the basis of his relation to concrete practical problems, it is also possible to predict approximately, knowing his general type of thought, how a given individual will approach one or another practical question. That is the incomparable educational value of the dialectical method of thought.

The ABC of Materialist Dialectics

Gangrenous skeptics like Souvarine believe that 'nobody knows' what the dialectic is. And there are 'Marxists' who kowtow reverently before Souvarine and hope to learn something from him. And these Marxists hide not only in the *Modern Monthly*. Unfortunately a current of Souvarinism exists in the present opposition of the SWP. And here it is necessary to warn young comrades: Beware of this malignant infection!

The dialectic is neither fiction nor mysticism, but a science of the forms of our thinking insofar as it is not limited to the daily problems of life but attempts to arrive at an understanding of more complicated and drawn-out processes. The dialectic and formal logic bear a relationship similar to that between higher and lower mathematics.

I will here attempt to sketch the substance of the problem in a very concise form. The Aristotelian logic of the simple syllogism starts from the proposition that 'A' is equal to 'A'. This postulate is accepted as an axiom for a multitude of practical human actions and elementary generalisations. But in reality 'A' is not equal to 'A'. This is easy to prove if we observe these two letters under a lens—they are quite different from each

other. But, one can object, the question is not of the size or the
form of the letters, since they are only symbols for equal
quantities, for instance, a pound of sugar. The objection is
beside the point; in reality a pound of sugar is never equal to a
pound of sugar—a more delicate scale always discloses a difference. Again one can object: but a pound of sugar is equal
to itself. Neither is this true—all bodies change uninterruptedly
in size, weight, colour, etc. They are never equal to themselves.
A sophist will respond that a pound of sugar is equal to itself 'at
any given moment.' Aside from the extremely dubious practical
value of this 'axiom', it does not withstand theoretical criticism
either. How should we really conceive the word 'moment'? If it
is an infinitesimal interval of time, then a pound of sugar is
subjected during the course of that 'moment' to inevitable
changes. Or is the 'moment' a purely mathematical abstraction,
that is, a zero of time? But everything exists in time; and existence itself is an uninterrupted process of transformation; time
is consequently a fundamental element of existence. Thus the
axiom 'A' is equal to 'A' signifies that a thing is equal to
itself if it does not change, that is, if it does not exist.

At first glance it could seem that these 'subtleties' are useless
In reality they are of decisive significance. The axiom 'A' is
equal to 'A' appears on one hand to be the point of departure
for all our knowledge, on the other hand the point of departure for
all the errors in our knowledge. To make use of the axiom 'A' is
equal to 'A' with impunity is possible only within certain *limits*.
When quantitative changes in 'A' are negligible for the task at
hand then we can presume that 'A' is equal to 'A'. This is, for
example, the manner in which a buyer and a seller consider a
pound of sugar. We consider the temperature of the sun likewise.
Until recently we considered the buying power of the dollar in the
same way. But quantitative changes beyond certain limits become
converted into qualitative. A pound of sugar subjected to the
action of water or kerosene ceases to be a pound of sugar. A
dollar in the embrace of a president ceases to be a dollar. To

determine at the right moment the critical point where quantity changes into quality is one of the most important and difficult tasks in all the spheres of knowledge including sociology.

Every worker knows that it is impossible to make two completely equal objects. In the elaboration of bearing-brass into cone bearings, a certain deviation is allowed for the cones which should not, however, go beyond certain limits (this is called tolerance). By observing the norms of tolerance, the cones are considered as being equal. ('A' is equal to 'A'.) When the tolerance is exceeded the quantity goes over into quality; in other words, the cone bearings become inferior or completely worthless.

Our scientific thinking is only a part of our general practice including techniques. For concepts there also exists 'tolerance' which is established not by formal logic issuing from the axiom 'A' is equal to 'A', but by the dialectical logic issuing from the axiom that everything is always changing. 'Common sense' is characterised by the fact that it systematically exceeds dialectical 'tolerance'.

Vulgar thought operates with such concepts as capitalism, morals, freedom, workers' state, etc. as fixed abstractions, presuming that capitalism is equal to capitalism, morals are equal to morals, etc. Dialectical thinking analyses all things and phenomena in their continuous change, while determining in the material conditions of those changes that critical limit beyond which 'A' ceases to be 'A', a workers' state ceases to be a workers' state.

The fundamental flaw of vulgar thought lies in the fact that it wishes to content itself with motionless imprints of a reality which consists of eternal motion. Dialectical thinking gives to concepts, by means of closer approximations, corrections, concretisation, a richness of content and flexibility; I would even say a succulence which to a certain extent brings them close to living phenomena. Not capitalism in general, but a given capitalism at a given stage of development. Not a workers' state in general, but a given workers' state in a backward country in an imperialist encirclement, etc.

Dialectical thinking is related to vulgar thinking in the same way that a motion picture is related to a still photograph. The motion picture does not outlaw the still photograph but combines a series of them according to the laws of motion. Dialectics does not deny the syllogism, but teaches us to combine syllogisms in such a way as to bring our understanding closer to the eternally changing reality. Hegel in his *Logic* established a series of laws: change of quantity into quality, development through contradictions, conflict of content and form, interruption of continuity, change of possibility into inevitability, etc., which are just as important for theoretical thought as is the simple syllogism for more elementary tasks.

Hegel wrote before Darwin and before Marx. Thanks to the powerful impulse given to thought by the French Revolution, Hegel anticipated the general movement of science. But because it was only an *anticipation,* although by a genius, it received from Hegel an idealistic character. Hegel operated with ideological shadows as the ultimate reality. Marx demonstrated that the movement of these ideological shadows reflected nothing but the movement of material bodies.

We call our dialectic, materialist, since its roots are neither in heaven nor in the depths of our 'free will', but in objective reality, in nature. Consciousness grew out of the unconscious, psychology out of physiology, the organic world out of the inorganic, the solar system out of nebulae. On all the rungs of this ladder of development, the quantitative changes were transformed into qualitative. Our thought, including dialectical thought, is only one of the forms of the expression of changing matter. There is place within this system for neither God, nor Devil, nor immortal soul, nor eternal norms of laws and morals. The dialectic of thinking, having grown out of the dialectic of nature, possesses consequently a thoroughly materialist character.

Darwinism, which explained the evolution of species through quantitative transformations passing into qualitative, was the highest triumph of the dialectic in the whole field of organic matter. Another great triumph was the discovery of the table of atomic weights of chemical elements and further the transformation of one element into another.

With these transformations (species, elements, etc.) is closely linked the question of classification, equally important in the natural as in the social sciences. Linnaeus' system (18th century), utilising as its starting point the immutability of species, was limited to the description and classification of plants according to their external characteristics. The infantile period of botany is analogous to the infantile period of logic, since the forms of our thought develop like everything that lives. Only decisive repudiation of the idea of fixed species, only the study of the history of the evolution of plants and their anatomy prepared the basis for a really scientific classification.

Marx, who in distinction from Darwin was a conscious dialectician, discovered a basis for the scientific classification of human societies in the development of their productive forces and the structure of the relations of ownership which constitute the anatomy of society. Marxism substituted for the vulgar descriptive classification of societies and states, which even up to now still flourishes in the universities, a materialistic dialectical classification. Only through using the method of Marx is it possible correctly to determine both the concept of a workers' state and the moment of its downfall.

All this, as we see, contains nothing 'metaphysical' or 'scholastic', as conceited ignorance affirms. Dialectic logic expresses the laws of motion in contemporary scientific thought. The struggle against materialist dialectics on the contrary expresses a distant past, conservatism of the petty-bourgeoisie, the self-conceit of university routinists and . . . a spark of hope for an after-life.

The Nature of the USSR
The definition of the USSR given by comrade Burnham, 'not a workers' and not a bourgeois state', is purely negative, wrenched from the chain of historical development, left dangling in mid-air, void of a single particle of sociology and represents simply a theoretical capitulation of pragmatism before a *contradictory* historical phenomenon.

If Burnham were a dialectical materialist, he would have probed the following three questions: (1) What is the historical origin of the USSR? (2) What changes has this state suffered during its existence? (3) Did these changes pass from the quantitative stage to the qualitative? That is, did they create a historically necessary domination by a new exploiting class? Answering these questions would have forced Burnham to draw the only possible conclusion—the USSR is still a degenerated workers' state.

The dialectic is not a magic master key for all questions. It does not replace concrete scientific analysis. But it directs this analysis along the correct road, securing it against sterile wanderings in the desert of subjectivism and scholasticism.

Bruno R. places both the Soviet and fascist regimes under the category of 'bureaucratic collectivism', because the USSR, Italy and Germany are all ruled by bureaucracies; here and there are the principles of planning; in one case private property is liquidated, in another limited, etc. Thus on the basis of the *relative* similarity of *certain* external characteristics of *different* origin, of *different* specific weight, of *different* class significance, a fundamental *identity* of social regimes is constructed, completely in the spirit of bourgeois professors who construct categories of 'controlled economy', 'centralised state', without taking into consideration whatsoever the class nature of one or the other. Bruno R. and his followers, or semi-followers like Burnham, at best remain in the sphere of social classification on the level of Linnaeus, in whose justification it should be remarked however that he lived before Hegel, Darwin and Marx.

Even worse and more dangerous, perhaps, are those eclectics who express the idea that the class character of the Soviet state 'does not matter', and that the direction of our policy is determined by the 'character of the war'. As if the war were an independent super-social substance; as if the character of the war were not determined by the character of the ruling class, that is, by the same social factor that also determines the character of the state. Astonishing how easily some comrades forget the ABC's of Marxism under the blows of events!

It is not surprising that the theoreticians of the opposition who reject dialectic thought capitulate lamentably before the contradictory nature of the USSR. However the contradiction between the social basis laid down by the revolution, and the character of the caste which arose out of the degeneration of the revolution is not only an irrefutable historical fact but also a motor force. In our struggle for the overthrow of the bureaucracy we base ourselves on this contradiction. Meanwhile some ultra-lefts have already reached the ultimate absurdity by affirming that it is necessary to sacrifice the social structure of the USSR in order to overthrow the Bonapartist oligarchy! They have no suspicion that the USSR minus the social structure founded by the October Revolution would be a fascist regime.

Evolution and Dialectics

Comrade Burnham will probably protest that as an evolutionist he is interested in the development of society and state forms not less than we dialecticians. We will not dispute this. Every educated person since Darwin has labelled himself an 'evolutionist'. But a real evolutionist must apply the idea of evolution to his own forms of thinking. Elementary logic, founded in the period when the idea of evolution itself did not yet exist,, is evidently insufficient for the analysis of evolutionary processes. Hegel's logic is the logic of evolution. Only one must not forget that the concept of 'evolution' itself has been completely corrupted and emasculated by university professors and liberal writers to mean peaceful 'progress'. Whoever has come to understand that evolution proceeds through the struggle of antagonistic forces; that a slow accumulation of changes at a certain moment explodes the old shell and brings about a catastrophe, revolution; whoever has learned finally to apply the general laws of evolution to thinking itself, he is a dialectician, as distinguished from vulgar evolutionists. Dialectic training of the mind, as necessary to a revolutionary fighter as finger exercises to a pianist, demands approaching all problems as *processes* and not as *motionless categories*. Whereas vulgar evolutionists, who limit themselves generally to recognising evolution in only certain spheres, content themselves in all other questions with the banalities of 'common sense'.

The American liberal, who has reconciled himself to the existence of the USSR, more precisely to the Moscow bureaucracy, believes, or at least believed until the Soviet-German pact, that the Soviet regime on the whole is a 'progressive thing', that the repugnant features of the bureaucracy ('well, naturally they exist!') will progressively slough away and that peaceful and painless 'progress' is thus assured.

A vulgar petty-bourgeois radical is similar to a liberal 'progressive' in that he takes the USSR as a whole, failing to understand its internal contradictions and dynamics. When Stalin concluded an alliance with Hitler, invaded Poland, and now Finland, the vulgar radicals triumphed; the identity of the methods of Stalinism and fascism was proved! They found themselves in difficulties however when the new authorities invited the population to expropriate the land-owners and capitalists—they had not foreseen this possibility at all! Meanwhile the social revolutionary measures, carried out via bureaucratic military means, not only did not disturb *our,* dialectic, definition of the USSR as a degenerated workers' state, but gave it the most incontrovertible corroboration. Instead of utilising this triumph of Marxian analysis for persevering agitation, the petty-bourgeois oppositionists began to shout with criminal light-mindedness that the events have refuted our prognosis, that our old formulas are no longer applicable, that new words are necessary. What words? They haven't decided yet themselves.

Defence of the USSR

We began with philosophy and then went to sociology. It became clear that in both spheres, of the two leading personalities of the opposition, one had taken an anti-Marxian, the other an eclectic position. If we now consider politics, particularly the question of the defence of the USSR, we will find that just as great surprises await us.

The opposition discovered that our formula of 'unconditional defence of the USSR', the formula of our programme, is 'vague, abstract and out-moded (!?)'. Unfortunately they do not explain under what future 'conditions' they are ready to defend the conquests of the revolution. In order to give at least an ounce of sense to their new formula, the opposition attempts to represent the matter as if up to now we had 'unconditionally' defended the international policy of the Kremlin government with its Red Army and GPU. Everything is turned upside down! In reality for a long time we have not defended the Kremlin's international policy, not even conditionally, particularly since the time that we openly proclaimed the necessity of crushing the Kremlin oligarchy through insurrection! A wrong policy not only mutilates the current tasks but also compels one to represent his own past in a false light.

In the above-quoted article in the *New International*, Burnham and Shachtman cleverly labelled the group of disillusioned intellectuals 'The League of Abandoned Hopes', and persistently asked what would be the position of this deplorable League in case of military conflict between a capitalistic country and the Soviet Union. 'We take this occasion, therefore,' they wrote, 'to demand from Hook, Eastman and Lyons *unambiguous* declarations on the question of defence of the Soviet Union from attack by Hitler or Japan—or for that matter by England. . . .' Burnham

and Shachtman did not lay down any 'conditions', they did not
specify any 'concrete' circumstances, and at the same time they
demanded an 'unambiguous' reply. '. . . Would the League
(of Abandoned Hopes) also refrain from taking a position or
would it declare itself neutral?' they continued; 'In a word, is it
for the defence of the Soviet Union from imperialist attack,
regardless and in spite of the Stalinist regime?' (My emphasis.)
A quotation to marvel at! And this is exactly what our programme declares. Burnham and Shachtman in January 1939
stood in favour of unconditional defence of the Soviet Union
and defined the significance of unconditional defence entirely
correctly as 'regardless and in spite of the Stalinist regime'.
And yet this article was written when the experience of the
Spanish Revolution had already been drained to completion.
Comrade Cannon is absolutely right when he says that the
role of Stalinism in Spain was incomparably more criminal than
in Poland or Finland. In the first case the bureaucracy through
hangman's methods strangled a socialist revolution. In the
second case it gives an impulse to the socialist revolution through
bureaucratic methods. Why did Burnham and Shachtman themselves so unexpectedly shift to the position of the 'League of
Abandoned Hopes'? Why? We cannot consider Shachtman's
super-abstract references to the 'concreteness of events' as an
explanation. Nevertheless, it is not difficult to find an explanation. The Kremlin's participation in the Republican camp in
Spain was supported by the bourgeois democrats all over the
world. Stalin's work in Poland and Finland is met with frantic
condemnation from the same democrats. In spite of all its
noisy formulae the opposition happens to be a reflection inside
the Socialist Workers Party of the moods of the 'left' petty
bourgeoisie. This fact unfortunately is incontrovertible.

'Our subjects,' wrote Burnham and Shachtman about the
League of Abandoned Hopes, 'take great pride in believing that
they are contributing something "fresh," that they are "re-
evaluating in the light of new experiences", that they are "not

dogmatists" ("conservatives"?—L.T.) who refuse to re-examine their "basic assumption", etc. What a pathetic self-deception! None of them has brought to light any new facts, given any new understanding of the present or future.' Astonishing quotation! Should we not add a new chapter to their article, 'Intellectuals in Retreat'? I offer comrade Shachtman my collaboration. . . .

How is it possible that outstanding individuals like Burnham and Shachtman, unconditionally devoted to the cause of the proletariat, could become so frightened of the not so frightening gentlemen of the League of Abandoned Hopes! On the purely theoretical plane the explanation in respect to Burnham rests in his incorrect method, in respect to Shachtman in his disregard for method. Correct method not only facilitates the attainment of a correct conclusion, but, connecting every new conclusion with the preceding conclusions in a consecutive chain, fixes the conclusions in one's memory. If political conclusions are made empirically, if inconsistency is proclaimed as a kind of advantage, then the Marxian system of politics is invariably replaced by impressionism—in so many ways characteristic of petty-bourgeois intellectuals. Every new turn of events catches the empiricist-impressionist unawares, compels him to forget what he himself wrote yesterday, and produces a consuming desire for new formulae before new ideas have appeared in his head.

The Soviet-Finnish War

The resolution of the opposition upon the question of the Soviet-Finnish war is a document which could be signed, perhaps with slight changes, by the Bordigists, Vereecken, Sneevliet, Fenner Brockway, Marceau Pivert and the like, but in no case by Bolshevik-Leninists. Based exclusively on features of the Soviet bureaucracy and on the mere fact of the 'invasion' the resolution is void of the slightest social content. It places Finland and the USSR on the same level and unequivocally 'condemns, rejects and opposes *both* governments and their armies'. Having noticed, however, that something was not in order, the resolution unexpectedly and without any connection with the text adds: 'In the application (!) of this perspective, the Fourth International will, of course (how marvellous is this "of course"), take into account (!) the differing economic relations in Finland and Russia.' Every word is a pearl. By 'concrete' circumstances our lovers of the 'concrete' mean the military situation, the moods of the masses and in the third place the opposed economic regimes. As to just how these three 'concrete' circumstances will be 'taken into account', the resolution doesn't give the slightest inkling. If the opposition opposes equally 'both governments and their armies' in relation to this war, how will it 'take into account' the differences in the military situation and the social regimes? Definitely nothing of this is comprehensible.

In order to punish the Stalinists for their unquestionable crimes, the resolution, following the petty-bourgeois democrats of all shadings, does not mention by so much as a word that the Red Army in Finland expropriates large land-owners and introduces workers' control while preparing for the expropriation of the capitalists.

Tomorrow the Stalinists will strangle the Finnish workers. But now they are giving—they are compelled to give—a tremendous impulse to the class struggle in its sharpest form. The leaders of the opposition construct their policy not upon the 'concrete' process that is taking place in Finland, but upon democratic abstractions and noble sentiments.

The Soviet-Finnish war is apparently beginning to be supplemented by a civil war in which the Red Army finds itself at the given stage in the same camp as the Finnish petty peasants and the workers, while the Finnish army enjoys the support of the owning classes, the conservative labour bureaucracy and the Anglo-Saxon imperialists. The hopes which the Red Army awakens among the Finnish poor will, unless international revolution intervenes, prove to be an illusion; the collaboration of the Red Army with the poor will be only temporary; the Kremlin will soon turn its weapons against the Finnish workers and peasants. We know all this now and we say it openly as a warning. But in this 'concrete' civil war that is taking place on Finnish territory, what 'concrete' position must the 'concrete' partisans of the Fourth International take? If they fought in Spain in the Republican camp in spite of the fact that the Stalinists were strangling the socialist revolution, all the more must they participate in Finland in that camp where the Stalinists are compelled to support the expropriation of the capitalists.

Our innovators cover the holes in their position with violent phrases. They label the policy of the USSR 'imperialist'. Vast enrichment of the sciences! Beginning from now on both the foreign policy of finance-capital and the policy of exterminating finance-capital will be called imperialism. This will help significantly in the clarification and class education of the workers! But simultaneously—will shout the, let us say, very hasty Stanley —the Kremlin supports the policy of finance-capital in Germany! This objection is based on the substitution of one problem for another, in the dissolving of the concrete into the abstract (the usual mistake of vulgar thought).

If Hitler tomorrow were forced to send arms to the insurrectionary Indians, must the revolutionary German workers oppose this concrete action by strikes or sabotage? On the contrary they must make sure that the insurrectionists receive the arms as soon as possible. We hope that *this* is clear to Stanley. But this example is purely hypothetical. We used it in order to show that even a fascist government of finance-capital can under certain conditions be forced to support a *national* revolutionary movement (in order to attempt to strangle it the next day). Hitler would never under any circumstances support a proletarian revolution for instance in France. As for the Kremlin it is at the present time forced—and this is not a hypothetical but a real situation—to provoke a social revolutionary movement in Finland (in order to attempt to strangle it politically tomorrow). To cover a given social revolutionary movement with the all-embracing term of imperialism only because it is provoked, mutilated and at the same time strangled by the Kremlin merely testifies to one's theoretical and political poverty.

It is necessary to add that the stretching of the concept of 'imperialism' lacks even the attraction of novelty.   At present not only the 'democrats' but also the bourgeoisie of the democratic countries describe Soviet policy as imperialist. The aim of the bourgeoisie is transparent—to erase the social contradictions between capitalistic and Soviet expansion, to hide the problem of property, and in this way to help genuine imperialism. What is the aim of Shachtman and the others? They don't know themselves. Their terminological novelty objectively leads them away from the Marxian terminology of the Fourth International a.)d brings them close to the terminology of the 'democrats'. This circumstance, alas, again testifies to the opposition's extreme sensitivity to the pressure of petty-bourgeois public opinion.

'The Organizational Question'
From the ranks of the opposition one begins to hear more frequently: 'The Russian question isn't of any decisive importance in and of itself; the most important task is to change the party regime.' Change in regime, it is necessary to understand, means a change in leadership, or more precisely, the elimination of Cannon and his close collaborators from directing posts. These clamorous voices demonstrate that the tendency towards a struggle against 'Cannon's faction' preceded that 'concreteness of events' to which Shachtman and others refer in explaining their change of position. At the same time these voices remind us of a whole series of past oppositional groups who took up a struggle on different occasions; and who, when the principled basis began to crumble under their feet, shifted to the so-called 'organisational question'—the case was identical with Molinier, Sneevliet, Vereecken and many others. As disagreeable as these precedents may appear, it is impossible to pass over them.

It would be incorrect, however, to believe that the shifting of the struggle to the 'organisational question' represents a simple 'manoeuvre' in the factional struggle. No, the inner feelings of the opposition tell them, in truth, however confusedly, that the issue concerns not only the 'Russian problem' but rather the entire approach to political problems in general, including also the methods of building the party. And this is in a certain sense correct.

We too have attempted above to prove that the issue concerns not only the Russian problem but even more the opposition's method of thought, which has its social roots. The opposition is under the sway of petty-bourgeois moods and tendencies. This is the essence of the whole matter.

We saw quite clearly the ideological influence of another class in the instances of Burnham (pragmatism) and Shachtman (eclecticism). We did not take into consideration other leaders such as comrade Abern because he generally does not participate in principled discussions, limiting himself to the plane of the 'organisational question'. This does not mean, however, that Abern has no importance. On the contrary, it is possible to say that Burnham and Shachtman are the amateurs of the opposition, while Abern is the unquestionable professional. Abern, and only he, has his own traditional group which grew out of the old Communist Party and became bound together during the first period of the independent existence of the 'Left Opposition'. All the others who hold various reasons for criticism and discontent cling to this group.

Any serious factional fight in a party is always in the final analysis a reflection of the class struggle. The Majority faction established from the beginning the ideological dependence of the opposition upon petty-bourgeois democracy. The opposition, on the contrary, precisely because of its petty-bourgeois character, does not even attempt to look for the social roots of the hostile camp.

The opposition opened up a severe factional fight which is now paralysing the party at a very critical moment. That such a fight could be justified and not pitilessly condemned, very serious

and deep foundations would be necessary. For a Marxist such
foundations can have only a *class* character. Before they began
their bitter struggle, the leaders of the opposition were obligated
to ask themselves this question: What non-proletarian class influence is reflected in the majority of the National Committee?
Nevertheless, the opposition has not made the slightest attempt
at such a class evaluation of the divergencies. It sees only 'conservatism', 'errors', 'bad methods' and similar psychological,
intellectual and technical deficiencies. The opposition is not
interested in the class nature of the opposition faction, just as it
is not interested in the class nature of the USSR. This fact alone
is sufficient to demonstrate the petty-bourgeois character of
the opposition, with its tinge of academic pedantry and journalistic impressionism.

In order to understand what classes or strata are reflected in
the factional fight, it is necessary to study the fight of both
factions historically. Those members of the opposition who affirm
that the present fight has 'nothing in common' with the old
factional struggles, demonstrate once again their superficial attitude toward the life of their own party. The fundamental core
of the opposition is the same which three years ago grouped
itself around Muste and Spector. The fundamental core of the
Majority is the same which grouped itself around Cannon. Of the
leading figures only Shachtman and Burnham have shifted from
one camp to the other. But these personal shifts, important
though they might be, do not change the general character of
the two groups. I will not go into the historical sequence of the
faction fight, referring the reader to the in every respect excellent article by Joseph Hansen, 'Organisational Methods and
Political Principles'.

If we subtract everything accidental, personal and episodical,
if we reduce the present groupings in struggle to their fundamental political types, then indubitably the struggle of comrade
Abern against comrade Cannon has been the most consistent.
In this struggle Abern represents a propagandistic group, petty-

bourgeois in its social composition, united by old personal ties and having almost the character of a family. Cannon represents the proletarian party in process of formation. The historical right in this struggle—independent of what errors and mistakes might have been made—rests wholly on the side of Cannon.

When the representatives of the opposition raised the hue and cry that the 'leadership is bankrupt', 'the prognoses did not turn out to be correct', 'the events caught us unawares', 'it is necessary to change our slogans', all this without the slightest effort to think the questions through seriously, they appeared fundamentally as party defeatists. This deplorable attitude is explained by the irritation and fright of the old propagandistic circle before the new tasks and the new party relations. The sentimentality of personal ties does not want to yield to the sense of duty and discipline. The task that stands before the party is to break up the old clique ties and to dissolve the best elements of the propagandistic past in the proletarian party. It is necessary to develop such a spirit of party patriotism that nobody dare say: 'The reality of the matter is not the Russian question but that we feel more easy and comfortable under Abern's leadership than under Cannon's'.

I personally did not arrive at this conclusion yesterday. I happened to have expressed it tens and hundreds of times in conversation with members of Abern's group. I invariably emphasised the petty-bourgeois composition of this group. I insistently and repeatedly proposed to transfer from membership to candidacy such petty-bourgeois fellow-travellers as proved incapable of recruiting workers for the party. Private letters, conversations and admonitions as has been shown by subsequent events have not led to anything—people rarely learn from someone else's experience. The antagonism between the two party layers and the two periods of its development rose to the surface and took on the character of bitter factional struggle. Nothing remains but to give an opinion, clearly and definitely, to the American section and the whole International. 'Friendship is friendship but duty is duty'—says a Russian proverb.

The following question can be posed: If the opposition is a petty-bourgeois tendency does that signify further unity is impossible? Then how reconcile the petty-bourgeois tendency with the proletarian? To pose the question like this means to judge one-sidedly, undialectically and thus falsely. In the present discussion the opposition has clearly manifested its petty-bourgeois features. But this does not mean that the opposition has no other features. The majority of the members of the opposition are doubly devoted to the cause of the proletariat and are capable of learning. Tied today to a petty-bourgeois milieu they can tomorrow tie themselves to the proletariat. The inconsistent ones, under the influence of experience, can become more consistent. When the party embraces thousands of workers even the professional factionalists can re-educate themselves in the spirit of proletarian discipline. It is necessary to give them time for this. That is why comrade Cannon's proposal to keep the discussion free from any threats of split, expulsions, etc., was absolutely correct and in place.

Nevertheless, it remains not less indubitable that if the party as a whole should take the road of the opposition it could suffer complete destruction. The present opposition is incapable of giving the party Marxian leadership. The majority of the present National Committee expresses more consistently, seriously and profoundly the proletarian tasks of the party than the Minority. Precisely because of this the Majority can have no interest in directing the struggle toward split—correct ideas will win. Nor can the healthy elements of the opposition wish a split—the experience of the past demonstrates very clearly that all the different kinds of improvised groups who split from the Fourth International condemned themselves to sterility and decomposition. That is why it is possible to envisage the next party convention without any fear. It will reject the anti-Marxian novelties of the opposition and guarantee party unity.

December 15, 1939.

A letter to John G. Wright

Dear Friend,   December 19, 1939.

I read your letter to Joe. I endorse completely your opinion about the necessity for a firm even implacable theoretical and political fight against the petty-bourgeois tendencies of the opposition. You will see from my last article, which will be air-mailed to you to-morrow, that I characterise the divergencies of the opposition even more sharply than has the majority. But at the same time, I believe that the implacable ideological fight should go parallel with very cautious and wise organisational tactics. You have not the slightest interest in a split, even if the opposition should become, accidentally, a majority at the next convention. You have not the slightest reason to give the heterogeneous and unbalanced army of the opposition a pretext for a split. Even as an eventual minority, you should in my opinion remain disciplined and loyal towards the party as a whole. It is extremely important for the education in genuine party patriotism, about the necessity of which Cannon wrote me one time very correctly.

A majority composed of this opposition would not last more than a few months. Then the proletarian tendency of the party will again become the majority with tremendously increased authority. Be extremely firm but don't lose your nerve—this applies now more than ever to the strategy of the proletarian wing of the party.

With best comradely greetings and wishes,

Yours,

Coyoacan, D. F.   LEON TROTSKY.

P.S.—The evils came from: (1) Bad composition especially of the most important New York branch; (2) Lack of experience especially by the members who came over from the Socialist Party (Youth). To overcome these difficulties inherited from the past is not possible by exceptional measures. Firmness and patience are necessary.   L.T.

A letter to Max Shachtman†

December 20, 1939.

Dear Comrade Shachtman,

I am sending you a copy of my last article.* You will see from my polemics that I consider the divergences as of decisive character. I believe that you are on the wrong side of the barricades, my dear friend. By your position you give courage to all the petty-bourgeois and anti-Marxist elements to fight our doctrine, our programme, and our tradition. I don't hope to convince you with these lines, but I do express the prognosis that if you refuse now to find a way towards collaboration with the Marxist wing against the petty-bourgeois revisionists, you will inevitably deplore for years and years the greatest error of your life.

If I had the possibility I would immediately take an aeroplane to New York City in order to discuss with you for 48 or 72 hours uninterruptedly. I regret very much that you don't feel in this situation the need to come here to discuss the questions with me. Or do you? I should be happy . . .

L. TROTSKY.

Coyoacan, D. F.

---

* The article referred to is 'A Petty Bourgeois Opposition in the Socialist Workers Party'. See page 56 of this volume.—Ed.

Four Letters to the National Committee Majority†

Coyoacan, D. F.
December 26, 1939.

Dear Friends,

I was previously disposed in favour of transmitting the discussion in the Socialist Appeal and the New International, but I must recognise that your arguments are very serious especially in connection with the arguments of Comrade Burnham.*

The New International and Socialist Appeal are not instruments of the discussion under the control of a special discussion committee, but rather instruments of the Party and its National Committee. In the discussion bulletin the opposition can ask for equal rights with the majority, but the official party publications have the duty to defend the point of view of the Party and the Fourth International until they are changed. A discussion on the pages of the official party publications can be conducted only within the limits established by the majority of the National Committee. It is so self-evident that arguments are not necessary.

The permanent juridical guarantees for the minority surely are not borrowed from the Bolshevik experience. But they are also not an invention of Comrade Burnham; the French Socialist Party has had for a long time such constitutional guarantees which correspond completely to the spirit of envious literary and parliamentary cliques, but never prevent the subjugation of the workers by the coalition of these cliques.

The organisational structure of the proletarian vanguard must be subordinated to the positive demands of the revolutionary fight and not to the negative guarantees against their degeneration. If the Party is not fit for the needs of the socialist revolution, it would degenerate in spite of the wisest juridical

---

* The minority of the National Committee demanded that the discussion be carried in the *Socialist Appeal* and the *New International*. This was rejected by the majority.—Ed.

stipulations. On the organisational field, Burnham shows a complete lack of revolutionary conception of the party, as he showed it on the political field in the small but very significant question of the Dies Committee. In both cases he proposes a purely negative attitude, as, in the question of the Soviet State, he gave a purely negative definition. It is not sufficient to dislike the capitalist society (a negative attitude), it is necessary to accept all the practical conclusions of a social revolutionary conception. Alas, this is not the case of Comrade Burnham.

My practical conclusions?

First, it is necessary to officially condemn before the Party the attempt to annihilate the party line by putting the party programme on the same level with every innovation not accepted by the Party.

Second, if the National Committee finds it necessary to devote one issue of the New International to the discussion (I don't propose it now), it should be done in such a way that the reader sees where the party position is and where the attempt at revision, and that the last word remain with the majority and not with the opposition.

Third, if the internal bulletins are not sufficient, it would be possible to publish a special symposium of articles devoted to the agenda of the convention.

The fullest loyalty in the discussion, but not the slightest concession to the petty-bourgeois, anarchistic spirit!

W. RORK [*Leon Trotsky*]

Coyoacan, D. F.
December 27, 1939

Dear Friends,

I must confess that your communication about the insistences of Comrade Burnham and Shachtman concerning the publication of the controversial articles in the New International and the Socialists Appeal in the first moment surprised me. What can be the reason, I asked myself. That they feel so sure of their position is completely excluded. Their arguments are of a very primitive nature, the contradictions between themselves are sharp and they cannot help but feel that the majority represents the tradition and the Marxist doctrine. They can't hope to issue victorious from a theoretical fight; not only Shachtman and Abern but also Burnham must understand it. What is then the source of their thirst for publicity? The explanation is very simple: they are impatient to justify themselves before the democratic public opinion, to shout to all the Eastmans, Hooks and the others that they, the opposition, are not so bad as we. This inner necessity must be especially imperative with Burnham. It is the same kind of inner capitulation which we observed in Zinoviev and Kamenev on the eve of the October Revolution and by many 'internationalists' under the pressure of the patriotic war wave. If we make abstractions from all the individual peculiarities, accidents or misunderstandings and errors, we have before us the first social patriotic sin-fall in our own party. You established this fact correctly from the beginning, but it appears to me in full clarity only now after they proclaimed their wish to announce—as the Poumists, Pivertists and many others—that they are not so bad as the 'Trotskyites'.

This consideration is a supplementary argument against any concession to them in this field. Under the given conditions, we have the full right to say to them: you must wait for the verdict of the party and not appeal before the verdict is pronounced to the democratic patriotic judges.

I considered the question previously too abstractly, namely, only from the point of view of the theoretical fight, and from this point of view I agree completely with Comrade Goldman that we could only win. But the larger political criterion indicates that we should eliminate the premature intervention of the democratic patriotic factor in our inner party fight and that the opposition should reckon in the discussion only on their own strength as the majority does. Under these conditions the test and the selection of different elements of the opposition would have a more efficient character and the results would be more favourable for the party.

Engels spoke one time about the mood of the enraged petty-bourgeois. It seems to me that a trace of this mood can be found in the ranks of the opposition. Yesterday many of them were hypnotised by the Bolshevik tradition. They never absorbed it innerly but didn't dare to challenge it openly. But Shachtman and Abern gave them this kind of courage and now they openly enjoy the mood of the enraged petty-bourgeois. This is the impression, for example, which I received from the last articles and letters of Stanley. He has lost totally his self-criticism and believes sincerely that every inspiration which visits his brain is worthy of being proclaimed and printed if only it is directed against the programme and tradition of the party. The crime of Shachtman and Abern consists especially in having provoked such an explosion of petty-bourgeois self-satisfaction.

W. RORK [*Leon Trotsky*]

P.S.—It is absolutely sure that the Stalinist agents are working in our midst with the purpose to sharpen the discussion and provoke a split. It would be necessary to check many factional 'fighters' from this special point of view.

W.R.

Jan. 3, 1940.

Dear Friends,

I received the two documents of the opposition,* studied that on bureaucratic conservatism and am now studying the second on the Russian question. What lamentable writings! It is difficult to find a sentence expressing a correct idea or placing a correct idea in the correct place. Intelligent and even talented

---

* These documents were 'The War and Bureaucratic Conservatism' and 'What Is at Issue in the Dispute on the Russian Question'.—Ed.

people occupied an evidently false position and push themselves more and more into a blind alley.

The phrase of Abern about the 'split' can have two senses: either he wishes to frighten you with a split as he did during the entry discussion† or he wishes really to commit political suicide. In the first case, he will of course not prevent our giving a Marxist appreciation of the opposition politics. In the second case, nothing can be done; if an adult person wishes to commit suicide it is difficult to hinder him.

The reaction of Burnham is a brutal challenge to all Marxists. If dialectics is a religion and if it is true that religion is the opium of the people, how can he refuse to fight for liberating his own party from this venom? I am now writing an open letter to Burnham on this question. I don't believe that the public opinion of the Fourth International would permit the editor of the theoretical Marxist magazine to limit himself to rather cynical aphorisms about the foundation of scientific socialism. In any case, I will not rest until the anti-Marxist conceptions of Burnham are unmasked to the end before the Party and the International. I hope to send the open letter, at least the Russian text, the day after tomorrow.

Simultaneously, I am writing an analysis of the two documents. Excellent is the explanation why they agree to disagree about the Russian question.

I grit my teeth upon losing my time in the reading of these absolutely stale documents. The errors are so elementary that it is necessary to make an effort to remember the necessary argument from the ABC of Marxism.

                                        W. RORK [*Leon Trotsky*]

Coyoacan, D. F.

----

† When the American Trotskyists were discussing entrance into the Socialist Party in the first months of 1936 Abern was bitterly opposed to the move.—Ed.

Jan. 4, 1940.

Dear Friends,

I enclose a copy of my letter to Shachtman which I sent more than two weeks ago.* Shachtman didn't even answer me. It shows the mood into which he has pushed himself by his unprincipled fight. He makes a bloc with the anti-Marxist Burnham and he refuses to answer my letters concerning this bloc. The fact in itself is of course of doubtful importance but it has an indisputable symptomatic vein. This is my reason for sending you a copy of my letter to Shachtman.

With best wishes,
L. TROTSKY

Coyoacan, D. F.

---

* See page 82 of this volume.—Ed.

A letter to Joseph Hansen†

Jan. 5, 1940.

Dear Joe,

Thank you for your interesting information. In the case of necessity or of advisability, Jim could publish our correspondence and that with Wright concerning the split matter. This correspondence shows our firm desire to preserve the unity of the party in spite of the sharp factional struggle. I mentioned in my letter to Wright* that even as a minority the Bolshevik wing of the party should in my opinion remain disciplined and Jim answered that he wholeheartedly agreed with that view. These two quotations are decisive for the matter.

Concerning my remarks about Finland in the article on the petty-bourgeois opposition, I will say here only a few words. Is there a principled difference between Finland and Poland—yes or no? Was the intervention of the Red Army in Poland accompanied by civil war—yes or no? The press of the Mensheviks who are very well informed thanks to their friendship with Bund and with PPS emigrés says openly that a revolutionary wave surrounded the advance of the Red Army. And not only in Poland but also in Rumania.

The Kremlin created the Kuusinen government with the evident purpose of supplementing the war by civil war. There was information about the beginning of the creation of a Finnish Red Army, about 'enthusiasm' of poor Finnish farmers in the occupied regions where the large land properties were confiscated, and so on. What is this if not the beginning of civil war?

The further development of the civil war depended completely upon the advance of the Red Army. The 'enthusiasm' of the people was evidently not hot enough to produce independent insurrections of peasants and workers under the sword of the hangman Mannerheim. The retreat of the Red Army necessarily halted the elements of the civil war at the very beginning.

---

* See page 81 of this volume.—Ed.

If the imperialists help the Finnish bourgeoisie efficiently in defending the capitalist regime, the civil war in Finland would become for the next period impossible. But if, as is more probable, the reinforced detachments of the Red Army more successfully penetrate into the country, we will inevitably observe the process of civil war paralleling the invasion.

We cannot foresee all the military episodes, the ups and downs of purely tactical interest, but they don't change the general 'strategical' line of events. In this case as in all others, the opposition makes a purely conjunctural and impressionistic policy instead of a principled one. (It is not necessary to repeat that the civil war in Finland as was the case in Poland would have a limited, semi-stifled nature and that it can, in the next stage, go over into a civil war between the Finnish masses and the Moscow bureaucracy. We know this at least as clearly as the opposition and we openly warn the masses. But we analyse the process as it is and we don't identify the first stage with the second one.)

With warm wishes and greetings for all friends,

L. TROTSKY

Coyoacan, D. F.

An Open Letter to Comrade Burnham

Dear Comrade:

You have expressed as your reaction to my article on the petty-bourgeois opposition, I have been informed, that you do not intend to argue over the dialectic with me and that you will discuss only the 'concrete questions'. 'I stopped arguing about religion long ago,' you added ironically. I once heard Max Eastman voice this same sentiment.

Is There Logic in Identifying Logic with Religion?

As I understand this, your words imply that the dialectic of Marx, Engels and Lenin belongs to the sphere of religion. What does this assertion signify? The dialectic, permit me to recall once again, is the *logic of evolution*. Just as a machine shop in a plant supplies instruments for all departments, so logic is indispensable for all spheres of human knowledge. If you do not consider logic in general to be a religious prejudice (sad to say, the self-contradictory writings of the opposition incline one more and more toward this lamentable idea), then just which logic do you accept? I know of two systems of logic worthy of attention: the logic of Aristotle (formal logic) and the logic of Hegel (the dialectic). Aristotelian logic takes as its starting point immutable objects and phenomena. The scientific thought of our epoch studies all phenomena in their origin, change and disintegration. Do you hold that the progress of the sciences, including Darwinism, Marxism, modern physics, chemistry, etc., has not influenced in any way the forms of our thought? In other words, do you hold that in a world where everything changes, the syllogism alone remains unchanging and eternal? The Gospel according to St. John begins with the words: 'In the beginning was the Word,' i.e., in the beginning was Reason or the Word (reason expressed in the word, namely, the syllogism). To St. John the syllogism is one of the literary pseudonyms for God. If you consider that the syllogism is immutable, i.e., has neither origin nor development, then it signifies that to you it is the product of divine revelation.

But if you acknowledge that the logical forms of our thought develop in the process of our adaptation to nature, then please take the trouble to inform us just who following Aristotle anaiysed and systematised the subsequent progress of logic. So long as you do not clarify this point, I shall take the liberty of asserting that to identify logic (the dialectic) with religion reveals utter ignorance and superficiality in the basic questions of human thought.

Is the Revolutionist Not Obliged to Fight Against Religion?

Let us grant however that your more than presumptuous innuendo is correct. But this does not improve affairs to your advantage. Religion, as I hope you will agree, diverts attention away from real to fictitious knowledge, away from the struggle for a better life to false hopes for reward in the Hereafter. Religion is the opium of the people. Whoever fails to struggle against religion is unworthy of bearing the name of revolutionist. On what grounds then do you justify your refusal to fight against the dialectic if you deem it one of the varieties of religion?

You stopped bothering yourself long ago, as you say, about the question of religion. But you stopped only *for yourself*. In addition to you, there exist all the others. Quite a few of them. We revolutionists never 'stop' bothering ourselves about religious questions, inasmuch as our task consists in emancipating from the influence of religion, not only ourselves but also the masses. If the dialectic is a religion, how is it possible to renounce the struggle against this opium within one's own party?

Or perhaps you intended to imply that religion is of no political importance? That it is possible to be religious and at the same time a consistent communist and revolutionary fighter? You will hardly venture so rash an assertion. Naturally, we maintain the most considerate attitude toward the religious prejudices of a backward worker. Should he desire to fight for our programme, we would accept him as a party member; but at the same time, our party would persistently educate him in the spirit of materialism and atheism. If you agree with this, how can you refuse to struggle against a 'religion', held, to my knowledge, by the overwhelming majority of those members of your own party who are interested in theoretical questions? You have obviously overlooked this most important aspect of the question.

Among the educated bourgeoisie there are not a few who have broken personally with religion, but whose atheism is solely for their own private consumption; they keep thoughts like these to themselves but in public often maintain that it is well the people have a religion. Is it possible that you hold such a point of view toward your own party? Is it possible that this explains your refusal to discuss with us the philosophic foundations of Marxism? If that is the case, under your scorn for the dialectic rings a note of contempt for the party.

Please do not make the objection that I have based myself on a phrase expressed by you in private conversation, and that you are not concerned with publicly refuting dialectic materialism. This is not true. Your winged phrase serves only as an illustration. Whenever there has been an occasion, for various reasons you have proclaimed your negative attitude toward the doctrine which constitutes the theoretical foundation of our programme. This is well known to everyone in the party. In the article 'Intellectuals in Retreat', written by you in collaboration with Shachtman and published in the party's theoretical organ, it is categorically affirmed that you reject dialectic materialism. Doesn't the party have the right after all to know just why? Do you really assume that in the Fourth International an editor of a theoretical organ can confine himself to the bare declaration: 'I decisively reject dialectical materialism'—as if it were a question of a proffered cigarette: 'Thank you, I don't smoke?' The question of a correct philosophical doctrine, that is, a correct method of thought, is of decisive significance to a revolutionary party just as a good machine shop is of decisive significance to production. It is still possible to defend the old society with the material and intellectual methods inherited from the past. It is absolutely unthinkable that this old society can be overthrown and a new one constructed without first critically analysing the current methods. If the party errs in the very foundations of its thinking it is your elementary duty to point out the correct road. Otherwise your conduct will be interpreted inevitably as the cavalier attitude of an academician toward a proletarian organisation which, after all, is incapable of grasping a real 'scientific' doctrine. What could be worse than that?

Instructive Examples

Anyone acquainted with the history of the struggles of tendencies within workers' parties knows that desertions to the camp of opportunism and even to the camp of bourgeois reaction began not infrequently with rejection of the dialectic. Petty-bourgeois intellectuals consider the dialectic the most vulnerable point in Marxism and at the same time they take advantage of the fact that it is much more difficult for workers to verify differences on the philosophical than on the political plane. This long known fact is backed by all the evidence of experience. Again, it is impermissible to discount an even more important fact, namely, that all the great and outstanding revolutionists—first and foremost, Marx, Engels, Lenin, Luxemburg, Franz Mehring—stood on the ground of dialectic materialism. Can it be assumed that all of them were incapable of distinguishing between science and religion? Isn't there too much presumptuousness on your part, comrade Burnham? The examples of Bernstein, Kautsky and Franz Mehring are extremely instructive. Bernstein categorically rejected the dialectic as 'scholasticism' and 'mysticism'. Kautsky maintained indifference toward the question of the dialectic, somewhat like comrade Shachtman. Mehring was a tireless propagandist and defender of dialectic materialism. For decades he followed all the innovations of philosophy and literature, indefatigably exposing the reactionary essence of idealism, neo-Kantianism, utilitarianism, all forms of mysticism, etc. The political fate of these three individuals is very well known. Bernstein ended his life as a smug petty-bourgeois democrat; Kautsky, from a centrist, became a vulgar opportunist. As for Mehring, he died a revolutionary communist.

In Russia three very prominent academic Marxists, Struve, Bulgakov and Berdyaev began by rejecting the philosophic doctrine of Marxism and ended in the camp of reaction and the orthodox church. In the United States, Eastman, Sidney Hook and their friends utilised opposition to the dialectic as cover for their transformation from fellow travellers of the proletariat to fellow travellers of the bourgeoisie. Similar examples by the score could be cited from other countries. The example of Plekhanov, which appears to be an exception, in reality only proves the rule. Plekhanov was a remarkable propagandist of dialectic materialism, but during his whole life he never had the opportunity of participating in the actual class struggle. His thinking was divorced from practice. The revolution of 1905 and subsequently the World War flung him into the camp of petty-bourgeois democracy and forced him in actuality to renounce dialectic materialism. During the World War Plekhanov came forward openly as the protagonist of the Kantian categorical imperative in the sphere of international relations: 'Do not do unto other as you would not have them do unto you.' The example of Plekhanov only proves that dialectic materialism *in and of itself* still does not make a man a revolutionist.

Shachtman on the other hand argues that Liebknecht left a posthumous work against dialectic materialism which he had written in prison. Many ideas enter a person's mind while in prison which cannot be checked by association with other people. Liebknecht, whom nobody, least of all himself, considered a theoretician, became a symbol of heroism in the world labour movement. Should any of the American opponents of the dialectic display similar self-sacrifice and independence from patriotism during war, we shall render what is due to him as a revolutionist. But that will not thereby resolve the question of the dialectic method.

It is impossible to say what Liebknecht's own final conclusions would have been had he remained at liberty. In any case before publishing his work, undoubtedly he would have shown it to his more competent friends, namely, Franz Mehring and Rosa Luxemburg. It is quite probable that on their advice he would have simply tossed the manuscript into the fire. Let us grant however that against the advice of people far excelling him in the sphere of theory he nevertheless had decided to publish his work. Mehring, Luxemburg, Lenin and others would not of course have proposed that he be expelled for this from the party; on the contrary, they would have intervened decisively in his behalf had anyone made such a foolish proposal. But at the same time they would not have formed a philosophical bloc with him, but rather would have differentiated themselves decisively from his theoretical mistakes.

Comrade Shachtman's behaviour, we note, is quite otherwise. 'You will observe,' he says—and this to teach the youth!— 'that Plekhanov was an outstanding theoretician of dialectic materialism but ended up an opportunist; Liebknecht was a remarkable revolutionist but he had his doubts about dialectic materialism.' This argument if it means anything at all signifies that dialectic materialism is of no use whatsoever to a revolutionist. With these examples of Liebknecht and Plekhanov, artificially torn out of history, Shachtman reinforces and 'deepens' the idea of his last year's article, namely, that politics does not depend on method, inasmuch as method is divorced from politics through the divine gift of inconsistency. By falsely interpreting two 'exceptions', Shachtman seeks to overthrow the rule. If this is the argument of a 'supporter' of Marxism, what can we expect from an opponent? The revision of Marxism passes here into its downright liquidation; more than that, into the liquidation of every doctrine and every method.

What Do You Propose Instead?

Dialectic materialism is not of course an eternal and immutable philosophy. To think otherwise is to contradict the spirit of the dialectic. Further development of scientific thought will undoubtedly create a more profound doctrine into which dialectic materialism will enter merely as structural material. However, there is no basis for expecting that this philosophic revolution will be accomplished under the decaying bourgeois regime, without mentioning the fact that a Marx is not born every year or every decade. The life-and-death task of the proletariat now consists not in *interpreting* the world anew but in *remaking* it from top to bottom. In the next epoch we can expect great revolutionists of action but hardly a new Marx. Only on the basis of socialist culture will mankind feel the need to review the ideological heritage of the past and undoubtedly will far surpass us not only in the sphere of economy but also in the sphere of intellectual creation. The regime of the Bonapartist bureaucracy in the USSR is criminal not only because it creates an ever-growing inequality in all spheres of life but also because it degrades the intellectual activity of the country to the depths of the unbridled blockheads of the GPU.

Let us grant however that contrary to our supposition the proletariat is so fortunate during the present epoch of wars and revolutions as to produce a new theoretician or a new constellation of theoreticians who will surpass Marxism and in particular advance logic beyond the materialistic dialectics. It goes without saying that all advanced workers will learn from the new teachers and the old men will have to re-educate themselves again. But in the meantime this remains the music of the future. Or am I mistaken? Perhaps you will call my attention to those works which should supplant the system of dialectic materialism for the proletariat? Were these at hand surely you would not have refused to conduct a struggle against the opium of the dialectic. But none exist. While attempting to discredit the philosophy of Marxism you do not propose anything with which to replace it.

Picture to yourself a young amateur physician who proceeds to argue with a surgeon using a scalpel that modern anatomy, neurology, etc. are worthless, that much in them remains unclear and incomplete and that only 'conservative bureaucrats' could set to work with a scalpel on the basis of these pseudo-sciences, etc. I believe that the surgeon would ask his irresponsible colleague to leave the operating room. We too, comrade Burnham, cannot yield to cheap innuendos about the philosophy of scientific socialism. On the contrary, since in the course of the factional struggle the question has been posed point-blank, we shall say, turning to all members of the party, especially the youth: Beware of the infiltration of bourgeois scepticism into your ranks. Remember that socialism to this day has not found higher scientific expression than Marxism. Bear in mind that the method of scientific socialism is dialectic materialism. Occupy yourselves with serious study! Study Marx, Engels, Plekhanov, Lenin and Franz Mehring. This is a hundred times more important for you than the study of tendentious, sterile and slightly ludicrous treatises on the conservatism of Cannon. Let the present discussion produce at least this positive result, that the youth attempt to imbed in their minds a serious theoretical foundation for revolutionary struggle!

False Political 'Realism'

In your case, however, the question is not confined to the dialectic. The remarks in your resolution to the effect that you do not now pose for the decision of the party the question of the nature of the Soviet state signify in reality that you *do pose* this question, if not juridically then theoretically and politically. Only infants can fail to understand this. This very statement likewise has another meaning, far more outrageous and pernicious. It means that you divorce politics from Marxist sociology. Yet for us the crux of the matter lies precisely in this. If it is possible to give a correct definition of the state without utilising the method of dialectic materialism; if it is possible correctly to determine politics without giving a class analysis of the state, then the question arises: is there any need whatsoever for Marxism?

Disagreeing among themselves on the class nature of the Soviet state, the leaders of the opposition agree on this, that the foreign policy of the Kremlin must be labelled 'imperialist' and that the USSR cannot be supported 'unconditionally'. (Vastly substantial platform!) When the opposing 'clique' raises the question of the nature of the Soviet state point-blank at the convention (what a crime!) you have in advance agreed . . . to disagree, i.e., to vote differently. In the British 'national' government this precedent occurs of ministers who 'agree to disagree', i.e., to vote differently. But His Majesty's ministers enjoy this advantage, that they are well aware of the nature of *their* state and can afford the luxury of disagreement on *secondary* questions. The leaders of the opposition are far less favourably situated. They permit themselves the luxury of differing on the fundamental question in order to solidarise on secondary questions. If this is Marxism and principled politics then I don't know what unprincipled combinationism means.

You seem to consider apparently that by refusing to discuss dialectic materialism and the class nature of the Soviet state and by sticking to 'concrete' questions you are acting the part of a realistic politician. This self-deception is a result of your inadequate acquantance with the history of the past 50 years of factional struggles in the labour movement. In every principled conflict, without a single exception, the Marxists invariably sought to face the party squarely with the fundamental problems of doctrine and programme, considering that only under this condition could the 'concrete' questions find their proper place and proportion. On the other hand the opportunists of every shade, especially those who had already suffered a few defeats in the sphere of principled discussion, invariably counterposed to the Marxist class analysis 'concrete' conjunctural appraisals which they, as is the custom, formulated under the pressure of bourgeois democracy. Through decades of factional struggle this division of roles has persisted. The opposition, permit me to assure you, has invented nothing new. It is continuing the tradition of revisionism in theory and opportunism in politics.

Toward the close of the last century the revisionist attempts of Bernstein, who in England came under the influence of Anglo-Saxon empiricism and utilitarianism—the most wretched of philosophies!— were mercilessly repulsed. Whereupon the German opportunists suddenly recoiled from philosophy and sociology. At conventions and in the press they did not cease to berate the Marxist 'pedants', who replaced the 'concrete political questions' with general principled considerations. Read over the records of the German social-democracy toward the close of the last and the beginning of the present century—and you will be astonished yourself at the degree to which, as the French say, *le mort saisit le vif* (the dead grip the living)!

You are not unacquainted with the great role played by *Iskra* in the development of Russian Marxism. *Iskra* began with the struggle against so-called 'Economism' in the labour movement and against the Narodniki (Party of the Social Revolutionists). The chief argument of the 'Economists' was that *Iskra* floats in the sphere of theory while they, the 'Economists', propose leading the concrete labour movement. The main argument of the Social Revolutionists was as follows: *Iskra* wants to found a school of dialectic materialism while we want to overthrow Czarist autocracy. It must be said that the Narodnik terrorists took their own words very seriously: bomb in hand they sacrificed their lives. We argued with them: 'Under certain circumstances a bomb is an excellent thing but we should first clarify our own minds.' It is historical experience that the greatest revolution in all history was not led by the party which started out with bombs but by the party which started out with dialectic materialism.

When the Bolsheviks and the Mensheviks were still members of the same party, the pre-convention periods and the convention itself invariably witnessed an embittered struggle over the agenda. Lenin used to propose as first on the agenda such questions as clarification of the nature of the Czarist monarchy, the analysis

of the class character of the revolution, the appraisal of the
stages of the revolution we were passing through, etc., Martov
and Dan, the leaders of the Mensheviks, invariably objected: We
are not a sociological club but a political party; we must come to
an agreement not on the class nature of Czarist economy but on
the 'concrete political tasks'. I cite this from memory but I do
not run any risk of error since these disputes were repeated
from year to year and became stereotyped in character. I
might add that I personally committed not a few sins on this
score myself. But I have learned something since then.

To those enamoured with 'concrete political questions' Lenin
invariably explained that our politics is not of conjunctural but
of principled character; that tactics are subordinate to strategy;
that for us the primary concern of every political campaign is
that it guide the workers from the particular question to the
general, that it teach them the nature of modern society and the
character of its fundamental forces. The Mensheviks always felt
the need urgently to slur over principled differences in their
unstable conglomeration by means of evasions, whereas Lenin
on the contrary posed principled questions point-blank. The
current arguments of the opposition against philosophy and
sociology in favour of 'concrete political questions' is a belated
repetition of Dan's arguments. Not a single new word! How
sad it is that Shachtman respects the principled politics of
Marxism only when it has aged long enough for the archives.

Especially awkward and inappropriate does the appeal to shift
from Marxist theory to 'concrete political questions' sound on
your lips, comrade Burnham, for it was not I but you who
raised the question of the character of the USSR, thereby forcing
me to pose the question of the method through which the class
character of the state is determined. True enough, you withdrew
your resolution. But this factional manoeuvre has no objective
meaning whatsoever. You draw your *political* conclusions from
your *sociological* premise, even if you have temporarily slipped
it into your briefcase. Shachtman draws exactly the same political

conclusions without a sociological premise: he adapts himself to you. Abern seeks to profit equally both from the hidden premise and the absence of a premise for his 'organisational' combinations. This is the real and not the diplomatic situation in the camp of the opposition. You proceed as an anti-Marxist; Shachtman and Abern—as *Platonic* Marxists. Who is worse, it is not easy to determine.

The Dialectic of the Present Discussion

When confronted with the diplomatic front covering the hidden premises and lack of premises of our opponents, we, the 'conservatives', naturally reply: A fruitful dispute over 'concrete questions' is possible only if you clearly specify what class premises you take as your starting point. We are not compelled to confine ourselves to those topics in this dispute which you have selected artificially. Should someone propose that we discuss as 'concrete' questions the invasion of Switzerland by the Soviet fleet or the length of a tail of a Bronx witch, then I am justified in posing in advance such questions as, does Switzerland have a sea coast? Are there witches at all?

Every serious discussion develops from the particular and even the accidental to the general and fundamental. The immediate causes and motives of a discussion are of interest, in most cases, only symptomatically. Of actual political significance are only those problems which the discussion raises in its development. To certain intellectuals, anxious to indict 'bureaucratic conservatism' and to display their 'dynamic spirit', it might seem that questions concerning the dialectic, Marxism, the nature of the state, centralism are raised 'artificially' and that the discussion has taken a 'false' direction. The nub of the matter however consists in this, that discussion has its own objective logic which does not coincide at all with the subjective logic of individuals and groupings. The *dialectic* character of the discussion proceeds from the fact that its objective course is determined by the living conflict of opposing tendencies and not by a preconceived logical plan. The *materialist* basis of the discussion consists in its reflecting the pressure of different classes. Thus, the present discussion in the SWP, like the historic process as a whole, develops—with or without your permission, comrade Burnham—according to the laws of dialectic materialism. There is no escape from these laws.

'Science' Against Marxism and 'Experiments' Against Programme

Accusing your opponents of 'bureaucratic conservatism' (a bare psychological abstraction insofar as no specific social interests are shown underlying this 'conservatism'), you demand in your document that conservative politics be replaced by 'critical and experimental politics—in a word, scientific politics'. (p. 32.) This statement, at first glance so innocent and meaningless with all its pompousness, is in itself a complete exposure. You don't speak of Marxist politics. You don't speak of proletarian politics. You speak of 'experimental', 'critical', 'scientific' politics. Why this pretentious and deliberately abstruse terminology so unusual in our ranks? I shall tell you. It is the product of your adaptation, comrade Burnham, to bourgeois public opinion, and the adaptation of Shachtman and Abern to your adaptation. Marxism is no longer fashionable among the broad circles of bourgeois intellectuals. Moreover if one should mention Marxism, God forbid, he might be taken for a dialectic materialist. It is better to avoid this discredited word. What to replace it with? Why, of course, with 'science', even with Science capitalised. And science, as everybody knows, is based on 'criticism' and 'experiments'. It has its own ring; so solid, so tolerant, so unsectarian, so professorial! With this formula one can enter any democratic salon.

Reread, please, your own statement once again: 'In place of conservative politics, we must put bold, flexible, critical and experimental politics—in a word, scientific politics'. You couldn't have improved it! But this is precisely the formula which all petty-bourgeois empiricists, all revisionists and, last but not least, all political adventurers have counterposed to 'narrow', 'limited', 'dogmatic' and 'conservative' Marxism.

Buffon once said: The style is the man. Political terminology is not only the man but the party. Terminology is one of the elements of the class struggle. Only lifeless pedants can fail to understand this. In your document you painstakingly expunge —yes, no one else but you, comrade Burnham—not only such terms as the dialectic and materialism but also Marxism. You are above all this. You are a man of 'critical', 'experimental' science. For exactly the same reason you culled the label 'imperialism' to describe the foreign policy of the Kremlin. This innovation differentiates you from the too embarrassing terminology of the Fourth International by creating less 'sectarian', less 'religious', less rigorous formulas, common to you and—oh happy coincidence!—bourgeois democracy.

You want to experiment? But permit me to remind you that the workers' movement possesses a long history with no lack of experience and, if you prefer, experiments. This experience so dearly bought has been crystallised in the shape of a definite doctrine, the very Marxism whose name you so carefully avoid. Before giving you the right to experiment, the party has the right to ask: What method will you use? Henry Ford would scarcely permit a man to experiment in his plant who had not assimilated the requisite conclusions of the past development of industry and the innumerable experiments already carried out. Furthermore experimental laboratories in factories are carefully segregated from mass production. Far more impermissible even are witch doctor experiments in the sphere of the labour movement—even though conducted under the banner of anonymous 'science'. For us the science of the workers' movement is Marxism. Nameless social science, Science with a capital letter, we leave these completely at the disposal of Eastman and his ilk.

I know that you have engaged in disputes with Eastman and in some questions you have argued very well. But you debate with him as a representative of your own circle and not as an agent of the class enemy. You revealed this conspicuously in your joint article with Shachtman when you ended up with the unexpected invitation to Eastman, Hook, Lyons and the rest that they take advantage of the pages of the *New International* to promulgate their views. It did not even concern you that they might pose the question of the dialectic and thus drive you out of your diplomatic silence.

On January 20 of last year, hence long prior to this discussion, in a letter to comrade Shachtman I insisted on the urgent necessity of attentively following the internal developments of the Stalinist party. I wrote: 'It would be a thousand times more important than inviting Eastman, Lyons and the others to present their personal sweatings. I was wondering a bit why you gave space to Eastman's last insignificant and arrogant article. He has at his disposal *Harper's Magazine, Modern Monthly, Common Sense,* etc. But I am absolutely perplexed that you personally *invited* these people to besmirch the not-so-numerous pages of the *New International*. The perpetuation of this polemic can interest some *petty-bourgeois intellectuals* but not the revolutionary elements. It is my firm conviction that a certain reorganisation of the *New International* and the *Socialist Appeal* is necessary: more distance from Eastman, Lyons, etc.; and nearer to the workers and, in this sense, to the Stalinist party.'

As always in such cases Shachtman replied inattentively and carelessly. In actuality, the question was resolved by the fact that the enemies of Marxism whom you invited refused to accept your invitation. This episode, however, deserves closer attention. On the one hand, you, comrade Burnham, bolstered by Shachtman, invite bourgeois democrats to send in friendly explanations to be printed in the pages of our party organ. On the other hand, you, bolstered by this same Shachtman, refuse to engage in a debate with me over the dialectic and the class nature of the Soviet state. Doesn't this signify that you, together with your ally Shachtman, have turned your faces somewhat toward the bourgeois semi-opponents and your backs toward your own party? Abern long ago came to the conclusion that Marxism is a doctrine to be honoured but a good oppositional combination is something far more substantial. Meanwhile, Shachtman slips and slides downward, consoling himself with wisecracks. I feel, however, that his heart is a trifle heavy. Upon reaching a certain point, Shachtman will, I hope, pull himself together and begin the upward climb again. Here is the hope that his 'experimental' factional politics will at least turn out to the profit of 'Science'.

'An Unconscious Dialectician'

Using as his text my remark concerning Darwin, Shachtman has stated, I have been informed, that you are an 'unconscious dialectician'. This ambiguous compliment contains an iota of truth. Every individual is a dialectician *to some extent or other,* in most cases, unconsciously. A housewife knows that a certain amount of salt flavours soup agreeably, but that added salt makes the soup unpalatable. Consequently, an illiterate peasant woman guides herself in cooking soup by the Hegelian law of the transformation of quantity into quality. Similar examples from daily life could be cited without end. Even animals arrive at their practical conclusions not only on the basis of the Aristotelian syllogism but also on the basis of the Hegelian dialectic. Thus a fox is aware that quadrupeds and birds are nutritious and tasty. On sighting a hare, a rabbit, or a hen, a fox concludes: this particular creature belongs to the tasty and nutritive type, and —chases after the prey. We have here a complete syllogism, although the fox, we may suppose, never read Aristotle. When the same fox, however, encounters the first animal which exceeds it in size, for example, a wolf, it quickly concludes that quantity passes into quality, and turns to flee. Clearly, the legs of a fox are equipped with Hegelian tendencies, even if not fully conscious ones. All this demonstrates, in passing, that our methods of thought, both formal logic and the dialectic, are not arbitrary constructions of our reason but rather expressions of the actual inter-relationships in nature itself. In this sense, the universe throughout is permeated with 'unconscious' dialectics. But nature did not stop there. No little development occurred before nature's inner relationships were converted into the language of the consciousness of foxes and men, and man was then enabled to generalise these forms of consciousness and transform them into logical (dialectical) categories, thus creating the possibility for probing more deeply into the world about us.

The most finished expression to date of the laws of the dialectic which prevail in nature and in society has been given by Hegel and Marx. Despite the fact that Darwin was not interested in verifying his logical methods, his empiricism—that of a genius —in the sphere of natural science reached the highest dialectic generalisations. In this sense, Darwin was, as I stated in my previous article, an 'unconscious dialectician'. We do not, however, value Darwin for his inability to rise to the dialectic, but for having, despite his philosophical backwardness, explained to us the origin of species. Engels was, it might be pointed out, exasperated by the narrow empiricism of the Darwinian method, although he, like Marx, immediately appreciated the greatness of the theory of natural selection. Darwin, on the contrary, remained, alas, ignorant of the meaning of Marx's sociology to the end of his life. Had Darwin come out in the press against the dialectic or materialism, Marx and Engels would have attacked him with redoubled force so as not to allow his authority to cloak ideological reaction.

In the attorney's plea of Shachtman to the effect that you are an 'unconscious dialectician', the stress must be laid on the word *unconscious*. Shachtman's aim (also partly unconscious) is to defend his bloc with you by degrading dialectic materialism. For in reality, Shachtman is saying: The difference between a 'conscious' and an 'unconscious' dialectician is not so great that one must quarrel about it. Shachtman thus attempts to discredit the Marxist method.

But the evil goes beyond even this. Very many unconscious or semi-unconscious dialecticians exist in this world. Some of them apply the materialist dialectic excellently to politics, even though they have never concerned themselves with questions of method. It would obviously be pedantic blockheadedness to attack such comrades. But it is otherwise with you, comrade Burnham. You are an editor of the theoretical organ whose task it is to educate the party in the spirit of the Marxist method. Yet you are a *conscious opponent of the dialectic* and are not at all an *unconscious dialectician.* Even if you had, as Shachtman insists, successfully followed the dialectic in political questions, i.e., even if you were endowed with a dialectic 'instinct', we would still be compelled to begin a struggle against you, because your dialectic instinct, like other individual qualities, cannot be transmitted to others, whereas the conscious dialectic method can, to one degree or another, be made accessible to the entire party.

The Dialectic and Mr. Dies

Even if you have a dialectic instinct—and I do not undertake to judge this—it is well nigh stifled by academic routine and intellectual hauteur. What we term the class instinct of the worker, accepts with relative ease the dialectic approach to questions. There can be no talk of such a class instinct in a bourgeois intellectual. Only by *consciously* surmounting his petty-bourgeois spirit can an intellectual divorced from the proletariat rise to Marxist politics. Unfortunately, Shachtman and Abern are doing everything in their power to bar this road to you. By their support they render you a very bad service, comrade Burnham.

Bolstered by your bloc, which might be designated as the 'League of Factional Abandon', you commit one blunder after another: in philosophy, in sociology, in politics, in the organisational sphere. Your errors are not accidental. You approach each question by isolating it, by splitting it away from its connection with other questions, away from its connection with social factors, and—independently of international experience. You lack the dialectic method. Despite all your education, in politics you proceed like a witch-doctor.

In the question of the Dies Committee your mumbo-jumbo manifested itself no less glaringly than in the question of Finland. To my arguments in favour of utilising this parliamentary body you replied that the question should be decided not by principled considerations but by some special circumstances known to you alone but which you refrained from specifying. Permit me to tell you what these circumstances were: your ideological dependence on bourgeois public opinion. Although bourgeois democracy, in all its sections, bears full responsibility for the capitalist regime, including the Dies Committee, it is compelled, in the interests of this very same capitalism, shamefacedly to distract attention away from the too naked organs of the regime. A simple division of labour! An old fraud which still continues, however, to operate effectively! As for the workers, to whom you refer vaguely, a section of them, and a very considerable section, is like yourself under the influence of bourgeois democracy. But the average worker, not infected with the prejudices of the labour aristocracy, would joyfully welcome every bold revolutionary word thrown in the very face of the class enemy. And the more reactionary the institution which serves as the arena for the combat, all the more complete is the satisfaction of the worker. This has been proved by historical experience. Dies himself, becoming frightened and jumping back in time, demonstrated how false your position was. It is always better to compel the enemy to retreat than to hide oneself without a battle.

But at this point I see the irate figure of Shachtman rising to stop me with a gesture of protest: 'The opposition bears no responsibility for Burnham's views on the Dies Committee. This question did not assume a factional character,' and so forth and so on. I know all this. As if the only thing that lacked was for the entire opposition to express itself in favour of the tactic of boycott, so utterly senseless in this instance! It is sufficient that the leader of the opposition, who has views and openly expressed them, came out in favour of boycott. If you happened to have outgrown the age when one argues about 'religion', then, let me confess, I had considered that the entire Fourth International had outgrown the age when abstentionism is accounted the most revolutionary of policies. Aside from your lack of method, you revealed in this instance an obvious lack of political sagacity. In the given situation, a revolutionist would not have needed to discuss long before springing through a door flung open by the enemy and making the most of the opportunity. For those members of the opposition who together with you spoke against participation in the Dies Committee—and their number is not so small—it is necessary in my opinion to arrange special elementary courses in order to explain to them the elementary truths of revolutionary tactics which have nothing in common with the pseudo-radical abstentionism of the intellectual circles.

'Concrete Political Questions'

The opposition is weakest precisely in the sphere where it imagines itself especially strong—the sphere of day-to-day revolutionary politics. This applies above all to you, comrade Burnham. Impotence in the face of great events manifested itself in you as well as in the entire opposition most glaringly in the questions of Poland, the Baltic states and Finland. Shachtman began by discovering a philosopher's stone: the achievement of a simultaneous insurrection against Hitler and Stalin in occupied Poland. The idea was splendid; it is only too bad that Shachtman was deprived of the opportunity of putting it into practice. The advanced workers in eastern Poland could justifiably say: 'A simultaneous insurrection against Hitler and Stalin in a country occupied by troops might perhaps be arranged very conveniently from the Bronx; but here, locally, it is more difficult. We should like to hear Burnham's and Shachtman's answer to a "concrete political question": What shall we do between now and the coming insurrection?' In the meantime, the commanding staff of the Soviet army called upon the peasants and workers to seize the land and the factories. This call, supported by armed force, played an enormous role in the life of the occupied country. Moscow papers were filled to overflowing with reports of the boundless 'enthusiasm' of workers and poor peasants. We should and must approach these reports with justifiable distrust: there is no lack of lies. But it is nevertheless impermissible to close one's eyes to facts. The call to settle accounts with the landlords and to drive out the capitalists could not have failed to rouse the spirit of the hounded and crushed Ukrainian and Byelo-Russian peasants and workers who saw in the Polish landlord a double enemy.

In the Parisian organ of the Mensheviks, who are in solidarity with the bourgeois democracy of France and not the Fourth International, it was stated categorically that the advance of the Red Army was accompanied by a wave of revolutionary upsurge, echoes of which penetrated even the peasant masses of Rumania. What adds special weight to the dispatches of this organ is the close connection with the Mensheviks and the leaders of the Jewish Bund, the Polish Socialist Party and other organisations who are hostile to the Kremlin and who fled from Poland. We were therefore completely correct when we said to the Bolsheviks in eastern Poland: 'Together with the workers and peasants, and in the forefront, you must conduct a struggle against the land-lords and the capitalists; do not tear yourself away from the masses, despite all their illusions, just as the Russian revolu-tionists did not tear themselves away from the masses who had not yet freed themselves from their hopes in the Czar (Bloody Sunday, January 22, 1905); educate the masses in the course of the struggle, warn them against naïve hopes in Moscow, but do not tear yourself away from them, fight in their camp, try to extend and deepen their struggle, and to give it the greatest possible independence. Only in this way will you prepare the coming insurrection against Stalin.' The course of events in Poland has completely confirmed this directive, which was a continuation and a development of all our previous policies, particularly in Spain.

Since there is no principled difference between the Polish and Finnish situations, we can have no grounds for changing our directive. But the opposition, who failed to understand the meaning of the Polish events, now tries to clutch at Finland as a new anchor of salvation. 'Where is the civil war in Finland? Trotsky talks of a civil war. We have seen nothing about it in the press,' and so on. The question of Finland appears to the opposition as in principle different from the question of western Ukraine and Byelo-Russia. Each question is isolated and viewed aside and apart from the general course of development. Confounded by the course of events, the opposition seeks each time to support itself on some accidental, secondary, temporary and conjunctural circumstances.

Do these cries about the absence of civil war in Finland signify that the opposition would adopt our policy if civil war were actually to unfold in Finland? Yes or no? If yes, then the opposition thereby condemns its own policy in relation to Poland, since there, despite the civil war, they limited themselves to refusal to participate in the events, while they waited for a simultaneous uprising against Stalin and Hitler. It is obvious, comrade Burnham, that you and your allies have not thought this question through to the end.

What about my assertion concerning a civil war in Finland? At the very inception of military hostilities, one might have conjectured that Moscow was seeking through a 'small' punitive expedition to bring about a change of government in Helsingfors and to establish the same relations with Finland as with the other Baltic states. But the appointment of the Kuusinen government in Terrijoki demonstrated that Moscow had other plans and aims. Dispatches then reported the creation of a Finnish 'Red Army'. Naturally, it was only a question of small formations set up from above. The programme of Kuusinen was issued. Next the dispatches appeared of the division of large estates among poor peasants. In their totality, these dispatches signified an attempt on the part of Moscow to organise a civil war. Naturally, this is a civil war of a special type. It does not arise spontaneously from the depths of the popular masses. It is not conducted under the leadership of the Finnish revolutionary party based on mass support. It is introduced on bayonets from without. It is controlled by the Moscow bureaucracy. All this we know, and we dealt with all this in discussing Poland. Nevertheless, it is precisely a question of civil war, of an appeal to the lowly, to the poor, a call to them to expropriate the rich, drive them out, arrest them, etc. I know of no other name for these actions except civil war.

'But, after all, the civil war in Finland did not unfold,' object the leaders of the opposition. 'This means that your predictions did not materialise,' With the defeat and the retreat of the Red Army, I reply, the civil war in Finland cannot, of course, unfold under the bayonets of Mannerheim. This fact is an argument not against me but against Shachtman; since it demonstrates that in the first stages of war, at a time when discipline in armies is still strong, it is much easier to organise insurrection, and on two fronts to boot, from the Bronx than from Terrijoki.

We did not foresee the defeats of the first detachments of the Red Army. We could not have foreseen the extent to which stupidity and demoralisation reign in the Kremlin and in the tops of the army beheaded by the Kremlin. Nevertheless, what is involved is only a military episode, which cannot determine our political line. Should Moscow, after its first unsuccessful attempt, refrain entirely from any further offensive against Finland, then the very question which today obscures the entire world situation to the eyes of the opposition would be removed from the order of the day. But there is little chance of this. On the other hand, if England, France and the United States, basing themselves on Scandinavia, were to aid Finland with military force, then the Finnish question would be submerged in a war between the USSR and the imperialist countries. In this case, we must assume that

even a majority of the oppositionists would remind themselves
of the programme of the Fourth International.

At the present time, however, the opposition is not interested
in these two variants: either the suspension of the offensive on
the part of the USSR, or the outbreak of hostilities between
the USSR and the imperialist democracies. The opposition is
interested only in the isolated question of the USSR's invasion
of Finland. Very well, let us take this as our starting point. If the
second offensive, as may be assumed, is better prepared and
conducted, then the advance of the Red Army into the country
will again place the question of civil war on the order of the
day, and moreover on a much broader scale than during the
first and ignominiously unsuccessful attempt. Our directive, consequently, remains completely valid so long as the question
itself remains on the agenda. But what does the opposition propose in the event that the Red Army successfully advances into
Finland and civil war unfolds there? The opposition apparently
doesn't think about this at all, for they live from one day to the
next, from one incident to another, clutching at episodes, clinging
to isolated phrases in an editorial, feeding on sympathies and
antipathies. The weakness of empiricists and impressionists is
always revealed most glaringly in their approach to 'concrete
political questions'.

Theoretical Bewilderment and Political Abstentionism

Throughout all the vacillations and convulsions of the opposition, contradictory though they may be, two general features run
like a guiding thread from the pinnacles of theory down to the
most trifling political episodes. The first general feature is the
absence of a unified conception. The opposition leaders split
sociology from dialectic materialism. They split politics from
sociology. In the sphere of politics they split our tasks in Poland
from our experience in Spain—our tasks in Finland from our position on Poland. History becomes transformed into a series of
exceptional incidents; politics becomes transformed into a series

of improvisations. We have here, in the full sense of the term, the disintegration of Marxism, the disintegration of theoretical thought, the disintegration of politics into its constituent elements. Empiricism and its foster-brother, impressionism, dominate from top to bottom. That is why the ideological leadership, comrade Burnham, rests with you as an opponent of the dialectic, as an empiricist, unabashed by his empiricism.

Throughout the vacillations and convulsions of the opposition, there is a second general feature intimately bound to the first, namely, a tendency to refrain from active participation, a tendency to self-elimination, to abstentionism, naturally under cover of ultra-radical phrases. You are in favour of overthrowing Hitler and Stalin in Poland; Stalin and Mannerheim in Finland. And until then, you reject both sides *equally*, in other words, you withdraw from the struggle, including the civil war. Your citing the absence of civil war in Finland is only an accidental conjunctural argument. Should the civil war unfold, the opposition will attempt not to notice it, as they tried not to notice it in Poland, or they will declare that inasmuch as the policy of the Moscow bureaucracy is 'imperialist' in character 'we' do not take part in this filthy business. Hot on the trail of 'concrete' political tasks in words, the opposition actually places itself outside the historical process. Your position, comrade Burnham, in relation to the Dies Committee merits attention precisely because it is a graphic expression of this same tendency of abstentionism and bewilderment. Your guiding principle still remains the same: 'Thank you, I don't smoke.'

Naturally, any man, any party and even any class can become bewildered. But with the petty bourgeoisie, bewilderment, especially in the face of great events, is an inescapable and, so to speak, congenital condition. The intellectuals attempt to express their state of bewilderment in the language of 'science'. The contradictory platform of the opposition reflects petty-bourgeois bewilderment expressed in the bombastic language of the intellectuals. There is nothing proletarian about it.

The Petty-Bourgeoisie and Centralism

In the organisational sphere, your views are just as schematic, empiric, non-revolutionary as in the sphere of theory and politics. A. Stolberg, lantern in hand, chases after an ideal revolution, unaccompanied by any excesses, and guaranteed against Thermidor and counter-revolution; you, likewise, seek an ideal party democracy which would secure for ever and for everybody the possibility of saying and doing whatever popped into his head, and which would insure the party against bureaucratic degeneration. You overlook a trifle, namely, that the party is not an arena for the assertion of free individuality, but an instrument of the proletarian revolution; that only a victorious revolution is capable of preventing the degeneration not only of the party but of the proletariat itself and of modern civilization as a whole. You do not see that our American section is not sick from too much centralism—it is laughable even to talk about it— but from a monstrous abuse and distortion of democracy on the part of petty-bourgeois elements. This is at the root of the present crisis.

A worker spends his day at the factory. He has comparatively few hours left for the party. At the meetings he is interested in learning the most important things: the correct evaluation of the situation and the political conclusions. He values those leaders who do this in the clearest and the most precise form and who keep in step with events. Petty-bourgeois, and especially declassed elements, divorced from the proletariat, vegetate in an artificial and shut-in environment. They have ample time to dabble in politics or its substitute. They pick out faults, exchange all sorts of titbits and gossip concerning happenings among the party 'tops'. They always locate a leader who initiates them into all the 'secrets'. Discussion is their native element. No amount of democracy is ever enough for them. For their war of words they seek the fourth dimension. They become jittery, they revolve in a vicious circle, and they quench their thirst with salt water. Do you want to know the organisational programme of the opposition? It consists of a mad hunt for the fourth dimension of party democracy. In practice this means burying politics beneath discussion; and burying centralism beneath the anarchy of the intellectual circles. When a few thousand workers join the party, they will call the petty-bourgeois anarchists severely to order. The sooner, the better.

Conclusions

Why do I address you and not the other leaders of the opposition? Because you are the ideological leader of the bloc. Comrade Abern's faction, destitute of a programme and a banner, is ever in need of cover. At one time Shachtman served as cover, then came Muste with Spector, and now you, with Shachtman adapting himself to you. Your ideology I consider the expression of bourgeois influence in the proletariat.

To some comrades, the tone of this letter may perhaps seem too sharp. Yet, let me confess, I did everything in my power to restrain myself. For, after all, it is a question of nothing more or less than an attempt to reject, disqualify and overthrow the theoretical foundations, the political principles and organisational methods of our movement.

In reaction to my previous article, comrade Abern, it has been reported, remarked: 'This means split.' Such a response merely demonstrates that Abern lacks devotion to the party and the Fourth International; he is a circle man. In any case, threats of split will not deter us from presenting a Marxist analysis of the differences. For us Marxists, it is a question not of split but of educating the party. It is my firm hope that the coming convention will ruthlesly repulse the revisionists.

The convention, in my opinion, must declare categorically that in their attempts to divorce sociology from dialectic materialism and politics from sociology, the leaders of the opposition have broken from Marxism and become the transmitting mechanism for petty-bourgeois empiricism. While reaffirming, decisively and completely, its loyalty to the Marxist doctrine and the political and organisational methods of Bolshevism, while binding the editorial boards of its official publications to promulgate and defend this doctrine and these methods, the party will, of course, extend the pages of its publications in the future to those of its members who consider themselves capable of adding something new to the doctrine of Marxism. But it will not permit a game of hide-and-seek with Marxism and light-minded gibes concerning it.

The politics of a party has a class character. Without a class analysis of the state, the parties and ideological tendencies, it is impossible to arrive at a correct political orientation. The party must condemn as vulgar opportunism the attempt to determine policies in relation to the USSR from incident to incident and independently of the class nature of the Soviet state.

The disintegration of capitalism, which engenders sharp dissatisfaction among the petty-bourgeoisie and drives its bottom layers to the left, opens up broad possibilities but it also contains grave dangers. The Fourth International needs only those emigrants from the petty bourgeoisie who have broken completely with their social past and who have come over decisively to the standpoint of the proletariat.

This theoretical and political transit must be accompanied by an actual break with the old environment and the establishment of intimate ties with workers, in particular, by participation in the recruitment and education of proletarians for their party. Emigrants from the petty-bourgeois milieu who prove incapable of settling in the proletarian milieu must after the lapse of a certain period of time be transferred from membership in the party to the status of sympathisers.

Members of the party untested in the class struggle must not be placed in responsible positions. No matter how talented and devoted to socialism an emigrant from the bourgeois milieu may be before becoming a teacher, he must first go to school in the working class. Young intellectuals must not be placed at the head of the intellectual youth but sent out into the provinces for a few years, into the purely proletarian centres, for hard practical work.

The class composition of the party must correspond to its class programme. The American section of the Fourth International will either become proletarian or it will cease to exist.

*   *   *

Comrade Burnham! If we can arrive at an agreement with you on the basis of these principles, then without difficulty we shall find a correct policy in relation to Poland, Finland and even India. At the same time, I pledge myself to help you conduct a struggle against any manifestations whatsoever of bureaucratism and conservatism. These in my opinion are the conditions necessary to end the present crisis.

With Bolshevik greetings,
L. TROTSKY

Coyoacan, D. F.
January 7, 1940.

A letter to James P. Cannon†

January 9, 1940

Dear Friend,

Yesterday I sent the Russian text of my new article written in the form of a letter to Burnham. Not all comrades possibly are content with the fact that I give the predominant place in the discussion to the matter of dialectics. But I am sure it is now the only way to begin the theoretical education of the Party, especially of the youth and to inject an aversion to empiricism and eclectics.

W. RORK [*Leon Trotsky*]

A letter to Farrell Dobbs†

January 10, 1940

Dear Friend,

In my article sent for translation to Wright I don't mention at all two questions:

First, that of bureaucratic conservatism. I believe we discussed the matter a bit with you here. As a political tendency, bureaucratic conservatism represents the material interests of a certain social stratum, namely of the privileged workers' bureaucracy in the capitalist, especially in the imperialist states and in an incomparably higher degree in the USSR. It would be fantastic, not to say stupid to search for such roots of the 'bureaucratic conservatism' of the majority. If bureaucratism and conservatism are not determined by social conditions then they represent traits in the personal characters of some leaders. Such things occur. But how explain in this case the formation of a faction? Is it a selection of conservative individualities? We have here a psychological and not a political explanation. If we admit (I personally don't do it) that Cannon for example, has bureaucratic tendencies, then we must inevitably reach the conclusion that the majority supports Cannon *in spite* of this trait and not *because* of it. It signifies that the question of the social foundations of the factional fight isn't even touched by the minority leaders.

Second, in order to compromise my 'defence' of Cannon they insist that I falsely defended Molinier.* I am the last to deny that I can commit mistakes of political nature as well as of personal appreciations. But in spite of all, the argument is not very profound. I never supported the false theories of Molinier. It was namely a question of his personal character: brutality, lack of discipline and his private financial affairs. Some comrades, among them Vereecken, insisted upon immediate separation from

---

* Molinier was one of the leading figures in the French Trotskyist movement. He was expelled from the movement for gross violation of discipline.—Ed.

Molinier. I insisted upon the necessity for the organisation to try to discipline Molinier. But in 1934 when Molinier tried to replace the party programme by 'four slogans' and created a paper on this basis, I was among those who proposed his expulsion. This is the whole story. One can be of different opinion about the wisdom of my patient conduct in regard to Molinier, however I was guided of course not by the personal interests of Molinier, but by the interests of the education of the party: our own sections inherited some Comintern venom in the sense that many comrades are inclined to the abuse of such measures as expulsion, split or threats of expulsions and splits. In the case of Molinier, as in the case of some American comrades (Field, Weisbord and some others), I was for a more patient attitude. In several cases I succeeded, in several others it was a failure. But I don't regret at all my more patient attitude towards some doubtful figures in our movement. In any case, my 'defence' of them was never a bloc at the expense of principles. If somebody should propose, for example, to expel Comrade Burnham, I would oppose it energetically. But at the same time, I find it necessary to conduct the most strenuous ideological fight against his anti-Marxist conceptions.

Yours fraternally,
L. TROTSKY

Coyoacan, D. F.

123

A letter to John G. Wright†

January 13, 1940

Dear Comrade Wright,

I agree completely with your appreciation of the pamphlet of Comrade Shachtman.* It is the *weak* Shachtman multiplied by factional passion. He lacks a small thing which is called the proletarian point of view. He lives in the realm of literary shadows: when he stands with his face toward the proletariat and Marxism, his shadows are useful because they correspond more or less with reality; now he turns his back to the proletarian majority of the party and to Marxism and as a result every word he writes is a fantastic misinterpretation of facts and ideas. I am obliged now to lose again a couple of days to submit his absolutely extravagant document to a more attentative analysis. I hope to show to the party members including the majority of the minority that Shachtman's document is in every line a pathetic rupture with Marxism and with Bolshevism.

Yours fraternally,
L. TROTSKY

---

* The pamphlet referred to is 'The Crisis in the American Party—An Open Letter to Comrade Leon Trotsky', published in Vol. II, No. 7 of the *Internal Bulletin*, dated January 1, 1940.

A letter to James P. Cannon†

January 16, 1940

Dear Friend,

*   *   *

What miserable writing is Shachtman's open letter. Its only merit is that it obliged me to tell him the full truth about his politics. My answer is already dictated, I have only to polish it. Unfortunately it will not be shorter than my letter to Burnham.

L.T.

A letter to William F. Warde†

January 16, 1940

Dear Comrade Warde,

* * *

You are one of the comparatively few comrades who are seriously interested in the methodological questions of our movement. Don't you believe that your intervention in the discussion from *this* point of view would be very useful?

Friends write me that the interest for dialectical materialism in our party, especially in the youth, is becoming very acute. Don't you believe that comrades who could orientate this interest should now create some purely theoretical association with the purpose of promoting in the party the doctrines of dialectical materialism? Yourself, Comrade Wright, Comrade Gerland (very well acquainted with the matter) could possibly form the first nucleus of such an association, of course, under the control of the propaganda department of the National Committee. It is, certainly, only a vague suggestion from afar which should be discussed with the responsible party institutions.

Yours comradely,
LEON TROTSKY

Coyoacan, D.F.

A letter to Joseph Hansen†

January 18, 1940

Dear Joe,

* * *

My article against Shachtman is already written. I need now to polish it for two days, and I will try to use some of your quotations.

But I wish to speak here about another more important question. Some of the leaders of the opposition are preparing a split; whereby they represent the opposition in the future as a persecuted minority. It is very characteristic of their state of mind. I believe we must answer them approximately as follows:

'You are already afraid of our future repressions? We propose to you mutual guarantees for the future minority, independently of who might be this minority, you or we. These guarantees could be formulated in four points: (1) No prohibition of factions; (2) No other restrictions on factional activity than those dictated by the necessity for common action; (3) The official publications must represent, of course, the line established by the new convention; (4) The future minority can have, if it wishes, an internal bulletin destined for party members, or a common discussion bulletin with the majority.'

The continuation of discussion bulletins immediately after a long discussion and a convention is, of course, not a rule but an exception, a rather deplorable one. But we are not bureaucrats at all. We don't have immutable rules. We are dialecticians also in the organisational field. If we have in the party an important minority which is dissatisfied with the decisions of the convention, it is incomparably more preferable to legalise the discussion after the convention than to have a split.

We can go, if necessary, even further and propose to them to publish, under the supervision of the new National Committee, special discussion symposiums, not only for party members, but for the public in general. We should go as far as possible in this respect in order to disarm their at least premature complaints and handicap them in provoking a split.

For my part I believe that the prolongation of the discussion, if it is channellised by the good will of both sides, can only serve in the present conditions the education of the party.

I believe that the majority should make these propositions officially in the National Committee in a written form. Whatever might be their answer, the party could only win.

With best greetings,
CORNELL [*Leon Trotsky*]

Coyoacan, D. F.

From a Scratch—To the Danger of Gangrene

The discussion is developing in accordance with its own internal logic. Each camp, corresponding to its social character and political physiognomy, seeks to strike at those points where its opponent is weakest and most vulnerable. It is precisely this that determines the course of the discusssion and not *a priori* plans of the leaders of the opposition. It is belated and sterile to lament now over the flaring up of the discussion. It is necessary only to keep a sharp eye on the role played by Stalinist provocateurs who are unquestionably in the party and who are under orders to poison the atmosphere of the discussion and to head the ideological struggle toward split. It is not so very difficult to recognise these gentlemen; their zeal is excessive and of course artificial; they replace ideas and arguments with gossip and slander. They must be exposed and thrown out through the joint efforts of both factions. But the principled struggle must be carried through to the end, that is, to serious clarification of the more important questions that have been posed. It is necessary to so utilise the discussion that it raises the theoretical level of the party.

A considerable proportion of the membership of the American section, as well as our entire young International, came to us either from the Comintern in its period of decline or from the Second International. These are bad schools. The discussion has revealed that wide circles of the party lack a sound theoretical education. It is sufficient, for instance, to refer to the circumstances that the New York branch of the party did not respond with a vigorous defensive reflex to the attempts at light-minded revision of Marxist doctrine and programme but on the contrary gave support in the majority to the revisionists. This is unfortunate, but remediable to the degree that our American section and the entire International consist of honest individuals sincerely seeking their way to the revolutionary road. They have the desire and the will to learn. But there is no time to lose. It is precisely the party's penetration into the trade unions and into the workers' milieu in general that demands heightening the theoretical qualification of our cadres. I do not mean by cadres the 'apparatus' but the party as a whole. Every party member should and must consider himself an officer in the proletarian army.

'Since when have you become specialists in the question of philosophy?' the oppositionists now ironically ask the majority representatives. Irony here is completely out of place. Scientific socialism is the conscious expression of the unconscious historical process; namely, the instinctive and elemental drive of the proletariat to reconstruct society on communist beginnings. These organic tendencies in the psychology of workers spring to life with utmost rapidity today in the epoch of crises and wars. The discussion has revealed beyond all question a clash in the party between a petty-bourgeois tendency and a proletarian tendency. The petty-bourgeois tendency reveals its confusion in its attempt to reduce the programme of the party to the small coin of 'concrete' questions. The proletarian tendency on the contrary strives to correlate all the partial questions into theoretical unity. At stake at the present time is not the extent to which individual members of the majority consciously apply the dialectic method. What is important is the fact that the majority as a whole pushes toward the proletarian posing of the questions and by very reason of this tends to assimilate the dialectic which is the 'algebra of the revolution'. The oppositionists, I am informed, greet with bursts of laughter the very mention of 'dialectics'. In vain. This unworthy method will not help. The dialectic of the historic process has more than once cruelly punished those who tried to jeer at it.

Comrade Shachtman's latest article, 'An Open Letter to Leon Trotsky', is an alarming symptom. It reveals that Shachtman refuses to learn from the discussion and persists instead in deepening his mistakes, exploiting thereby not only the inadequate theoretical level of the party but also the specific prejudices of its petty-bourgeois wing. Everybody is aware of the facility with which Shachtman is able to weave various historical episodes around one or another axis. This ability makes Shachtman a talented journalist. Unfortunately, this by itself is not enough. The main question is what axis to select. Shachtman is absorbed always by the reflection of politics in literature and in the press. He lacks interest in the actual processes of the class struggle, the life of the masses, the inter-relationships between the different layers within the working class itself, etc. I have read not a few excellent and even brilliant articles by Shachtman but I have never seen a single commentary of his which actually probed into the life of the American working class or its vanguard.

A qualification must be made to this extent—that not only Shachtman's personal failing is embodied therein, but the fate of a whole revolutionary generation which because of a special conjucture of historical conditions grew up outside the labour movement. More than once in the past I have had occasion to speak and write about the danger of these valuable elements degenerating *despite* their devotion to the revolution. What was an inescapable characteristic of adolescence in its day has become a weakness. Weakness invites disease. If neglected, the disease can become fatal. To escape this danger it is necessary to open a new chapter consciously in the development of the party. The propagandists and journalists of the Fourth International must begin a new chapter in their own consciousness. It is necessary to re-arm. It is necessary to make an about-face on one's own axis: to turn one's back to the petty-bourgeois intellectuals, and to face toward the workers.

To view as the cause of the present party crisis—the conservatism of its worker section; to seek a solution to the crisis through the victory of the petty-bourgeois bloc—it would be difficult to conceive a mistake more dangerous to the party. As a matter of fact, the gist of the present crisis consists in the conservatism of the petty-bourgeois elements who have passed through a purely propagandistic school and who have not yet found a pathway to the road of the class struggle. The present crisis is the final battle of these elements for self-preservation. Every oppositionist as an individual can, if he firmly desires, find a worthy place for himself in the revolutionary movement. As a faction they are doomed. In the struggle that is developing Shachtman is not in the camp where he ought to be. As always in such cases, his strong sides have receded into the background while his weak traits on the other hand have assumed an especially finished expression. His 'Open Letter' represents, so to speak, a crystallisation of his weak traits.

Shachtman has left out a trifle: his class position. Hence his extraordinary zigzags, his improvisations and leaps. He replaces class analysis with disconnected historical anecdotes for the sole purpose of covering up his own shift, for camouflaging the contradiction between his yesterday and today. This is Shachtman's procedure with the history of Marxism, the history of his own party, and the history of the Russian Opposition. In carrying this out he heaps mistakes upon mistakes. All the historical analogies to which he resorts speak, as we shall see, against him.

It is much more difficult to correct mistakes than to commit them. I must ask patience from the reader in following with me step by step all the zigzags of Shachtman's mental operations. For my part I promise not to confine myself merely to exposing mistakes and contradictions, but to counterpose from beginning to end the proletarian position against the petty-bourgeois, the Marxist position against the eclectic. In this way all of us perhaps may learn something from the discussion.

'Precedents'

'How did we, irreconcilable revolutionists, so suddenly become a petty-bourgeois tendency?' Shachtman demands indignantly. Where are the proofs? 'Wherein (has) this tendency manifested itself in the last year (!) or two among the representative spokesmen of the Minority?' (*Internal Bulletin*, Vol. 2, No. 7, Jan. 1940, p. 11.) Why didn't we yield in the past to the influence of the petty-bourgeois democracy? Why during the Spanish Civil War did we .. and so forth and so on. This is Shachtman's trump argument in beginning his polemic against me and the one on which he plays variations in all keys, apparently investing it with exceptional importance. It does not so much as enter Shachtman's mind that I can turn this very argument against him.

The opposition document, 'War and Bureaucratic Conservatism', concedes that Trotsky is right nine times out of ten, perhaps ninety-nine times out of a hundred. I understand only too well the qualified and extremely magnanimous character of this concession. The proportion of my mistakes is in reality considerably greater. How to explain then the fact that two or three weeks after this document was written, Shachtman suddenly decided that Trotsky:

(a) Is incapable of a critical attitude toward information supplied him although one of his informants for ten years has been Shachtman himself.

(b) Is incapable of distinguishing a proletarian tendency from a petty-bourgeois tendency—a Bolshevik tendency from a Menshevik tendency.

(c) Is champion of the absurd conception of 'bureaucratic revolution' in place of revolution by the masses.

(d) Is incapable of working out a correct answer to concrete questions in Poland, Finland, etc.

(e) Is manifesting a tendency to capitulate to Stalinism.

(f) Is unable to comprehend the meaning of democratic centralism—and so on *ad infinitum*.

In a word, during the space of two or three weeks Shachtman has discovered that I make mistakes ninety-nine times out of a hundred, especially where Shachtman himself happens to become involved. It occurs to me that the latest percentage also suffers from slight exaggeration—but this time in the opposite direction. In any event Shachtman discovered my tendency to replace revolution by the masses with 'bureaucratic revolution' far more abruptly than I discovered his petty-bourgeois deviation.

Comrade Shachtman invites me to present proof of the existence of a 'petty-bourgeois tendency' in the party during the past year; or even two-three years. Shachtman is completely justified in not wishing to refer to the more distant past. But in accordance with Shachtman's invitation, I shall confine myself to the last three years. Please pay attention. To the rhetorical questions of my unsparing critic I shall reply with a few exact documents.

I.

On May 25, 1937, I wrote to New York concerning the policy of the Bolshevik-Leninist faction in the Socialist Party:

'. . . I must cite two recent documents: (a) the private letter of "Max" about the convention, and (b) Shachtman's article "Towards a Revolutionary Socialist Party". The title of this article alone characterises a false perspective. It seems to me established by the developments, including the last convention, that the party is evolving, not into a "revolutionary" party, but into a kind of ILP, that is, a miserable centrist political abortion without any perspective.

'The affirmation that the American Socialist Party is now "closer to the position of revolutionary Marxism than any party of the Second or Third Internationals" is an absolutely unmerited compliment: the American Socialist Party is only more backward than the analogous formations in Europe—the POUM, ILP, SAP, etc. . . . Our duty is to unmask this negative advantage of Norman Thomas and Co., and not speak about the "superiority (of the war resolution) over any resolution ever adopted before by the party. . . ." This is a *purely literary appreciation,* because every resolution must be taken in connection with historical events, with the political situation and its imperative needs. . . .'

In both of the documents mentioned in the above letter, Shachtman revealed excessive adaptability toward the left wing of the petty-bourgeois democrats—political mimicry—a very dangerous symptom in a revolutionary politician! It is extremely

important to take note of his high appraisal of the 'radical'
position of Norman Thomas in relation to war . . . in Europe.
Opportunists, as is well known, tend to all the greater radicalism
the further removed they are from events. With this law in mind
it is not difficult to appraise at its true value the fact that
Shachtman and his allies accuse us of a tendency to 'capitulate
to Stalinism'. Alas, sitting in the Bronx, it is much easier to
display irreconcilability toward the Kremlin than toward the
American petty bourgeoisie.

II

To believe comrade Shachtman, I dragged the question of the
class composition of the factions into the dispute by the hair.
Here too, let us refer to the recent past.

On October 3, 1937, I wrote to New York:

'I have remarked hundreds of times that the worker who
remains unnoticed in the "normal" conditions of party life
reveals remarkable qualities in a change of the situation when
general formulas and fluent pens are not sufficient, where acquaintance with life of workers and practical capacities are necessary.
Under such conditions a gifted worker reveals a sureness of
himself and reveals also his general political capabilities.

'Predominance in the organisation of intellectuals is inevitable
in the first period of the development of the organisation. It is
at the same time a big handicap to the political education of
the more gifted workers. . . . It is absolutely necessary at the
next convention to introduce in the local and central committees
as many workers as possible. To a worker, activity in the leading
party body is at the same time a high political school. . . .

'The difficulty is that in every organisation there are traditional committee members and that different secondary, factional
and personal considerations play a too great role in the composition of the list of candidates.'

I have never met either attention or interest from comrade
Shachtman in questions of this kind.

III

To believe comrade Shachtman, I injected the question of comrade Abern's faction as a concentration of petty-bourgeois individuals artificially and without any basis in fact. Yet on October 10, 1937, at a time when Shachtman marched shoulder to shoulder with Cannon and it was considered officially that Abern had no faction, I wrote to Cannon:

'The party has only a minority of genuine factory workers. . . . The non-proletarian elements represent a very necessary yeast, and I believe that we can be proud of the good quality of these elements. . . . But. . . . Our party can be inundated by non-proletarian elements and can even lose its revolutionary character. The task is naturally not to prevent the influx of intellectuals by artificial methods, . . . but to orientate practically all the organisation toward the factories, the strikes, the unions. . . .

'A concrete example: We cannot devote enough or equal forces to all the factories. Our local organisation can choose for its activity in the next period one, two or three factories in its area and concentrate all its forces upon these factories. If we have in one of them two or three workers we can create a special help commission of five non-workers with the purpose of enlarging our influence in these factories.

'The same can be done among the trade unions. We cannot introduce non-worker members in workers' unions. But we can with success build up help commissions for oral and literary action in connection with our comrades in the union. The un-breakable conditions should be: *not to command the workers but only to help them,* to give them suggestions, to arm them with the facts, ideas, factory papers, special leaflets, and so on.

'Such collaboration would have a tremendous educational importance from one side for the worker comrades, from the other side for the non-workers who need a solid re-education.

'You have for example an important number of Jewish non-worker elements in your ranks. They can be a very valuable yeast *if the party suceeds by and by in extracting them from a closed milieu* and ties them to the factory workers by daily activity. I believe *such an orientation would also assure a more healthy atmosphere inside the party.*

'One general rule we can establish immediately: a party member who doesn't win during three or six months a new worker for the party is not a good party member.

'If we establish seriously such a general orientation and if we verified every week the practical results, we will avoid *a great danger;* namely, that the intellectuals and white collar workers might suppress the worker minority, condemn it to silence, *transform the party into a very intelligent discussion club but absolutely not habitable for workers.*

'The same rules should be in a corresponding form elaborated for the working and recruiting of the *youth organisation, otherwise we run the danger of educating good young elements into revolutionary dillettantes and not revolutionary fighters.'*

From this letter it is obvious, I trust, that I did not mention the danger of a petty-bourgeois deviation the day following the Stalin-Hitler pact or the day following the dismemberment of Poland, but brought it forward persistently two years ago and more. Furthermore, as I then pointed out, bearing in mind primarily the 'non-existent' Abern faction, it was absolutely requisite in order to cleanse the atmosphere of the party, that the Jewish petty-bourgeois elements of the New York local be shifted from their habitual conservative milieu and dissolved in the real labour movement. It is precisely because of this that the above letter (not the first of its kind), written more than two years before the present discussion began, is of far greater weight as evidence than all the writings of the opposition leaders on the motives which impelled me to come out in defence of the 'Cannon clique'.

IV

Shachtman's inclination to yield to petty-bourgeois influence, especially the academic and literary, has never been a secret to me. During the time of the Dewey Commission I wrote, on October 14, 1937, to Cannon, Shachtman and Warde:

'. . . I insisted upon the necessity to surround the Committee by delegates of workers' groups in order to create channels from the Committee in the masses. . . . Comrades Warde, Shachtman and others declared themselves in agreement with me on this point. Together we analysed the practical possibilities to realise this plan. . . . But later, in spite of repeated questions from me, I never could have information about the matter and only accidentally I heard that comrade Shachtman was opposed to it. Why? I don't know.'

Shachtman never did divulge his reasons to me. In my letter I expressed myself with the utmost diplomacy but I did not have the slightest doubt that while agreeing with me in words Shachtman in reality was afraid of wounding the excessive political sensibilities of our temporary liberal allies: in *this* direction Shachtman demonstrates exceptional 'delicacy'.

V

On April 15, 1938, I wrote to New York:

'I am a bit astonished about the kind of publicity given to Eastman's letter in the *New International*. The publication of the letter is all right, but the prominence given it on the cover, combined with the silence about Eastman's article in *Harper's*, seems to me a bit compromising for the *New International*. Many people will interpret this fact as our willingness to close our eyes on principles when friendship is concerned.'

VI

On June 1, 1938, I wrote comrade Shachtman:

'It is difficult to understand here why you are so tolerant and even friendly toward Mr. Eugene Lyons. He speaks, it seems, at your banquets; at the same time he speaks at the banquets of the White Guards.'

This letter continued the struggle for a more independent and resolute policy toward the so-called 'liberals', who, while waging a struggle against the revolution, wish to maintain 'friendly relations' with the proletariat, for this doubles their market value in the eyes of bourgeois public opinion.

VII

On October 6, 1938, almost a year before the discussion began, I wrote about the necessity of our party press turning its face decisively toward the workers:

'Very important in this respect is the attitude of the *Socialist Appeal*. It is undoubtedly a very good Marxist paper, but it is not a genuine instrument of political action. . . . I tried to interest the editorial board of the *Socialist Appeal* in this question, but without success.'

A note of complaint is evident in these words. And it is not accidental. Comrade Shachtman as has been mentioned already displays far more interest in isolated episodes of long-ago-concluded struggles than in the social composition of his own party or the readers of his own paper.

VIII

On January 20, 1939, in a letter which I have already cited in connection with dialectic materialism, I once again touched on the question of comrade Shachtman's gravitation toward the milieu of the petty-bourgeois literary fraternity.

'I cannot understand why the *Socialist Appeal* is almost neglecting the Stalinist Party. This party now represents a mass of contradictions. Splits are inevitable. The next important acquisitions will surely come from the Stalinist Party. Our political attention should be concentrated on it. We should follow the development of its contradictions day by day and hour by hour. Someone on the staff ought to devote the bulk of his time to the Stalinists' ideas and actions. We could provoke a discussion and, if possible, publish the letters of hesitating Stalinists.

'It would be a thousand times more important than inviting Eastman, Lyons and the others to present their individual sweatings. I was wondering a bit at why you gave place to Eastman's last insignificant and arrogant article. . . . But I am absolutely perplexed that you, personally, *invite* these people to besmirch the not so numerous pages of the *New International*. The perpetuation of this polemic can interest some *petty-bourgeois intellectuals,* but not the revolutionary elements.

'It is my firm conviction that a certain reorganisation of the *New International* and the *Socialist Appeal* is necessary: more distance from Eastman, Lyons and so on; and nearer the workers and, in this sense, to the Stalinist Party.'

Recent events have demonstrated, sad to say, that Shachtman did not turn away from Eastman and Co. but on the contrary drew closer to them.

IX

On May 27, 1939, I again wrote concerning the character of the *Socialist Appeal* in connection with the social composition of the party:

'From the minutes I see that you are having difficulty with the *Socialist Appeal.* The paper is very well done from the journalistic point of view; but it is a paper for the workers and not a workers' paper. . . .

'As it is, the paper is divided among various writers, each of whom is very good, but collectively they do not permit the workers to penetrate to the pages of the *Appeal*. Each of them speaks for the workers (and speaks very well) but nobody will hear the workers. In spite of its literary brilliance, to a certain degree the paper becomes a victim of journalistic routine. You do not hear at all how the workers live, fight, clash with the police or drink whiskey. It is very dangerous for the paper as a revolutionary instrument of the party. The task is not to make a paper through the joint forces of a skilled editorial board but to encourage the workers to speak for themselves.

'A radical and courageous change is necessary as a condition of success. . . .

'Of course it is not only a question of the paper, but of the whole course of policy. I continue to be of the opinion that you have *too many petty-bourgeois boys and girls* who are very good and devoted to the party, but who do not fully realise that their duty is not to discuss among themselves, but to penetrate into the fresh milieu of workers. I repeat my proposition: Every petty-bourgeois member of the party who, during a certain time, let us say three or six months, does not win a worker for the party, should be demoted to the rank of candidate and after another three months expelled from the party. In some cases it might be unjust, but the party as a whole would receive a salutary shock which it needs very much. A very radical change is necessary.'

In proposing such Draconian measures as the expulsion of those petty-bourgeois elements incapable of linking themselves to the workers, I had in mind not the 'defence' of Cannon's faction but the rescue of the party from degeneration.

X

Commenting on sceptical voices from the Socialist Workers Party which had reached my ears, I wrote comrade Cannon on June 16, 1939:

'The pre-war situation, the aggravation of nationalism and so on is a natural hindrance to our development and the profound cause of the depression in our ranks. But it must now be underlined that *the more the party is petty-bourgeois in its composition, the more it is dependent upon the changes in the official public opinion.* It is a supplementary argument for the necessity for a courageous and active re-orientation toward the masses.

'The pessimistic reasonings you mention in your article are, of course, a reflection of the patriotic, nationalistic pressure of the official public opinion. "If fascism is victorious in France, . . ." "If fascism is victorious in England. . . ." And so on. The victories of fascism are important, but the death agony of capitalism is more important.'

The question of the dependence of the petty-bourgeois wing of the party upon official public opinion consequently was posed several months before the present discussion began and was not at all dragged in artificially in order to discredit the opposition.

*   *   *

Comrade Shachtman demanded that I furnish 'precedents' of petty-bourgeois tendencies among the leaders of the opposition during the past period. I went so far in answering this demand as to single out from the leaders of the opposition comrade Shachtman himself. I am far from having exhausted the material at my disposal. Two letters—one of Shachtman's, the other mine—which are perhaps still more interesting as 'precedents', I shall cite presently in another connection. Let Shachtman not object that the lapses and mistakes in which the correspondence is concerned likewise can be brought against other comrades, including representatives of the present majority. Possibly. Probably. But Shachtman's name is not repeated in this correspondence accidentally. Where others have committed episodic mistakes, Shachtman has evinced a tendency.

In any event, completely opposite to what Shachtman now claims concerning my alleged 'sudden' and 'unexpected' appraisals, I am able, documents in hand, to prove—and I believe have proved—that my article on the 'Petty-Bourgeois Opposition' did no more than summarise my correspondence with New York during the last three years. (In reality the past ten.) Shachtman has very demonstratively asked for 'precedents'. I have given him 'precedents'. They speak entirely against Shachtman.

The Philosophic Bloc Against Marxism
The opposition circles consider it possible to assert that the question of dialectic materialism was introduced by me only

because I lacked an answer to the 'concrete' questions of Finland,
Latvia, India, Afghanistan, Baluchistan and so on. This argument, void of all merit in itself, is of interest however in that it
characterises the level of certain individuals in the opposition,
their attitude toward theory and toward elementary ideological
loyalty. It would not be amiss, therefore, to refer to the fact
that my first serious conversation with comrades Shachtman
and Warde, in the train immediately after my arrival in Mexico
in January 1937, was devoted to the necessity of persistently
propagating dialectic materialism. After our American section
split from the Socialist Party I insisted most strongly on the
earliest possible publication of a theoretical organ, having again
in mind the need to educate the party, first and foremost its new
members, in the spirit of dialectic materialism. In the United
States, I wrote at that time, where the bourgeoisie systematically
instills vulgar empiricism in the workers, more than anywhere
else is it necessary to speed the elevation of the movement to a
proper theoretical level. On January 20, 1939, I wrote to comrade
Shachtman concerning his joint article with comrade Burnham,
'Intellectuals in Retreat':

'The section on the dialectic is the greatest blow that you,
personally, as the editor of the *New International,* could have
delivered to Marxist theory. . . . Good! We will speak about
it publicly.'

Thus a year ago I gave an open notice in advance to Shachtman
that I intended to wage a public struggle against his eclectic
tendencies. At that time there was no talk whatever of the
coming opposition; in any case furthest from my mind was the
supposition that the philosophic bloc against Marxism prepared
the ground for a political bloc against the programme of the
Fourth International.

The character of the differences which have risen to the
surface has only confirmed my former fears both in regard to
the social composition of the party and in regard to the theoretical
education of the cadres. There was nothing that required a

change of mind or 'artificial' introduction. This is how matters stand in actuality. Let me also add that I feel somewhat abashed over the fact that it is almost necessary to justify coming out in defence of Marxism within one of the sections of the Fourth International!

In his 'Open Letter', Shachtman refers particularly to the fact that comrade Vincent Dunne expressed satisfaction over the article on the intellectuals. But I too praised it: 'Many parts are excellent'. However, as the Russian proverb puts it, a spoonful of tar can spoil a barrel of honey. It is precisely this spoonful of tar that is involved. The section devoted to dialectic materialism expresses a number of conceptions monstrous from the Marxist standpoint, whose aim, it is now clear, was to prepare the ground for a political bloc. In view of the stubbornness with which Shachtman persists that I seized upon the article as a pretext, let me once again quote the central passage in the section of interest to us:

'. . . nor has anyone yet demonstrated that agreement or disagreement on the more abstract doctrines of dialectic materialism necessarily affects (!) today's and tomorrow's concrete political issues—and political parties, programmes and struggles are based on such concrete issues.' (The *New International*, January 1939, p. 7.) Isn't this alone sufficient? What is above all astonishing is this formula, unworthy of revolutionists:
. . . political parties, programmes and struggles are based on such concrete issues'. What parties? What programmes? What struggles? All parties and all programmes are here lumped together. The party of the proletariat is a party unlike all the rest. It is not at all based upon 'such concrete issues'. In its very foundation it is diametrically opposed to the parties of bourgeois horse-traders and petty-bourgeois rag patchers. Its task is the preparation of a social revolution and the regeneration of mankind on new material and moral foundations. In order not to give way under the pressure of bourgeois public opinion and police repression, the proletarian revolutionists, a

leader all the more, requires a clear, far-sighted, completely thought-out world outlook. Only upon the basis of a unified Marxist conception is it possible to correctly approach 'concrete' questions.

Precisely here begins Shachtman's betrayal—not a mere mistake as I wished to believe last year; but, it is now clear, an outright theoretical betrayal. Following in the footsteps of Burnham, Shachtman teaches the young revolutionary party that 'no one has yet demonstrated' presumably that dialectic materialism affects the political activity of the party. 'No one has yet demonstrated', in other words, that Marxism is of any use in the struggle of the proletariat. The party consequently does not have the least motive for acquiring and defending dialectic materialism. This is nothing else than reunuciation of Marxism, of scientific method in general, a wretched capitulation to empiricism. Precisely this constitutes the philosophic bloc of Shachtman with Burnham and through Burnham with the priests of bourgeois 'Science'. It is precisely this and only this to which I referred in my January 20 letter of last year.

On March 5, Shachtman replied: 'I have reread the January article of Burnham and Shachtman to which you referred, and while in the light of what you have written I might have proposed a different formulation here (!) and there (!) if the article were to be done over again, I cannot agree with the substance of your criticism'.

This reply, as is always the case with Shachtman in a serious situation, in reality expresses nothing whatsoever; but it still gives the impression that Shachtman has left a bridge open for retreat. Today, seized with factional frenzy, he promises to 'do it again and again tomorrow'. Do what? Capitulate to bourgeois 'Science'? Renounce Marxism?

Shachtman explains at length to me (we shall see presently with what foundation) the utility of this or that *political bloc*. I am speaking about the deadliness of *theoretical betrayal*. A bloc can be justified or not depending upon its content and the circumstances. Theoretical betrayal cannot be justified by any bloc. Shachtman refers to the fact that his article is of purely political character. I do not speak of the article but of that section which renounces Marxism. If a text book on physics contained only two lines on God as the first cause it would be my right to conclude the author is an obscurantist.

Shachtman does not reply to the accusation but tries to distract attention by turning to irrelevant matters. 'Wherein does what you call my "bloc with Burnham in the sphere of philosophy" differ,' he asks, 'from Lenin's bloc with Bogdanov? Why was the latter principled and ours unprincipled? I should be very much interested to know the answer to this question.' I shall deal presently with the political difference, or rather the political polar opposite between the two blocs. We are here interested in the question of Marxist method. Wherein is the difference you ask? In this, that Lenin never declaimed for Bogdanov's profit that dialectic materialism is superflous in solving 'concrete political questions'. In this, that Lenin never theoretically confounded the Bolshevik party with parties in general. He was organically incapable of uttering such abominations. And not he alone but not a single one of the serious Bolsheviks. That is the difference. Do you understand? Shachtman sarcastically promised me that he would be 'interested' in a clear answer. The answer, I trust, has been given. I don't demand the 'interest'.

The Abstract and the Concrete; Economics and Politics

The most lamentable section of Shachtman's lamentable opus is the chapter, 'The State and the Character of the War'. 'What then is our position?' asks the author. 'Simply this: It is impossible to deduce *directly* our policy towards a *specific* war from an *abstract* characterisation of the class character of the state involved in the war, more particularly, from the property forms prevailing in that state. Our policy must flow from a *concrete* examination of the character of the war in relation to the interests of the international socialist revolution.' (Loc. cit.,

p. 13. My emphasis.) What a muddle! What a tangle of sophistry! If it is impossible to deduce our policy *directly* from the class character of a state, then why can't this be done *non-directly?* Why must the analysis of the character of the state be *abstract* whereas the analysis of the character of the war is *concrete?* Formally speaking, one can say with equal, in fact with much more right, that our policy in relation to the USSR can be deduced not from an *abstract* characterisation of war as 'imperialist', but only from a *concrete* analysis of the character of the state in the given historical situation. The fundamental sophistry upon which Shachtman constructs everything else is simple enough: Inasmuch as the economic basis determines events in the super-structure not *immediately;* inasmuch as the mere class characterization of the state is *not enough* to solve the practical tasks, therefore . . . therefore we can get along without examining economics and the class nature of the state; by replacing them, as Shachtman phrases it in his journalistic jargon, with the 'realities of living events'. (Loc. cit., p. 14.)

The very same artifice circulated by Shachtman to justify his philosophic bloc with Burnham (dialectic materialism determines our politics not immediately, consequently . . . it does not *in general* affect the 'concrete political tasks'), is repeated here word for word in relation to Marxist sociology: Inasmuch as property forms determine the policy of a state not immediately it is possible therefore to throw Marxist sociology overboard in general in determining 'concrete political tasks'.

But why stop there? Since the law of labour value determines prices not 'directly' and not 'immediately'; since the laws of natural selection determine not 'directly' and not 'immediately' the birth of a suckling pig; since the laws of gravity determine not 'directly' and not 'immediately' the tumble of a drunken policeman down a flight of stairs, therefore . . . therefore let us leave Marx, Darwin, Newton, and all the other lovers of 'abstractions' to collect dust on a shelf. This is nothing less than the solemn burial of science for, after all, the entire course of the development of science proceeds from 'direct' and 'immediate' causes to the more remote and profound ones, from multiple varieties and kaleidoscopic events—to the unity of the driving forces.

The law of labour value determines prices not 'immediately', but it nevertheless does determine them. Such 'concrete' phenomena as the bankruptcy of the New Deal find their explanation in the final analysis in the 'abstract' law of value. Roosevelt does not know this, but a Marxist dare not proceed without knowing it. Not immediately but through a whole series of intermediate factors and their reciprocal interaction, property forms determine not only politics but also morality. A proletarian politician seeking to ignore the class nature of the state would invariably end up like the policeman who ignores the laws of gravitation; that is, by smashing his nose.

Shachtman obviously does not take into account the distinction between the abstract and the concrete. Striving toward concreteness our mind operates with abstractions. Even 'this', 'given', 'concrete' dog is an abstraction because it proceeds to change, for example, by dropping its tail the 'moment' we point a finger at it. Concreteness is a relative concept and not an absolute one: what is concrete in one case turns out to be abstract in another: that is, insufficiently defined for a given purpose. In order to obtain a concept 'concrete' enough *for a given need* it is necessary to correlate several abstractions into one—just as in reproducing a segment of life upon the screen, which is a picture in movement, it is necessary to combine a number of still photographs.

The concrete is a combination of abstractions—not an arbitrary or subjective combination but one that corresponds to the laws of the movement of a given phenomenon.

'The interests of the international socialist revolution,' to which Shachtman appeals against the class nature of the state, represent in this given instance the vaguest of all abstractions.

After all, the question which occupies us is precisely this, in what concrete way can we further the interests of the revolution? Nor would it be amiss to remember, too, that the task of the socialist revolution is to create a workers' state. Before talking about the socialist revolution it is necessary consequently to learn how to distinguish between such 'abstractions' as the bourgeoisie and the proletariat, the capitalist state and the workers' state.

Shachtman indeed squanders his own time and that of others in proving that nationalized property does not determine 'in and of itself', 'automatically', 'directly', 'immediately' the policies of the Kremlin. On the question as to how the economic 'base' determines the political, juridical, philosophical, artistic and so on 'super-structure' there exists a rich Marxist literature. The opinion that economics presumably determines directly and immediately the creativeness of a composer or even the verdict of a judge represents a hoary caricature of Marxism, which the bourgeois professordom of all countries has circulated time out of end to mask their intellectual impotence.*

As for the question which immediately concerns us, the inter-relationship between the social foundations of the Soviet state and the policy of the Kremlin, let me remind the absent-minded Shachtman that for seventeen years we have already been establishing, publicly, the growing *contradiction* between the foundation laid down by the October Revolution and the tendencies of the state 'super-structure'. We have followed step by step the increasing independence of the bureaucracy from the Soviet proletariat and the growth of its dependence upon other classes and groups both inside and outside the country. Just what does Shachtman wish to add in this sphere to the analysis already made?

However, although economics determines politics not directly or immediately, but only in the last analysis, *nevertheless econo-*

---

* To young comrades I recommend that they study on this question the works of Engels (Anti-Dühring), Plekhanov and Antonio Labriola.

mics does determine politics. The Marxists affirm precisely this in contrast to the bourgeois professors and their disciples. While analysing and exposing the growing political independence of the bureaucracy from the proletariat, we have never lost sight of the objective social boundaries of this 'independence'; namely, nationalized property supplemented by the monopoly of foreign trade.

It is astonishing! Shachtman continues to support the slogan for a political revolution against the Soviet bureaucracy. Has he ever seriously thought out the meaning of this slogan? If we hold that the social foundations laid down by the October Revolution were 'automatically' reflected in the policy of the state, then why would a *revolution* against the bureaucracy be necessary? If the USSR, on the other hand, has completely ceased being a workers' state, not a *political* revolution would be required but a *social* revolution. Shachtman consequently continues to defend the slogan which follows (1) from the character of the USSR as a workers' state and (2) from the irreconcilable antagonism between the social foundations of the state and the bureaucracy. But as he repeats this slogan, he tries to undermine its theoretical foundation. Is it perhaps in order to demonstrate once again the independence of his politics from scientific 'abstractions'?

Under the guise of waging a struggle against the bourgeois caricature of dialectic materialism, Shachtman throws the doors wide open to historical idealism. Property forms and the class character of the state are a matter of *indifference* to him in analysing the policy of a government. The state itself appears to him an animal of indiscriminate sex. Both feet planted firmly on this bed of chicken feathers, Shachtman pompously explains to us—today in the year 1940!—that in addition to the nationalised property there is also the Bonapartist filth and their reactionary politics. How new! Did Shachtman perchance think that he was speaking in a nursery?

Shachtman Makes a Bloc—Also with Lenin

To camouflage his failure to understand the essence of the problem of the nature of the Soviet state, Shachtman leaped upon the words of Lenin directed against me on December 30, 1920, during the so-called Trade Union Discussion. 'Comrade Trotsky speaks of the workers' state. Permit me, this is an abstraction. . . . Our state is in reality not a workers' state but a workers' and peasants' state. . . . Our present state is such that the inclusively-organised proletariat must defend itself, and we must utilise these workers' organisations for the defence of the workers against their state and for the defence of our state by the workers.' Pointing to this quotation and hastening to proclaim that I have repeated my 'mistake' of 1920, Shachtman in his precipitance failed to notice a major error in the quotation concerning the definition of the nature of the Soviet state. On January 19, Lenin himself wrote the following about his speech of December 30: 'I stated, "our state is in reality not a workers' state but a workers' and peasants' state." . . . On reading the report of the discussion, I now see that I was wrong. . . . I should have said: "The workers' state is an abstraction. In reality we have a workers' state with the following peculiar features, (1) it is the peasants and not the workers who predominate in the population and (2) it is a workers' state with bureaucratic deformations." ' From this episode two conclusions follow: Lenin placed such great importance upon the precise sociological definition of the state that he considered it necessary to correct himself in the very heat of a polemic! But Shachtman is so little interested in the class nature of the Soviet state that twenty years later he noticed neither Lenin's mistake nor Lenin's correction!

I shall not dwell here on the question as to just how correctly Lenin aimed his argument against me. I believe he did so incorrectly—there was no difference of opinion between us on the definition of the state. But that is not the question now. The theoretical formulation on the question of the state, made by

Lenin in the above-cited quotation—in conjunction with the major correction which he himself introduced a few days later—is absolutely correct. But let us hear what incredible use Shachtman makes of Lenin's definition: 'Just as it was possible twenty years ago,' he writes, 'to speak of the term "workers' state" as an abstraction, so is it possible to speak of the term "degenerated workers' state" as an abstraction.' (Loc. cit., p. 14.) It is self-evident that Shachtman fails completely to understand Lenin. Twenty years ago the term 'workers' state' could not be considered in any way an abstraction *in general*: that is, something not real or not existing. The definition 'workers' state', while correct in and of itself, was *inadequate* in relation to the *particular* task; namely, the defence of the workers through their trade unions, and only in this sense was it abstract. However, in relation to the defence of the USSR against imperialism this self-same definition was in 1920, just as it still is today, unshakably concrete, making it obligatory for workers to defend the given state.

Shachtman does not agree. He writes: 'Just as it was once necessary in connection with the trade union problem to speak concretely of what *kind* of workers' state exists in the Soviet Union, so it is necessary to establish in connection with the present war the *degree* of degeneration of the Soviet state. . . . And the *degree* of the degeneration of the regime cannot be established by abstract reference to the existence of nationalized property, but only by observing the realities (!) of living (!) events (!).' From this it is completely incomprehensible why in 1920 the question of the character of the USSR was brought up in connection with the trade unions, i.e., particular internal questions of the regime, while today it is brought up in connection with the defence of the USSR, that is, in connection with the entire fate of the state. In the former case the workers' state was counterposed to the workers, in the latter case—to the imperialists. Small wonder that the analogy limps on both legs; what Lenin counterposed, Shachtman identifies.

Nevertheless, even if we take Shachtman's words at face value, it follows that the question over which he is concerned is only the *degree of the degeneration* (of what? a workers' state?); that is, of quantitative differences in the evaluation. Let us grant that Shachtman has worked out (where?) the 'degree' more precisely than we have. But in what way can purely quantitative differences in the evaluation of the degeneration of the *workers'* state affect our decision as to the defence of the USSR? It is impossible to make head or tail out of this. As a matter of fact, Shachtman, remaining true to eclecticism, that is, to himself, dragged in the question of 'degree' only in an effort to maintain his equilibrium between Abern and Burnham. What is in dispute actually is not at all the *degree* determined by 'the realities of living events' (what a precise, 'scientific', 'concrete', 'experimental' terminology!) but whether these *quantitative* changes have been transformed into *qualitative* changes; i.e., whether the USSR is still a workers' state, even though degenerated, or whether it has been transformed into a new type of exploitive state.

To this basic question Shachtman has no answer; feels no need for an answer. His argument is merely verbal mimicry of Lenin's words which were spoken in a different connection, which had a different content and included an outright error. Lenin in his corrected version declares: 'The given state is not merely a workers' state but a workers' state with bureaucratic deformations'. Shachtman declares: 'The given state is not merely a degenerated workers' state but. . . .' . . . but? Shachtman has nothing further to say. Both the orator and the audience stare at each other, mouths wide open.

What does 'degenerated workers' state' signify in our programme? To this question our programme responds with a degree of concreteness which is wholly adequate for solving the question of the defence of the USSR; namely: (1) those traits which in 1920 were a 'bureaucratic deformation' of the soviet system have now become an independent bureaucratic regime which has devoured the soviets; (2) the dictatorship of the bureaucracy, in-compatible with the internal and international tasks of socialism, has introduced and continues to introduce profound deformations in the economic life of the country as well; (3) basically, however, the system of planned economy, on the foundation of state owner-ship of the means of production, has been preserved and con-tinues to remain a colossal conquest of mankind. The defeat of the USSR in a war with imperialism would signify not solely the liquidation of the bureaucratic dictatorship, but of the planned economy; and the dismemberment of the country into spheres of influence; and a new stabilization of imperialism; and a new weakening of the world proletariat.

From the circumstance that the 'bureaucratic' deformation has grown into a regime of bureaucratic autocracy we draw the conclusion that the defence of the workers through their trade unions (which have undergone the self-same degeneration as the state) is today in contrast to 1920 completely unrealistic; it is necessary to overthrow the bureaucracy; this task can be carried out only by creating an illegal Bolshevik party in the USSR.

From the circumstance that the degeneration of the political system has not yet led to the destruction of planned state economy, we draw the conclusion that it is still the duty of the world proletariat to defend the USSR against imperialism and to aid the Soviet proletariat in its struggle against the bureaucracy.

Just what in our definition of the USSR does Shachtman find abstract? What concrete amendments does he propose? If the dialectic teaches us that 'truth is always concrete' then this law applies with equal force to criticism. It is not enough to label a definition abstract. It is necessary to point out exactly what it lacks. Otherwise criticism itself becomes sterile. Instead of concretising or changing the definition which he claims is abstract, Shachtman replaces it with a vacuum. That's not enough. A vacuum, even the most pretentious vacuum, must be recognised as the worst of all abstractions—it can be filled with any content. Small wonder that the theoretical vacuum, in displacing the class analysis, has sucked in the politics of impressionism and adventurism.

'Concentrated Economics'

Shachtman goes on to quote Lenin's words that 'politics is concentrated economics' and that in this sense 'politics cannot but take primacy over economics'. From Lenin's words Shachtman directs at me the moral that I, if you please, am interested only in 'economics' (nationalized means of production) and skip over 'politics'. This second effort to exploit Lenin is not superior to the first. Shachtman's mistake here assumes truly vast proportions! Lenin meant: when economic processes, tasks and interests acquire a *conscious* and *generalised* ('concentrated') character, they enter the sphere of politics by virtue of this very fact, and constitute the essence of politics. In this sense politics as concentrated economics rises above the day-to-day atomised, unconscious and ungeneralised economic activity.

The correctness of politics from the Marxist standpoint is determined precisely to the extent that it profoundly and allsidedly 'concentrates' economics; that is, expresses the progressive tendencies of its development. That is why we base our politics first and foremost upon our analysis of property forms and class relationships. A more detailed and concrete analysis of the factors in the 'super-structure' is possible for us only on this theoretical basis. Thus, for example, were we to accuse an opposing faction of 'bureacratic conservatism' we would immediately seek the social, i.e., class roots of this phenomenon. Any other procedure would brand us as 'Platonic' Marxists, if not simply noisy mimics.

'Politics is concentrated economics.' This proposition one should think applies to the Kremlin too. Or, in exception to the general law, is the policy of the Moscow government not 'concentrated economics' but a manifestation of the bureaucracy's free will? Our attempt to reduce the politics of the Kremlin to nationalized economy, refracted through the interests of the bureaucracy, provokes frantic resistance from Shachtman. He takes his guidance in relation to the USSR not from the conscious generalisation of economics but from 'observing the realities of living events'; i.e., from rule of thumb, improvisations, sympathies and antipathies. He counterposes this impressionistic policy to our sociologically grounded policy and accuses us at the same time of . . . ignoring politics. Incredible but true! To be sure, in the final analysis Shachtman's weak-kneed and capricious politics is likewise the 'concentrated' expression of economics but, alas, it is the economics of the declassed petty bourgeoisie.

Comparison with Bourgeois Wars

Shachtman reminds us that bourgeois wars were at one time progressive and that in another period they became reactionary and that therefore it is not enough to give the class definition of a state engaged in war. This proposition does not clarify the question but muddles it. Bourgeois wars could be progressive only at a time when the entire bourgeois regime was progressive; in other words, at a time when *bourgeois property* in contradistinction to feudal property was a progressive and constructive factor. Bourgeois wars became reactionary when bourgeois property became a brake on development. Does Shachtman wish to say in relation to the USSR that the state ownership of the means of production has become a brake upon development and that the extension of this form of property to other countries constitutes economic reaction? Shachtman obviously does not want to say this. He simply does not draw the logical conclusion to his own thoughts.

The example of national bourgeois wars does indeed offer a very instructive lesson, but Shachtman passes it by unconcernedly. Marx and Engels were striving for a unified German republic. In the war of 1870-71 they stood on the side of the Germans despite the fact that the struggle for unification was exploited and distorted by the dynastic parasites.

Shachtman refers to the fact that Marx and Engels immediately turned against Prussia upon the annexation of Alsace-Lorraine. But this turn only illustrates our standpoint all the more lucidly. It is impermissible to forget for a moment that what was in question was a war between two *bourgeois* states. Thus both camps had a common class denominator. To decide which of the two sides was the 'lesser evil'—insofar as history generally left any room for choice—was possible only on the basis of supplementary factors. On the German side it was a question of creating a *national* bourgeois state as an economic and cultural arena. The *national* state during that period was a progressive historical factor. To that extent Marx and Engels stood on the side of the Germans despite Hohenzollern and his junkers. The annexation of Alsace-Lorraine violated the principle of the national state in regard to France as well as Germany and laid the basis for a war of revenge. Marx and Engels, naturally, turned sharply against Prussia. They did not thereby at all incur the risk of rendering service to an inferior system of economy as against a superior one since in both camps, we repeat, bourgeois relations prevailed. If France had been a workers' state in 1870, then Marx and Engels would have been for France from the very beginning, inasmuch as they—one feels abashed again that this must be mentioned—guided themselves in all their activity by the class criterion.

Today in the old capitalist countries the solving of national tasks is no longer at stake at all. On the contrary mankind is suffering from the contradiction between the productive forces and the too-narrow framework of the national state. Planned economy on the basis of socialised property freed from national boundaries is the task of the international proletariat, above all —in Europe. It is precisely this task which is expressed in our slogan, 'For the Socialist United States of Europe!' The expropriation of the property owners in Poland as in Finland is a progressive factor in and of itself. The bureaucratic methods of the Kremlin occupy the very same place in this process as did the dynastic methods of Hohenzollern—in the unification of Germany. Whenever we are confronted with the necessity of choosing between the defence of reactionary property forms through reactionary measures and the introduction of progressive property forms through bureaucratic measures, we do not at all place both sides on the same plane, but choose the lesser evil. In this there is no more 'capitulation' to Stalinism than there was capitulation to Hohenzollern in the policy of Marx and Engels. It is scarcely necessary to add that the role of Hohenzollern in the war of 1870-71 justified neither the general historical role of the dynasty nor so much as its existence.

Conjunctural Defeatism, or Columbus and the Egg

Let us now check up on how Shachtman, aided by a theoretical vacuum, operates with the 'realities of living events' in an especially vital question. He writes: 'We have never supported the Kremlin's international policy . . . but what is war? War is the continuation of politics by other means. Then why should we support the war which is the continuation of the international policy which we *did not* and do not support?' (Loc. cit., p. 15.) The completeness of this argument cannot be denied; in the shape of a naked syllogism we are presented here with a rounded-out theory of *defeatism*. It is as simple as Columbus and the egg! Since we have never supported the Kremlin's international policy, therefore we ought *never* to support the USSR. Then why not say it?

We rejected the internal and international policies of the Kremlin prior to the German-Soviet pact and prior to the invasion of Poland by the Red Army. This means that the 'realities of living events' of last year do not have the slightest bearing on the case. If we were defencists in the past in connection with the USSR, it was only out of inconsistency. Shachtman revises not only the present policy of the Fourth International

but also the past. Since we are against Stalin we must therefore
be against the USSR too. Stalin has long held this opinion.
Shachtman has arrived at it only recently. From his rejection of
the Kremlin's politics flows complete and indivisible defeatism.
Then why not say so?

But Shachtman can't bring himself to say so. In a previous
passage he writes: 'We said—the Minority continues to say it—
that if the imperialists assail the Soviet Union with the aim
of crushing the last conquest of the October Revolution and
reducing Russia to a bunch of colonies we will support the
Soviet Union unconditionally.' (Loc. cit., p. 15.) Permit me,
permit me, permit me! The Kremlin's international policy is
reactionary; the war is the continuation of its reactionary politics;
we cannot support a reactionary war. How then does it unexpectedly turn out that if the pernicious imperialists 'assail'
the USSR and if the pernicious imperialists pursue the un-
commendable aim of transforming it into a colony, that under
these exceptional 'conditions', Shachtman will defend the USSR
. . . 'unconditionally'? How does this make sense? Where is the
logic? Or has Shachtman, following Burnham's example, also
relegated logic to the sphere of religion and other museum
exhibits?

The key to this tangle of confusion rests in the fact that
the statement, 'We have never supported the Kremlin's international policy', is an abstraction. It must be dissected and
concretised. In its present foreign as well as domestic policy,
the bureaucracy places first and foremost for defence its own
parasitic interests. To that extent we wage mortal struggle
against it, but in the final analysis, through the interests of the
bureaucracy, in a very distorted form the interests of the
workers' state are reflected. These interests we defend—with
our own methods. Thus we do not at all wage a struggle
against the fact that the bureaucracy safeguards (in its own way!)
state property, the monopoly of foreign trade or refuses to pay
Czarist debts. Yet in a war between the USSR and the capi-

talist world—independently of the incidents leading up to that war or the 'aims' of this or that government—what is involved is the fate of precisely those historical conquests which we defend unconditionally, i.e., despite the reactionary policy of the bureaucracy. The question consequently boils down—*in the last and decisive instance*—to the class nature of the USSR.

Lenin deduced the policy of defeatism from the imperialist character of the war; but he did not stop there. He deduced the imperialist character of the war from a specific stage in the development of the capitalist regime and its ruling class. Since the character of the war is determined precisely by the class character of society and the state, Lenin recommended that in determining our policy in regard to imperialist war we abstract ourselves from such 'concrete' circumstances as democracy and monarchy, as aggression and national defence. In opposition to this Shachtman proposes that we deduce defeatism from conjunctural conditions. This defeatism is indifferent to the class character of the USSR and of Finland. Enough for it are the reactionary features of the bureaucracy and the 'aggression'. If France, England or the United States sends airplanes and guns to Finland, this has no bearing in the determination of Shachtman's politics. But if British troops land in Finland, then Shachtman will place a thermometer under Chamberlain's tongue and determine Chamberlain's intentions—whether he aims only to save Finland from the Kremlin's imperialistic politics or whether in addition he aims to overthrow the 'last conquest of the October Revolution'. Strictly in accordance with the readings with the readings of the thermometer, Shachtman, the defeatist, is ready to change himself into a defencist. This is what it means to replace abstract principles with the 'realities of living events'.

Shachtman, as we have already seen, persistently demands the citation of precedents: when and where in the past have the leaders of the opposition manifested petty-bourgeois opportunism? The reply which I have already given him on this score must be supplemented here with two letters which we sent each other on the question of defencism and methods of defencism in connection with the events of the Spanish Revolution. On September 18, 1937, Shachtman wrote me:

'. . . You say, "If we would have a member in the Cortes he would vote *against* the military budget of Negrin." Unless this is a typographical error it seems to us to be a non-sequitur. If, as we all contend, *the element of an imperialist war* is not dominant at the present time in the Spanish struggle, and if instead the decisive element is still the struggle between the decaying bourgeois democracy, with all that it involves, on the one side, and fascism on the other, and further if we are obliged to give military assistance to the struggle against fascism, we don't see how it would be possible to vote in the Cortes against the military budget. . . . If a Bolshevik-Leninist on the Huesca front were asked by a Socialist comrade why his representative in the Cortes voted against the proposal by Negrin to devote a million pesetas to the purchase of rifles for the front, what would this Bolshevik-Leninist reply? It doesn't seem to us that he would have an effective answer. . . .' (My emphasis.)

This letter astounded me. Shachtman was willing to express confidence in the perfidious Negrin government on the purely negative basis that the 'element of an imperialist war' was not dominant in Spain.

On September 20, 1937, I replied to Shachtman:

'To vote the military budget of the Negrin government signifies to vote him *political* confidence. . . . To do it would be a crime. How we explain our vote to the anarchist workers? Very simply: We have not the slightest confidence in the capacity of this government to conduct the war and assure victory. We accuse this government of protecting the rich and starving the poor. This government must be smashed. So long as we are not strong enough to replace it, we are fighting under its command. But on every occasion we express openly our non-confidence in it: it is the only one possibility to mobilise the masses *politically* against this government and to prepare its overthrow. Any other politics would be a betrayal of the revolution.'

The tone of my reply only feebly reflects the . . . amazement which Shachtman's opportunist position produced in me. Isolated mistakes are of course unavoidable but today, two and a half years later, this correspondence is illuminated with new light. Since we defend bourgeois democracy against fascism, Shachtman reasons, we therefore cannot refuse confidence to the bourgeois government. In applying this very theorem to the USSR it is transformed into its converse—since we place no confidence in the Kremlin government, we cannot, therefore, defend the workers' state. Pseudo-radicalism in this instance, too, is only the obverse side of opportunism.

Renunciation of the Class Criterion

Let us return once more to the ABC's. In Marxist sociology the initial point of analysis is the *class* definition of a given phenomenon, e.g., state, party, philosophic trend, literary school, etc. In most cases, however the mere class definition is inadequate, for a class consists of different strata, passes through different stages of development, comes under different conditions, is subjected to the influence of other classes. It becomes necessary to bring up these second and third rate factors in order to round out the analysis, and they are taken either partially or completely, depending upon the specific aim. But for a Marxist, analysis is impossible without a class characterisation of the phenomenon under consideration.

The skeletal and muscular systems do not exhaust the anatomy of an animal; nevertheless an anatomical treatise which attempted to 'abstract' itself from bones and muscles would dangle in mid-air. War is not an organ but a function of society, i.e., its ruling class. It is impossible to define and study a function without understanding the organ, i.e., the state; it is impossible to gain scientific understanding of the organ without understanding the general structure of the organism, i.e., society. The bones and muscles of society consist of the productive forces and the class (property) relations. Shachtman holds it possible that a function, namely, war, can be studied 'concretely' independently of the organ to which it pertains, i.e., the state. Isn't this monstrous?

This fundamental error is supplemented by another equally glaring. After splitting function away from organ, Shachtman in studying the function itself, contrary to all his promises, proceeds not from the abstract to the concrete but on the contrary dissolves the concrete in the abstract. *Imperialist* war is one of the functions of finance capital, i.e., the bourgeoisie at a certain stage of development resting upon capitalism of a specific structure, namely, monopoly capital. This definition is sufficiently concrete for our basic political conclusions. But by extending the term *imperialist* war to cover the Soviet state too, Shachtman cuts the ground away from under his own feet. In order to reach even a superficial justification for applying one and the same designation to the expansion of finance capital and the expansion of the workers' state, Shachtman is compelled to detach himself from the social structure of both states altogether by proclaiming it to be—an abstraction. Thus playing hide and seek with Marxism, Shachtman labels the concrete as abstract and palms off the abstract as concrete!

This outrageous toying with theory is not accidental. Every petty bourgeois in the United States without exception is ready to call every seizure of territory 'imperialist', especially today when the United States does not happen to be occupied with acquiring territories. But if this very same petty bourgeois is told that the entire foreign policy of finance capital is imperialist regardless of whether it be occupied at the given moment in carrying out an annexation or in 'defending' Finland against annexation—then our petty bourgeois jumps back in pious indignation. Naturally the leaders of the opposition differ considerably from an average petty bourgeois in their aim and in their political level. But alas they have common roots of thought. A petty bourgeois invariably seeks to tear political events away from their social foundation, since there is an organic conflict between a class approach to facts and the social position and education of the petty bourgeoisie.

Once Again: Poland

My remark that the Kremlin with its bureaucratic methods gave an impulse to the socialist revolution in Poland, is converted by Shachtman into an assertion that in my opinion a 'bureaucratic revolution' of the proletariat is presumably possible. This is not only incorrect but disloyal. My expression was rigidly limited. It is not the question of 'bureaucratic revolution' but only a bureautic impulse. To deny this impulse is to deny reality. The popular masses in western Ukraine and Byelo Russia, in any event, felt this impulse, understood its meaning, and used it to accomplish a drastic overturn in property relations. A revolutionary party which failed to notice this impulse in time and refused to utilize it would be fit for nothing but the ash can.

This impulse in the direction of socialist revolution was possible only because the bureaucracy of the USSR straddles and has its roots in the economy of a workers' state. The revolutionary utilisation of this 'impulse' by the Ukrainian Byelo Russians was possible only through the class struggle in the occupied territories and through the power of the example of the October Revolution. Finally, the swift strangulation or semi-strangulation of this revolutionary mass movement was made possible through the isolation of this movement and the might of the Moscow bureaucracy. Whoever failed to understand the dialectic interaction of these three factors: the workers' state, the oppressed masses and the Bonapartist bureaucracy, had best restrain himself from idle talk about events in Poland.

At the elections for the National Assembly of western Ukraine and western Byelo Russia the electoral programme, dictated of course by the Kremlin, included three extremely important points: inclusion of both provinces in the Federation of the USSR; confiscation of landlords' estates in favour of the peasants; nationalisation of large industry and the banks. The Ukranian democrats, judging from their conduct, deem it a lesser evil to be unified under the rule of a single state. And from the standpoint of the future struggle for independence, they are correct. As for the other two points in the programme one would think that there could be no doubt in our midst as to their progressiveness. Seeking to get around reality, namely that nothing else but the social foundations of the USSR forced a social revolutionary programme upon the Kremlin, Shachtman refers to Lithuania, Esthonia and Latvia where everything has remained as of old. An incredible argument! No one has said that the Soviet bureaucracy *always* and *everywhere* either wishes or is able to accomplish the expropriation of the bourgeoisie. We only say that no other government could have accomplished that social overturn which the Kremlin bureaucracy notwithstanding its alliance with Hitler found itself compelled to sanction in eastern Poland. Failing this, it could not include the territory in the Federation of the USSR.

Shachtman is aware of the overturn itself. He cannot deny it. He is incapable of explaining it. But he nevertheless attempts to save face. He writes: 'In the Polish Ukraine and White Russia, where class exploitation was intensified by national oppression . . . the peasants began to take over the land themselves, to drive off the landlords who were already half-in-flight,' etc. (Loc. cit., p. 16.) The Red Army it turns out had no connection whatever with all this. It came into Poland only as a 'counter-revolutionary force' in order to suppress the movement. But why didn't the workers and peasants in western Poland seized by Hitler arrange a revolution? Why was it chiefly revolutionists, 'democrats', and Jews who fled from there, while in eastern

Poland—it was chiefly the landlords and capitalists who fled? Shachtman lacks the time to think this out—he is in a hurry to explain to me that the conception of 'bureaucratic revolution' is absurd, for the emancipation of the workers can be carried out only by the workers themselves. Am I not justified in repeating that Shachtman obviously feels he is standing in a nursery?

In the Parisian organ of the Mensheviks—who, if that is possible, are even more 'irreconcilable' in their attitude toward the Kremlin's foreign policy than Shachtman—it is reported that 'in the villages—very frequently at the very approach of the Soviet troops (i.e., even prior to their entering a given district—L.T.)—peasant committees sprang up everywhere, the elementary organs of revolutionary peasant self-rule. . . .' The military authorities hastened of course to subordinate these committees to the bureaucratic organs established by them in the urban centres. Nevertheless they were compelled to rest upon the peasant committees since without them it was impossible to carry out the agrarian revolution.

The leader of the Mensheviks, Dan, wrote on October 19: '*According to the unanimous testimony of all observers* the appearance of the Soviet army and the Soviet bureaucracy provides not only in the territory occupied by them but beyond its confines—an impulse (!!!) to social turmoil and social transformations.' The 'impulse', it will be observed, was invented not by me but by 'the unanimous testimony of all observers' who possessed eyes and ears. Dan goes even further and expresses the supposition that 'the waves engendered by this impulse will not only hit Germany powerfully in a comparatively short period of time but also to one degree or another roll on to other states'.

Another Menshevik author writes: 'However they may have attempted in the Kremlin to avoid anything which might smack of the great revolution, the very fact of the entry of Soviet troops into the territories of eastern Poland with its

long outlived semi-feudal agrarian relations, had to provoke
a stormy agrarian movement. With the approach of Soviet
troops the peasants began to seize landlords' estates and to
form peasant committees.' You will observe: with the *approach*
of Soviet troops and not at all with their *withdrawal* as should
follow in accordance with Shachtman's words. I cite the testimony of the Mensheviks because they are very well informed,
their sources of information coming through Polish and Jewish
émigrés friendly to them who have gathered in France, and also
because having capitulated to the French bourgeoisie, these
gentlemen cannot possibly be suspected of capitulation to
Stalinism.

The testimony of the Mensheviks furthermore is confirmed
by the reports of the bourgeois press:

'The agrarian revolution in Soviet Poland has had the force
of a spontaneous movement. As soon as the report spread that
the Red Army had crossed the river Zbrucz the peasants began
to share out amongst themselves the landlords' acres. Land was
given first to small holders and in this way about thirty per cent
of agricultural land was expropriated.' (New York *Times,*
January 17, 1940.)

Under the guise of a new argument Shachtman hands me
my own words to the effect that the expropriation of property
owners in eastern Poland cannot alter our appraisal of the
general policies of the Kremlin. Of course it cannot! No one
has proposed this. With the aid of the Comintern the Kremlin
has disorientated and demoralised the working class so that it
has not only facilitated the outbreak of a new imperialist war
but has also made extremely difficult the utilisation of this war
for revolution. Compared with those crimes the social overturn
in the two provinces, which was paid for moreover by the
enslavement of Poland, is of course of secondary importance
and does not alter the general reactionary character of the
Kremlin's policy. But upon the initiative of the opposition itself,
the question now posed is not one of general policy but of its

concrete refraction under specific conditions of time and place. To the peasants of Galicia and western Byelo Russia the agrarian overturn was of highest importance. The Fourth International could not have boycotted this overturn on the ground that the initiative was taken by the reactionary bureaucracy. Our outright duty was to participate in the overturn on the side of the workers and peasants and *to that extent* on the side of the Red Army. At the same time it was indispensable to warn the masses tirelessly of the generally reactionary character of the Kremlin's policy and of those dangers it bears for the occupied territories. To know how to combine these two tasks or more precisely two sides of one and the same task—just this is Bolshevik politics.

Once Again: Finland

Having revealed such odd perspicacity in understanding the events in Poland, Shachtman descends upon me with redoubled authority in connection with events in Finland. In my article 'A Petty-Bourgeois Opposition,' I wrote that 'the Soviet-Finnish War is *apparently beginning* to be *supplemented* by a civil war in which the Red Army finds itself at a given stage in the same camp as the Finnish petty peasants and the workers. . . .' This extremely cautious formula did not meet with the approval of my unsparing judge. My evaluation of events in Poland had already taken him off balance. 'I find even less (proof) for your—how shall I put it? astonishing remarks about Finland,' writes Shachtman on page 16 of his 'Letter.' I am very sorry that Shachtman chooses to become astonished rather than think things out.

In the Baltic states the Kremlin confined its tasks to making strategical gains with the unquestionable calculation that in the future these strategic military bases will permit the sovietisation of these former sections of the Czarist empire too. These successes in the Baltic, achieved by diplomatic threat, met with resistance, however, from Finland. To reconcile itself to

this resistance would have meant that the Kremlin placed in
jeopardy its 'prestige' and thereby its successes in Esthonia,
Latvia and Lithuania. Thus contrary to its initial plans the
Kremlin felt compelled to resort to armed force. From this
fact every thinking person posed to himself the following
question: Does the Kremlin wish only to frighten the Finnish
bourgeoisie and force them to make concessions or must it now
go further? To this question naturally there could be no
'automatic' answer. It was necessary—in the light of general
tendencies—to orient oneself upon concrete symptoms. The
leaders of the opposition are incapable of this.

Military operations began on November 30. That very same
day the Central Committee of the Finnish Communist Party,
undoubtedly located in either Leningrad or Moscow, issued a
radio manifesto to the toiling people of Finland. This manifesto
proclaimed: 'For the second time in the history of Finland
the Finnish working class is beginning a struggle against the
yoke of the plutocracy. The first experience of the workers
and peasants in 1918 terminated in the victory of the capitalists
and the landlords. But this time . . . the toiling people must
win!' This manifesto alone clearly indicated that not an
attempt to scare the bourgeois government of Finland was involved, but a plan to provoke insurrection in the country and to
supplement the invasion of the Red Army with civil war.

The declaration of the so-called People's Government published on December 2 states: 'In different parts of the country
the people have already risen and proclaimed the creation of a
democratic republic'. This assertion is obviously a fabrication,
otherwise the manifesto would have mentioned the places where
the attempts at insurrection took place. It is possible, however,
that isolated attempts, prepared from without, ended in failure
and that precisely because of this it was deemed best not to
go into details. In any case, the news concerning 'insurrections'
constituted a call to insurrection. Moreover, the declaration
carried information concerning the formation of 'the first

Finnish corps which in the course of coming battles will be enlarged by volunteers from the ranks of revolutionary workers and peasants'. Whether there were one thousand men in this 'corps' or only one hundred, the meaning of the 'corps' in determining the policies of the Kremlin was incontestable. At the same time cable dispatches reported the expropriation of large landholders in the border regions. There is not the slightest ground to doubt that this is just what took place during the first advance of the Red Army. But even if these dispatches are considered fabrications, they completely preserve their meaning as a call for an agrarian revolution. Thus I had every justification to declare that 'The Soviet-Finnish War is apparently beginning to be supplemented by a civil war'. At the beginning of December, true enough, I had at my disposal only a part of these facts. But against the background of the general situation, and I take the liberty to add, with the aid of an understanding of its internal logic, the isolated symptoms enabled me to draw the necessary conclusions concerning the direction of the entire struggle. Without such semi-*a priori* conclusions one can be a rationalising observer but in no case an active participant in events. But why did the appeal of the 'People's Government' fail to bring immediate mass response? For three reasons: first, Finland is dominated completely by a reactionary military machine which is supported not only by the bourgeoisie but by the top layers of the peasantry and the labour bureaucracy; secondly, the policy of the Kremlin succeeded in transforming the Finnish Communist Party into an insignificant factor; thirdly, the regime of the USSR is in no way capable of arousing enthusiasm among the Finnish toiling masses. Even in the Ukraine from 1918 to 1920 the peasants responded very slowly to appeals to seize the estates of the landlords because the local soviet power was still weak and every success of the Whites brought about ruthless punitive expeditions. All the less reason is there for surprise that the Finnish poor peasants delay in responding to an appeal for an agrarian revolution. To set the peasants in motion, serious successes of the Red Army are required. But during the first badly prepared advance the Red Army suffered only failures. Under such conditions there could not even be talk of the peasants rising. It was impossible to expect an independent civil war in Finland at the given stage: my calculations spoke quite precisely of *supplementing* military operations by measures of civil war. I have in mind—at least until the Finnish army is annihilated—only the occupied territory and the nearby regions. Today on January 17 as I write these lines dispatches from a Finnish source report that one of the border provinces has been invaded by detachments of Finnish émigrés and that brother is literally killing brother there. What is this if not an episode in a civil war? In any case there can be no doubt that a new advance of the Red Army into Finland will confirm at every step our general appraisal of the war. Shachtman has neither an analysis of the events nor the hint of a prognosis. He confines himself to noble indignation and for this reason at every step he sinks deeper into the mire.

The appeal of the 'People's Government' calls for workers' control. What can this mean! exclaims Shachtman. There is no workers' control in the USSR; whence will it come in Finland? Sad to say, Shachtman reveals complete lack of understanding of the situation. In the USSR workers' control is a stage long ago completed. From control over the bourgeoisie there they passed to management of nationalized production. From the management of workers—to the command of the bureaucracy. New workers' control would now signify control over the bureaucracy. This cannot be established except as the result of a successful uprising against the bureaucracy. In Finland, workers' control still signifies nothing more than crowding out the native bourgeoisie, whose place the bureaucracy proposes to take. Furthermore one should not think that the Kremlin is so stupid as to attempt ruling eastern Poland or Finland by means of imported commissars. Of greatest urgency to the

Kremlin is the extraction of a new administration apparatus from among the toiling population of the occupied areas. This task can be solved only in several stages. The first stage is the peasant committees and the committees of workers' control.*

Shachtman clutches eagerly even at the fact that Kuusinen's programme 'is, formally, the programme of a bourgeois "democracy" '. Does he mean to say by this that the Kremlin is more interested in establishing bourgeois democracy in Finland than in drawing Finland into the framework of the USSR? Shachtman himself doesn't know what he wants to say. In Spain, which Moscow did not prepare for union with the USSR, it was actually a question of demonstrating the ability of the Kremlin to safeguard bourgeois democracy against proletarian revolution. This task flowed from the interests of the Kremlin bureaucracy in that particular international situation. Today the situation is a different one. The Kremlin is not preparing to demonstrate its usefulness to France, England and the United States. As its actions have proved, it has firmly decided to sovietise Finland—at once or in two stages. The programme of the Kuusinen government, even if approached from a 'formal' point of view does not differ from the programme of the Bolsheviks in November 1917. True enough, Shachtman makes

---

* This article was already written when I read in the New York *Times* of January 17 the following lines relating to former eastern Poland: 'In industry, drastic acts of expropriation have not yet been carried out on a large scale. The main centres of the banking system, the railway system and a number of large industrial undertakings were State-owned for years before the Russian occupation. In small and medium-sized industries workmen now exercise control over production.

'The industrialists nominally retain a full right of ownership in their own establishments, but they are compelled to submit statements of costs of production, and so on, for the consideration of the workmen's delegates. The latter, jointly, with the employers, fix wages, conditions of work, and a "just rate of profit" for the industrialist.'

Thus we see that 'the realities of living events' do not at all submit themselves to the pedantic and lifeless patterns of the leaders of the opposition. Meanwhile our 'abstractions' are becoming transformed into flesh and blood.

much of the fact that I generally place significance on the manifesto of the 'idiot' Kuusinen. However, I shall take the liberty of considering that the 'idiot' Kuusinen acting on the ukase of the Kremlin and with the support of the Red Army represents a far more serious political factor than scores of superficial wise-acres who refuse to think through the internal logic (dialectics) of events.

As a result of his remarkable analysis, Shachtman this time openly proposes a *defeatist* policy in relation to the USSR, adding (for emergency use) that he does not at all cease to be a 'patriot of his class'. We are happy to get the information. But the trouble is that Dan, the leader of the Mensheviks, as far back as November 12 wrote that in the event the Soviet Union invaded Finland the world proletariat 'must take a definitive defeatist position in relation to this violation'. (*Sozialisticheski Vestnik,* No. 19-20, p. 43.) It is necessary to add that throughout the Kerensky regime, Dan was a rabid defencist; he failed to be a defeatist even under the Czar. Only the invasion of Finland by the Red Army has turned Dan into a defeatist. Naturally he does not thereby cease to be a 'patriot of his class'. What class? This question is not an uninteresting one. So far as the analysis of events is concerned Shachtman disagrees with Dan who is closer to the theatre of action and cannot replace facts with fiction; by way of compensation, where the 'concrete political conclusions' are concerned, Shachtman has turned out to be a 'patriot' of the very same class as Dan. In Marxist sociology this class, if the opposition will permit me, this class is called the *petty bourgeoisie.*

The Theory of 'Blocs'

To justify his bloc with Burnham and Abern—against the proletarian wing of the party, against the programme of the Fourth International, and against the Marxist method—Shachtman has not spared the history of the revolutionary movement which he—according to his own words—studied especially in order to transmit great traditions to the younger generation. The goal itself is of course excellent. But it demands a scientific method. Meanwhile, Shachtman has begun by sacrificing scientific method for the sake of a bloc. His historical examples are arbitrary, not thought out and downright false.

Not every collaboration is a bloc in the proper sense of the term. By no means infrequent are episodic agreements which are not at all transformed and do not seek to be transformed into a protracted bloc. On the other hand membership in one and the same party can hardly be called a bloc. We together with comrade Burnham have belonged (and I hope will continue to belong to the end) to one and the same international party; but this is still not a bloc. Two parties can conclude a long term bloc with each other against a common enemy: such was the policy of the 'People's Front'. Within one and the same party close but not congruent tendencies can conclude a bloc against a third faction.

For the evaluation of inner-party blocs two questions are of decisive significance: (1) First and foremost against whom or what is the bloc directed? (2) What is the relationship of forces within the bloc? Thus for a struggle against chauvinism within one's own party a bloc between internationalists and centrists is wholly permissible. The result of the bloc would in this case depend upon the clarity of the programme of the internationalists, upon their cohesiveness and discipline, for these traits are not infrequently more important in determining the relationship of forces than their numerical strength.

Shachtman as we said before appeals to Lenin's bloc with Bogdanov. I have already stated that Lenin did not make the slightest theoretical concessions to Bogdanov. Now we shall examine the political side of the 'bloc'. It is first of all necessary to state that what was actually in question was not a bloc but a collaboration in a common organisation. The Bolshevik faction led an independent existence. Lenin did not form a 'bloc' with Bogdanov against other tendencies within his own organisation. On the contrary he formed a bloc even with the Bolshevik-conciliators (Dubrovinsky, Rykov and others) against the theoretical heresies of Bogdanov. In essence, the question so far as Lenin was concerned was whether it was possible to remain with Bogdanov in one and the same organisation which although called a 'faction' bore all the traits of a party. If Shachtman does not look upon the opposition as an independent organisation then his reference to the Lenin-Bogdanov 'bloc' falls to pieces.

But the mistake in the analogy is not restricted to this. The Bolshevik faction-party carried on a struggle against Menshevism which at that time had already revealed itself completely as a petty-bourgeois agency of the liberal bourgeoisie. This was far more serious than the accusation of so-called 'bureaucratic conservatism', the class roots of which Shachtman does not even attempt to define. Lenin's collaboration with Bogdanov was collaboration between a proletarian tendency and a sectarian centrist tendency against petty-bourgeois opportunism. The class lines are clear. The 'bloc' (if one uses this term in the given instance) was justified.

The subsequent history of the 'bloc' is not lacking in significance. In the letter to Gorky cited by Shachtman, Lenin expressed the hope that it would be possible to separate the political questions from the purely philosophic ones. Shachtman forgets to add that Lenin's hope did not at all materialise. Differences developed from the heights of philosophy down the line of all the other questions, including the most current ones. If the 'bloc' did not discredit Bolshevism it was only because Lenin had a finished programme, a correct method, a firmly welded faction in which Bogdanov's group composed a small unstable minority.

Shachtman concluded a bloc with Burnham and Abern against the proletarian wing of his own party. It is impossilbe to evade this. The relationship of forces within the bloc is completely against Shachtman. Abern has his own faction. Burnham with

Shachtman's assistance can create the semblance of a faction constituting intellectuals disillusioned with Bolshevism. Shachtman has no independent programme, no independent method, no independent faction. The eclectic character of the opposition 'programme' is determine by the contradictory tendencies within the bloc. In the event the bloc collapses—and the collapse is inevitable—Shachtman will emerge from the struggle with nothing but injury to the party and to himself.

Shachtman further appeals to the fact that in 1917 Lenin and Trotsky united after a long struggle and it would therefore be incorrect to remind them of their past differences. This example is slightly compromised by the fact that Shachtman has already utilised it once before to explain his bloc with—Cannon against Abern. But aside from this unpleasant circumstance the historical analogy is false to the core. Upon joining the Bolshevik party, Trotsky recognised completely and wholeheartedly the correctness of the Leninist methods of building the party. At the same time the irreconcilable class tendency of Bolshevism had corrected an incorrect prognosis. If I did not again raise the question of 'permanent revolution' in 1917 it was because it had already been decided for both sides by the march of events. The basis for joint work was constituted not by subjective or episodic combinations but by the proletarian revolution. This is a solid basis. Furthermore in question here was not a 'bloc' but unification in a single party—against the bourgeoisie and its petty-bourgeois agents. Inside the party the October bloc of Lenin and Trotsky was directed against petty-bourgeois vacillations on the question of insurrection.

Equally superficial is Shachtman's reference to Trotsky's bloc with Zinoviev in 1926. The struggle at that time was conducted not against 'bureaucratic conservatism' as the psychological trait of a few unsympathetic individuals but against the mightiest bureaucracy in the world, its privileges, its arbitrary rule and its reactionary policy. The scope of permissible differences in a bloc is determined by the character of the adversary.

The relationship of elements within the bloc was likewise altogether different. The opposition of 1923 had its own programme and its own cadres composed not at all of intellectuals as Shachtman asserts, echoing the Stalinists, but primarily workers. The Zinoviev-Kamenev opposition on our demand acknowledged in a special document that the 1923 opposition was correct on all fundamental questions. Nevertheless since we had different traditions and since we were far from agreeing in everything, the merger never did take place; both groups remained independent factions. In certain important questions, it is true, the 1923 opposition made principled concessions to the opposition in 1926—against my vote—concessions which I considered and still consider impermissible. The circumstance that I did not protest openly against these concessions was rather a mistake. But there was generally not much room for open protests—we were working illegally. In any event, both sides were very well acquainted with my views on the controversial questions. Within the 1923 opposition, nine hundred and ninety-nine out of a thousand if not more stood on my point of view and not on the point of view of Zinoviev or Radek. With such a relation between the two groups in the bloc there might have been these or other partial mistakes but there was not so much as a semblance of adventurism.

With Shachtman the case is completely different. Who was right in the past and just when and where? Why did Shachtman stand first with Abern, then with Cannon and now back again with Abern? Shachtman's own explanation concerning the past bitter factional struggles is worthy not of a responsible political figure but of a nurse-maid: Johnny was a little wrong, Max a little, all were a little wrong, and now we are all a little right. Who was in the wrong and in what, not a word of this. There is no tradition. Yesterday is expunged from the calculations —and what is the reason for all this? Because in the organism of the party comrade Shachtman plays the role of a floating kidney.

Seeking historical analogies, Shachtman avoids one example to which his present bloc does actually bear a resemblance. I have in mind the so-called August bloc of 1912. I participated actively in this bloc. In a certain sense I created it. Politically I differed with the Mensheviks on all fundamental questions. I also differed with the ultra-left Bolsheviks, the *Vperyodists*. In the general tendency of politics I stood far more closely to the Bolsheviks. But I was against the Leninist 'regime' because I had not yet learned to understand that in order to realise the revolutionary goal a firmly welded centralised party is indispensable. And so I formed this episodic bloc consisting of heterogeneous elements which was directed against the proletarian wing of the party.

In the August bloc the liquidators had their own faction, the *Vperyodists* also had something resembling a faction. I stood isolated, having co-thinkers but no faction. Most of the documents were written by me and through avoiding principled differences had as their aim the creation of a semblance of unanimity upon 'concrete political questions'. Not a word about the past! Lenin subjected the August bloc to merciless criticism and the harshest blows fell to my lot. Lenin proved that inasmuch as I did not agree politically with either the Mensheviks or the *Vperyodists* my policy was adventurism. This was severe but it was true.

As 'mitigating circumstances' let me mention the fact that I had set as my task not to support the right or ultra-left factions against the Bolsheviks but to unite the whole party as a whole. The Bolsheviks too were invited to the August conference. But since Lenin flatly refused to unite with the Mensheviks (in which he was completely correct) I was left in an unnatural bloc with the Mensheviks and the *Vperyodists*. The second mitigating circumstance is this, that the very phenomenon of Bolshevism as the genuine revolutionary party was then developing for the first time—in the practice of the Second International there were no precedents. But I do not thereby seek in the least to absolve myself from guilt. Notwithstanding the conception of permanent revolution which undoubtedly disclosed the correct perspective, I had not freed myself at that period especially in the organisational sphere from the traits of a petty-bourgeois revolutionist. I was sick with the disease of conciliat-tionism toward Menshevism and with a distrustful attitude toward Leninist centralism. Immediately after the August conference the bloc began to disintegrate into its component parts. Within a few months I was not only in principle but organisationally outside the bloc.

I address Shachtman today with the very same rebuke which Lenin addressed to me 27 years ago: 'Your bloc is unprincipled'. 'Your policy is adventurism'. With all my heart I express the hope that from these accusations Shachtman will draw some conclusions which I once drew.

The Factions in the Struggle

Shachtman expresses surprise over the fact that Trotsky, 'the leader of the 1923 opposition', is capable of supporting the bureaucratic faction of Cannon. In this as in the question of workers' control Shachtman again reveals his lack of feeling for historical perspective. True, in justifying their dictatorship the Soviet bureaucracy exploited the principles of Bolshevik centralism but in the very process it transformed them into their exact opposite. But this does not discredit in the least the methods of Bolshevism. Over a period of many years Lenin educated the party in the spirit of proletarian discipline and severe centralism. In so doing he suffered scores of times the attack of petty-bourgeois factions and cliques. Bolshevik centralism was a profoundly progressive factor and in the end secured the triumph of the revolution. It is not difficult to understand that the struggle of the present opposition in the Socialist Workers Party has nothing in common with the struggle of the Russian opposition of 1923 against the privileged bureaucratic caste but it does instead bear great resemblance to the struggle of the Mensheviks against Bolshevik centralism.

Cannon and his group are according to the opposition 'an expression of a type of politics which can be best described as bureaucratic conservatism'. What does this mean? The domination of a conservative labour bureaucracy, share-holder in the profits of the national bourgeoisie, would be unthinkable without direct or indirect support of the capitalist state. The rule of the Stalinist bureaucracy would be unthinkable without the GPU, the army, the courts, etc. The Soviet bureaucracy supports Stalin precisely because he is the bureaucrat who defends their interests better than anybody else. The trade union bureaucracy supports Green and Lewis precisely because their vices, as able and dexterous bureaucrats, safeguard the material interests of the labour aristocracy. But upon what base does 'bureaucratic conservatism' rest in the SWP? Obviously not on material interests but on a selection of bureaucratic types in contrast to another camp where innovators, initiators and dynamic spirits have been gathered together. The opposition does not point to any objective, i.e., social basis for 'bureaucratic conservatism'. Everything is reduced to pure psychology. Under such conditions every thinking worker will say: It is possible that comrade Cannon actually does sin in the line of bureaucratic tendencies—it is hard for me to judge at a distance—but if the majority of the National Committee and of the entire party who are not at all interested in bureaucratic 'privileges' support Cannon they do so not because of his bureaucratic tendencies but in spite of them. This means that he has some other virtues which far outweigh his personal failing. That is what a serious party member will say. And in my opinion he would be correct.

To substantiate their complaints and accusations the leaders of the opposition bring up disjointed episodes and anecdotes which can be counted by the hundred and the thousand in every party and which moreover are impossible to verify objectively in most instances. Furthest from my mind is indulgence in a criticism of the story-telling section of the opposition documents. But there is one episode about which I wish to express myself as a participant and a witness. The leaders of the opposition very superciliously relate how easily, presumably without criticism and without deliberation, Cannon and his group accepted the programme of transitional demands. Here is what I wrote on April 15, 1938 to comrade Cannon concerning the elaboration of this programme:

'We have sent you the transitional programme draft and a short statement about the labour party. Without your visit to Mexico I could never have written the programme draft because I learned during the discussions many important things which permitted me to be more explicit and concrete. . . .'

Shachtman is thoroughly acquainted with these circumstances since he was one of those who took part in the discussion.

Rumours, personal speculations and simple gossip cannot help but occupy an important place in petty-bourgeois circles where people are bound together not by party ties but by personal relationships and where no habit has been acquired of a class approach to events. It is passed from ear to ear that I have been visited exclusively by representatives of the majority and that I have been led astray from the path of truth. Dear comrades, don't believe this nonsense! I collect political information through the very same methods that I use in my work generally. A critical attitude toward information is an organic part of the political physiognomy of every politician. If I were incapable of distinguishing false communications from true ones what value could my judgments have in general?

I am personally acquainted with no less than twenty members of Abern's faction. To several of them I am obligated for their friendly help in my work and I consider all of them, or almost all, as valuable party members. But at the same time I must say that what distinguishes each of them to one degree or another is the aura of a petty-bourgeois milieu, lack of experience in the class struggle and to a certain extent lack of the requisite connection with the proletarian movement. Their positive features link them to the Fourth International. Their negative features bind them to the most conservative of all factions.

'An "anti-intellectual" and "anti-intellectuals" attitude is drummed into the minds of party members,' complains the document on 'Bureaucratic Conservatism'. (*Internal Bulletin,* Vol. 2, No. 6, January 1940, p. 12.) This argument is dragged in by the hair. It is not those intellectuals who have completely gone over to the side of the proletariat who are in question, but those elements who are seeking to shift our party to the position of petty-bourgeois eclecticism. This same document declares: 'An anti-New York propaganda is spread which is at bottom a catering to prejudices that are not always healthy' (idem). What prejudices are referred to here? Apparently anti-Semitism. If anti-Semitic or other race prejudices exist in our party, it is necessary to wage a ruthless struggle against them through open blows and not through vague insinuations. But the question of the Jewish intellectuals and semi-intellectuals of New York is a *social* not a *national* question. In New York there are a great many Jewish proletarians, but Abern's faction is not built up of them. The petty-bourgeois elements of this faction have proved incapable to this day of finding a road to the Jewish workers. They are contented with their own milieu.

There has been more than one instance in history—more precisely it does not happen otherwise in history—that with the transition of the party from one period to the next those elements which played a progressive role in the past but who proved incapable of adapting themselves with timeliness to new tasks have drawn closer together in the face of danger and revealed not their positive but almost exclusively their negative traits. That is precisely the role today of Abern's faction in which Shachtman plays the role of journalist and Burnham the role of theoretical brain trust. 'Cannon knows,' persists Shachtman, 'how spurious it is to inject in the present discussion the "Abern question." He knows what every informed party leader, and many members know, namely, that for the past several years at least there has been no such thing as an "Abern Group".' I take the liberty of remarking that if anybody is here distorting reality it is none other than Shachtman himself. I have been following the development of the internal relations in the American section for about ten years. The specific composition and the special role played by the New York organisation became clear to me before anything else. Shachtman will perhaps recall that while I was still in Prinkipo I advised the National Committee to move away from New York and its atmosphere of petty-bourgeois squabbles for a while to some industrial centre in the provinces. Upon arriving in Mexico I gained the opportunity of becoming better acquainted with the English language and thanks to many visits from my northern friends, of arriving at a more vivid picture of the social composition and the political psychology of the various groupings. On the basis of my own personal and immediate observations during the past three years I assert that the Abern faction has existed uninterruptedly, statically if not 'dynamically'.

The members of the Abern faction, given a modicum of political experience, are easily recognisable not only by their social traits but by their approach to all questions. These comrades have always formally denied the existence of their faction. There was a period when some of them actually did try to dissolve themselves into the party. But they attempted this by doing violence to themselves, and on all critical questions they came out in relation to the party as a group. They were far less interested in prinicipled questions, in particular the question of changing the social composition of the party, than in combinations at the top, personal conflicts and generally occurrences in the 'general staff'. This is the Abern school. I persistently warned many of these comrades that soaking in this artificial existence would unfailingly bring them sooner or later to a new factional explosion.

The leaders of the opposition speak ironically and disparagingly of the proletarian composition of the Cannon faction; in their eyes this incidental 'detail' carries no importance. What is this if not petty-bourgeois disdain combined with blindness? At the Second Congress of the Russian Social-Democrats in 1903 where the split took place between the Bolsheviks and the Mensheviks there were only three workers among several scores of delegates. All three of them turned up with the majority. The Mensheviks jeered at Lenin for investing this fact with great symptomatic significance. The Mensheviks themselves explained the position the three workers took by their lack of 'maturity'. But as is well known it was Lenin who proved correct.

If the proletarian section of our American party is 'politically backward', then the first task of those who are 'advanced' should have consisted in raising the workers to a higher level. But why has the present opposition failed to find its way to these workers? Why did they leave this work to the 'Cannon clique'? What is involved here? Aren't the workers good enough for the opposition? Or is the opposition unsuitable for workers?

It would be asinine to think that the workers' section of the party is perfect. The workers are only gradually reaching clear class consciousness. The trade unions always create a culture medium for opportunist deviations. Inevitably we will run up against this question in one of the next stages. More than once the party will have to remind its own trade unionists that a *pedagogical adaptation to the more backward layers of the proletariat must not become transformed into a political adaptation to the conservative bureaucracy of the trade unions.* Every new stage of development, every increase in the party ranks and the complication of the methods of its work open up not only new possibilities but also new dangers. Workers in the trade unions, even those trained in the most revolutionary school, often display a tendency to free themselves from party control. At the present time, however, this is not at all in question. At the present time the non-proletarian opposition, dragging behind it the majority of the non-proletarian youth, is attempting to revise our theory, our programme, our tradition—and it does all this light-mindedly, in passing, for greater convenience in the struggle against the 'Cannon clique'. At the present time disrespect for the party is shown not by the trade unionists but by the petty-bourgeois oppositionists. It is precisely in order to prevent the trade unionists from turning their backs to the party in the future that it is necessary to decisively repulse these petty-bourgeois oppositionists.

It is moreover impermissible to forget that the actual or possible mistakes of those comrades working in the trade unions reflect the pressure of the American proletariat as it is today. This is our class. We are not preparing to capitulate to its pressure. But this pressure at the same time shows us our main historic road. The mistakes of the opposition on the other hand reflect the pressure of another and alien class. An ideological break with that class is the elementary condition for our future successes.

The reasonings of the opposition in regard to the youth are false in the extreme. Assuredly, without the conquest of the proletarian youth the revolutionary party cannot develop. But the trouble is that we have almost an entirely petty-bourgeois youth, to a considerable degree with a social-democratic, i.e., opportunist past. The leaders of this youth have indubitable virtues and ability but, alas, they have been educated in the spirit of petty-bourgeois combinationism and if they are not wrenched out of their habitual milieu, if they are not sent without high-sounding titles into working-class districts for day-to-day dirty work among the proletariat, they can forever perish for the revolutionary movement. In relation to the youth as in all the other questions, Shachtman unfortunately has taken a position that is false to the core.

It Is Time to Halt!

To what extent Shachtman's thought from a false starting point has become debased is to be seen from the fact that he depicts my position as a defence of the 'Cannon clique' and he harps several times on the fact that in France I supported just as mistakenly the 'Molinier clique'. Everything is reduced to my supporting isolated individuals or groups entirely independently of their programme. The example of Molinier only thickens the fog. I shall attempt to dispel it. Molinier was accused not of retreating from our programme but of being undisciplined, arbitrary and of venturing into all sorts of financial adventures to support the party and his faction. Since Molinier is a very energetic man and has unquestionable practical capacities I found it necessary—not only in the interests of Molinier but above all in the interests of the organisation itself—to exhaust all the possibilities of convincing and re-educating him in the spirit of proletarian discipline. Since many of his adversaries possessed all of his failings but none of his virtues I did everything to convince them not to hasten a split but to test Molinier over and over again. It was this that constituted my 'defence' of Molinier in the adolescent period of the existence of our French section.

Considering a patient attitude toward blundering or undisciplined comrades and repeated efforts to re-educate them in the revolutionary spirit as absolutely compulsory I applied these methods by no means solely to Molinier. I made attempts to draw closer into the party and save Kurt Landau, Field, Weisbord, the Austrian Frey, and the Frenchman Treint, and a number of others. In many cases my efforts proved fruitless; in a few cases it was possible to rescue valuable comrades.

In any case I did not make the slightest principled concession to Molinier. When he decided to found a paper on the basis of 'four slogans' instead of our programme, and set out independently to execute this plan, I was among those who insisted upon his immediate expulsion. But I will not hide the fact that at the Founding Congress of the Fourth International I was in favour of once again testing Molinier and his group within the framework of the International to see if they had become convinced of the erroneousness of their policy. This time, too, the attempt led to nothing. But I do not renounce repeating it under suitable conditions once again. It is most curious that among the bitterest opponents of Molinier there were people like Vereecken and Sneevliet, who after they had broken with the Fourth International successfully united with him.

A number of comrades upon acquainting themselves with my archives have reproached me in a friendly way with having wasted and still continuing to waste so much time on convincing 'hopeless people'. I replied that many times I have had the occasion to observe how people change with circumstances and that I am therefore not ready to pronounce people as 'hopeless' on the basis of a few even though serious mistakes.

When it became clear to me that Shachtman was driving himself and a certain section of the party into a blind alley I wrote him that if the opportunity were mine I would immediately take an airplane and fly to New York in order to discuss with him for seventy-two hour stretches at a time. I asked him if he didn't wish to make it possible somehow for us to get together. Shachtman did not reply. This is wholly within his right. It is quite possible that those comrades who may become acquainted with my archives in the future will say in this case too that my letter to Shachtman was a false step on my part and they will cite this 'mistake' of mine in connection with my over-persistent 'defence' of Molinier. They will not convince me. It is an extremely difficult task to form an international proletarian vanguard under present conditions. To chase after individuals at the expense of principles would of course be a crime. But to do everything possible to bring back outstanding yet mistaken comrades to our programme I have considered and still consider my duty.

From that very Trade Union Discussion which Shachtman utilised with such glaring irrelevance, I quote the words of Lenin which Shachtman should engrave on his mind: 'A mistake always begins by being small and growing greater. Differences always begin with trifles. Everyone has at times suffered a tiny wound but should this tiny wound become infected, a mortal disease may follow.' Thus spoke Lenin on January 23, 1921. It is impossible not to make mistakes; some err more frequently, others less frequently. The duty of a proletarian revolutionist is not to persist in mistakes, not to place ambition above the interests of the cause but to call a halt in time. It is time for comrade Shachtman to call a halt! Otherwise the scratch which has already developed into an ulcer can lead to gangrene.

January 24, 1940. *Coyoacan, D. F.*

A letter to Martin Abern

January 29, 1940

Dear Comrade Abern:

I received the communication about your alleged expression 'This means split' from Comrade Cannon. He wrote on December 28th, 1939:

> Your document has already been widely distributed in the party. So far I have heard only two definite comments from leaders of the minority. Abern, after he had read the title and the first few paragraphs, remarked to Goldman, 'This means a split'.

I know Cannon as a trustworthy comrade and I didn't have the slightest reason to doubt the veracity of his communication.

You say this report 'is a lie'. I know by long experience that during the sharp fight, misunderstandings of such a kind are very often without bad will from one side or the other.

You ask me whether I made any effort to check the veracity of this report. None at all. If I had spread it in private correspondence as a fact known to me, it would not have been loyal. But I published it with a remark 'it has been reported' and so gave you the full possibility to confirm or deny the report. I believe this to be the best checking possible in a party discussion.

You say in the beginning of your letter: 'I have disregarded in the past a number of false statements, but I note among other things, in your open letter . . .' etc. What signifies here the phrase, 'a number of false statements'? From whom? What signifies the expression, 'among other things'? What kind of things? Don't you believe that your expressions can be understood by inexperienced comrades as vague insinuations? If, in my article, there are 'a number of false statements' and 'other things', it would be better to enumerate them exactly. If the false statements are not from me, I don't understand why you introduce them in your letter to me. I can also hardly understand how one can 'disregard' a number of false statements if they have any political importance: it could be interpreted as a lack of attention toward the party.

In any case I note with satisfaction that you categorically deny the sentence 'this means split'. I interpret the energetic tone of your letter in this sense, that your denial is not a formal one, that is, that you deny not only the quotation, but that you consider as I do, the idea of split itself as a despicable betrayal of the Fourth International.

Fraternally yours,
LEON TROTSKY

Coyoacan, D. F.
Copy to Cannon

Two Letters to Albert Goldman†

February 10, 1940

Dear Comrade Goldman,

I agree completely with your letter of February 5th. If I published Abern's remark about the split, it was with the purpose of provoking a clear and unambiguous statement from Comrade Abern and other leaders of the opposition—not about the alleged hidden intentions of the majority leaders in this respect but about their own.

I have already heard the aphorism about the 'second class citizens'. I would ask the leaders of the opposition: when they call the opposing group, 'Cannon's clique' or 'conservative bureaucrats' and so on, do they wish to make second class citizens of them? I can only add that extreme sensitiveness is one of the most salient features of every petty bourgeois faction. I don't know if Shachtman, for example, wishes by his *Open Letter* to make me a second class citizen. I am interested only in his ideas, not in his psychoanalytical guessing.

I am a bit under the impression that, unnerved by a series of mistakes, the leaders of the opposition push each other into a hysterical mood and then in order to justify their factional hysteria in their own eyes, they attribute to their adversaries the darkest and most incredible designs. When they say my exchange of letters with Cannon was a camouflage, I can only shrug my shoulders.

The best treatment for petty bourgeois hysteria is Marxist objectivism. We will continue to discuss dialectics, Marxian sociology, the class nature of the Soviet State, the character of the war, not with the absurd and criminal purpose of provoking a split, but with the more reasonable purpose of convincing an important part of the party and of helping it pass over from a petty bourgeois position to a proletarian one.

With warmest comradely greetings,
L. TROTSKY.

February 19, 1940

Dear Comrade Goldman,

A convention of the minority is only a caucus on a national scale.* This is why it does not signify, in itself, a principled change of the situation. It is only a new step on the same road, a bad step on the road of split, but not necessarily the split itself. Possibly, even surely, there are two or three tendencies inside the opposition in respect to the split question and the aim of the convention is to unify them. On what basis? Probably some leaders don't see in their desperation any other way than a split.

Under these conditions a vigorous intervention in favour of unity by the majority could possibly make more difficult the task of the conscious splitters. Could not your caucus or possibly even better, the official majority of the N. C. or the P. C. address the Cleveland convention with a message concerning one question only, namely the unity of the party. In such a letter I wouldn't introduce the question of the character of the Soviet Union or of the mixed war, otherwise it could be understood that their position on these questions must be abandoned as a precondition for remaining in the party. Not at all. You accept them as they are, if they have a real devotion to the party and the 4th International and are ready to accept discipline in action.

With best greetings,

LEON TROTSKY

---

* The minority convoked a conference of their group in Cleveland on February 24-25, 1940. This conference resolved that there existed two politically irreconcilable tendencies in the party and that 'the party must extend to whichever group is the minority at the convention the right to publish a public political journal of its own defending the general programme of the Fourth International [and which] would at the same time present in an objective manner the special position of its tendency on the disputed Russian question'. The majority rejected the demands of the minority.—Ed.

Back to the Party!†

February 21, 1940

Dear Comrades,

The leaders of the Minority have not as yet answered any theoretical or political argument from our part. The inconsistency of their own arguments was unmasked in the writings of the Majority. Now the opposition leaders seem to have passed over to guerrilla warfare: It is the fate of many other defeated armies. Comrade A. Goldman characterised aptly the new method of the opposition in his circular letter of February 12th. One of the most curious examples of this new warfare is the more valiant than sensible attack of Comrade MacDonald in connection with my LIBERTY article. He didn't find, you see, in this article an analysis of the contradictory character of the Soviet state and of the 'progressive role' of the Red Army. With the same logic which he shows in the editing of PARTISAN REVIEW as in his analysis of the Kronstadt uprising, he discovers that I am 'in reality' a minorityite, a Shachtmanite, or a MacDonaldist, at least when I speak for the bourgeois press and that my contrary declarations, capitulatory toward Stalinism, are made only in the internal bulletins for the purpose of helping Cannon. If we should express MacDonald's discovery in a more articulate manner, it would signify: When Trotsky wishes to adapt himself to the bourgeois public opinion, to make himself agreeable to the readers of LIBERTY, he writes like Shachtman, and almost like Mac-Donald; but when he speaks to the Party, he becomes terribly anti-minority. The PARTISAN REVIEW is very interested in psychoanalysis and I permit myself to say that the editor of this reveiw, if he analyses himself a bit, would recognise that he has uncovered his own subconscious.

Nobody asks from the Minority that they analyse in every article and in every speech the contradictory nature of the Soviet state and the contradictory role of the Red Army. What we ask of them is that they understand this nature and this role and that they apply their understanding adequately at every occasion. My article was devoted to Stalin's politics and not to the nature of the Soviet state. In the Mexican bourgeois press, there was published an anonymous statement asserting 'from sources near to Trotsky' that I approve Stalin's international politics and that I am seeking a reconciliation with Stalin. I don't know whether such statements appeared also in the United States' press. It is clear that the Mexican press reproduced only in its own manner the terribly serious accusation of MacDonald and Company about my capitulation to Stalinism. In order to prevent such a misuse of the internal discussion by the world bourgeois press, I devoted my article in LIBERTY to the unmasking of Stalin's role in international politics and not at all to the sociological analysis of the nature of the Soviet state. I wrote what I found more urgent for that moment. Politics consists not in saying at each occasion everything one knows, but in saying at the given occasion just what is necessary. Possibly I coincided thereby with some assertions of the opposition, but surely the corresponding assertions of the opposition were only a repetition of thoughts that we expressed a thousand times before MacDonald appeared on our horizon.

But we will pass to more serious things. Comrade Abern's letter to me is an absolutely clear enunciation of his will to split. The justification he gives is simultaneously lamentable and scandalous: these are the two mildest words I can find. If 'Cannon's clique' should have the majority in the convention, it will, you see, transform Abern and his associates into 'second class' citizens. This is why he, Abern, prefers to have his own state where he will be like Weisbord, Field and Oehler, the first of the first class citizens. Who can decide about the places of different 'citizens' inside the Party? The Party itself. How can the Party come to a decision? Through a free discussion. Who took the initiative in this discussion? Abern and his associates. Where or are they limited in the use of their pen or their tongue? Not at all. They didn't succeed, it seems from Abern's letter, in convincing the Party. Worse than that: they discredited themselves a bit in the eyes of the Party and the International. This is very regrettable because they are valuable people. They could re-establish their authority now only by assiduous and serious work in the Party. It needs time, patience and firmness. But it seems that Abern lost hope in ever convincing the Party based on the principles of the Fourth International. The split tendency is a kind of desertion. This is why it is so lamentable.

But it is also scandalous! The underlying tone is the contempt of petty-bourgeois elements for the proletarian majority: We are such excellent writers, speakers, organisers, and they, the un-cultivated people, are incapable of appreciating us at face value. Better to build our own league of elevated souls!

In the Third International we persisted with all our power to remain a tendency or a faction. They persecuted us, they deprived us of all the means of legal expression, they invented the worst calumnies, in the USSR they arrested and shot our comrades—in spite of all we didn't wish to separate ourselves from the workers. We considered ourselves as a faction to the very last possibility. And all that—in spite of the corrupt totalitarian bureaucracy of the Third International. The Fourth International is the only honest revolutionary organisation in the world. We don't have a professional bureaucracy. Our 'apparatus' has no means of co-ercion. Every question is decided and every comrade is appre-ciated through methods of the most complete party democracy. If the majority of party members are mistaken, the minority can, by and by, educate them. If not before the next convention, then after it. The minority can attract new members to the Party and transform itself into a majority. It is necessary only to have a bit of confidence in the workers and a bit of hope that the workers can be imbued with confidence in the leaders of the opposition. But these leaders created in their own milieu an atmosphere of hysteric impatience. They adapt themselves to bourgeois public opinion, but they don't wish to adapt themselves to the rhythm of development of the Fourth International. Their impatience has a class character, it is the reverse side of the contempt of petty-bourgeois intellectuals toward the workers. This is why the split tendency expressed by Abern is so scandalous!

Comrade Abern in his appreciation as in his perspective is moved by hatred. And personal hatred is an abominable feeling in politics. I am sure that Abern's attitude and his split objectives can only repulse every sound member of the opposition. Back to the Party, comrades! Abern's way is a blind alley. There is no other way than that of the Fourth International.

LEON TROTSKY

Coyoacan, D. F.

'Science and Style'

Dear Comrades,

I received Burnham's 'Science and Style'. The abscess is open and this is an important political advantage. The theoretical backwardness of the American 'radical' opinion is expressed by the fact that Burnham repeats only—with some 'modernised' illustrations—what Struve wrote in Russia more than forty years ago and to a great degree what Dühring tried to teach German Social Democracy three-quarters of a century ago. So much from the point of view of 'science'. As far as 'style' is concerned, I frankly prefer Eastman.

The interest of the document is not at all of a theoretical character: the thousand and first professorial refutation of dialectics has no more worth than all its precedents. But, from the political point of view the importance of the document is indisputable. It shows that the theoretical inspirer of the opposition is not at all nearer to scientific socialism than was Muste, the former associate of Abern. Shachtman mentioned Bogdanov's philosophy. But it is absolutely impossible to imagine Bogdanov's signature under such a document, even after his definite rupture with Bolshevism. I believe the Party should ask Comrades Abern and Shachtman, as I do at this moment: What do you think of Burnham's 'science' and of Burnham's 'style'? The question of Finland is important but it is finally only an episode and the change of the international situation, revealing the genuine factors of events, can at once dissipate the divergences on this concrete issue. But can Comrades Abern and Shachtman now, after the appearance of 'Science and Style', continue to carry the slightest responsibility, not for the poor document as such, but for Burnham's entire conception on science, Marxism, politics, and 'morals'. Those Minorityites who prepared themselves for a split should consider that they would be connected not for a week and not for the duration of the Soviet-Finnish War, but for years with a 'leader' who has in his entire conception nothing in common with the proletarian revolution.

The abscess is open. Abern and Shachtman can no longer repeat that they wish only to discuss Finland and Cannon a bit. They can no longer play blind man's buff with Marxism and with the Fourth International. Should the Socialist Workers Party remain in the tradition of Marx, Engels, Franz Mehring, Lenin and Rosa Luxemburg—a tradition which Burnham proclaims 'reactionary' —or should it accept Burnham's conceptions which are only a belated reproduction of pre-Marxian petty-bourgeois socialism?

We know too well what such revisionism signified *politically* in the past. Now in the epoch of the death-agony of the bourgeois society, the political consequences of Burnhamism would be incomparably more immediate and anti-revolutionary. Comrades Abern and Shachtman, you have the floor!

LEON TROTSKY

Coyoacan, D. F.

A letter to James P. Cannon†

Dear Friend,   February 27, 1940

I am answering your letter of February 20th. The Minority convention is now as I suppose, over and I believe that in the concrete tactical question which you analyse in your letter, your *immediate* moves depend at least to 51 per cent on the results of this convention.

You are convinced that the Minority as a whole is preparing for a split and that you cannot win over anyone else. I accept this premise. But the more was it necessary to accomplish before the Cleveland convention an energetic gesture of peace in order to change radically your line after their negative answer. I appreciate completely your considerations in favour of the necessity to publish an issue of the NEW INTERNATIONAL preparing public opinion for the split. But the Minority convention took place on the 24th-25th of February and the Party convention will not be until the beginning of April. You have enough time at your disposal for the proposal of peace, for the denunciation of the Minority's refusal, and for the publication of the issue of the NEW INTERNATIONAL. We must do everything in order to convince also the other sections* that the Majority exhausted all the possibilities in favour of unity. This is why we three made the proposition to the International Executive Committee: it is necessary also to put to test every member of this not unimportant body.

I understand well the impatience of many Majority comrades (I suppose that this impatience is not infrequently connected with theoretical indifference), but they should be reminded that the happenings in the Socialist Workers Party have now a great international importance and that you must act not only on the basis of your subjective appreciations, as correct as they may be, but on the basis of objective facts available to everyone.

Coyoacan, D. F.   W. RORK [*Leon Trotsky*]

---

* Trotsky refers to other sections of the Fourth International.—Ed.

A letter to Joseph Hansen†

February 29, 1940

My dear Joe,

If Shachtman affirms that the letter quoted by me about Spain was signed not only by him but also by Cannon and Carter, then he is completely mistaken. I would of course not have hidden the other signatures but they did not exist. As you will see from the photographs, the letter was signed only by Max Shachtman.

In my article I admitted that in different questions the Majority comrades could have shared the errors of Shachtman but they never made a system of them, they never transformed them into a factional platform. And that is the whole question.

Abern and Burnham are indignant that I quote their oral declarations without a previous 'verification'. They mean obviously that instead of publishing these alleged declarations and of giving to both of them the full possibility to confirm or to deny them, I should send an investigating committee from here with 5 or 7 impartial persons and a couple of stenographers. And why the terrible moral noise? Burnham several times identified dialectics with religion. Yes, it is a fact. But on this special occasion he didn't pronounce the sentence I quote (as reported to me). Oh, horror! Oh, Bolshevik cynicism, etc.!

The same with Abern.* In his letter to me he shows clearly that he is preparing for a split. But you see, he never pronounced to Goldman the sentence about split. It is a slander! A dishonest invention! A calumny, etc.!

As far as I remember, my article on morals begins with a remark about the moral sweatings of the disorientated petty-bourgeois. We have now a new occurrence of the same phenomenon in our own party.

The new moralists quote, I heard, my terrible crime concerning

---

* See Trotsky's letter to Abern, January 29, 1940, on page 188.—Ed.

Eastman and Lenin's Testament.* What despicable hypocrites! Eastman published the document on his own initiative in a moment when our faction decided to interrupt all public activity in order to avoid a premature split. Don't forget it was before the famous Ang'o-Russian Trade Union Committee and before the Chinese Revolution, even before the appearance of the Zinoviev opposition. We were obliged to manoeuvre in order to win time. On the contrary, the Troika wished to utilise Eastman's publication in order to provoke a kind of oppositional abortion. They presented an ultimatum: Either I must sign the declaration written by the Troika in my name or they will immediately open the fight on the matter. The opposition centre decided unanimously that *this* issue at *this* moment is absolutely unfavourable, that I must accept the ultimatum and sign my name under a declaration written by the Politburo. The transforming of this political necessity into an abstract moral question is only possible for petty-bourgeois fakers who are ready to proclaim: Pereat mundus, fiat justicia! (the world can perish, long live justice!), but who have a far more indulgent bookkeeping for their own daily procedures. And these people imagine that they are revolutionaries! Our old Mensheviks were real heroes in comparison with them.

W. RORK [*Leon Trotsky*]

Coyoacan, D. F.

---

* In 1925 Max Eastman released for publication in the New York *Times* the text of Lenin's Testament and also included it in his book *Since Lenin Died.*

At the hearings of the Dewey Commission, Trotsky gave the following explanation for disavowing Eastman at the time:

'Eastman published this document without consulting me and the others, and by these means he sharpened terribly the inner struggle in the Soviet Union, in the Politburo, which was the beginning of the split. We tried on our side to avoid a split. The majority of the Politburo asked me, demanded of me, to take a position toward this. It was a very diplomatic document that I signed at that time.' (*The Case of Leon Trotsky*, p. 429.)

Three Letters to Farrell Dobbs†

March 4, 1940

Dear Comrade Dobbs,

It is of course difficult for me to follow from here the feverish political evolution of the opposition. But I agree that they produce more and more the impression of people who are hastening to burn all the bridges behind them. Burnham's article 'Science and Style' is not unexpected in itself. But the calm acceptance of the article by Shachtman, Abern and the others is the most disappointing symptom, not only from the theoretical and political point of view, but also from that of their genuine ideas concerning the unity of the Party.

So far as I can judge from here, they wish a split under the name of unity. Shachtman finds, or better to say invents 'historical precedents'. In the Bolshevik Party the opposition had its own public papers, etc. He forgets only that the Party at that time had hundreds of thousands of members, that the discussion had as its task to reach these hundreds of thousands and to convince them. Under such conditions it was not easy to confine the discussion to internal circles. On the other hand the danger of the co-existence of the Party and the opposition papers was mitigated by the fact that the final decision depended upon hundreds of thousands of workers and not upon two small groups. The American Party has only a comparatively small number of members, the discussion was and is more than abundant. The demarcation lines seem to be firm enough, at least for the next period. Under such conditions for the opposition to have their own public paper or magazine is a means not to convince the Party but to appeal against the Party to the external world.

The homogeneity and cohesion of a revolutionary propaganda organisation such as the SWP must be incomparably greater than that of a mass party. I agree with you that under such conditions the Fourth International should and could not admit a purely fictitious unity under the cover of which two independent organisations address the external world with different theories, different programmes, different slogans and different organisational principles. Under these conditions an open split would be a thousand times preferable to such a hypocritical unity.

The opposition refers also to the fact that we had in certain periods two parallel groups in the same country. But such abnormal situations were temporarily admitted only in two cases: When the political physiognomy of both groups or of one of them was not clear enough and the Fourth International needed time in order to make up its own mind about the matter; or a coexistence of two groups was admitted in the case of a very sharp but limited concrete disagreement (entrance in the PSOP,* etc.). The situation in the United States is absolutely different. We had a united party with a serious tradition, now we have two organisations one of which, thanks to its social composition and external pressure, entered, during a period of a couple of months, into an irreconcilable conflict with our theory, our programme, our politics, our organisational methods.

If they agree to work with you on the basis of democratic centralism, you can hope to convince and to win over the best elements by common practice. (They have the same right to hope to convince you.) But as an independent organisation with their own publication they can only develop in Burnham's direction. In this case the Fourth International cannot have, in my opinion, the slightest interest in granting them its cover, i.e., to camouflage before the workers their inevitable degeneration. On the contrary, the interests of the Fourth International would be in this case to force the opposition to have its experience absolutely independently from us, not only without the protection of our banner, but on the contrary, with the sharpest warning openly addressed by us to the masses.

This is why the convention has not only the right but the duty to formulate a sharp and clear alternative: Either a genuine unity

---
* PSOP—Socialist Party of Workers and Peasants of France.—Ed.

on the principle of democratic centralism (with serious and large guarantees for the Minority *inside* the Party) or an open, clear and demonstrative break before the forum of the working class.*

With best greetings,

W. RORK [*Leon Trotsky*]

P.S. I just received the Cleveland resolution on Party unity. My impression: The rank and file of the Minority do not wish a split. The leaders are interested not in a political but a purely journalistic activity. The leaders presented a resolution on Party split under the name of a resolution on Party unity with the purpose of involving their followers in a split. The resolution says: 'Minorities of the Bolshevik Party both before and during the First World War' had their own public political journals. What minorities? At what time? What journals? The leaders induce their followers into an error in order to camouflage their split intentions.

All hopes of the Minority leaders are based on their literary capacities. They assure one another that their paper would surely excel that of the Majority. Such was always the hope of the Russian Mensheviks who as a petty-bourgeois faction had more intellectuals and able journalists. But their hopes were in vain. A fluent pen is not sufficient to create a revolutionary party: a granite theoretical base is necessary, a scientific programme, a consistency in political thinking and firm organisational principles. The opposition as an opposition has nothing of all that; it is the opposite of all that. This is why I agree with you completely: If they wish to present Burnham's theories, Shachtman's politics and Abern's organisational methods to the external public opinion, they should do it in their own name without any responsibility of the Party or of the Fourth International.

W.R.

---

* The International Executive Committee should, a long time ago, have presented such an alternative, but unfortunately the IEC does not exist.

April 4, 1940

Dear Comrade Dobbs,

When you receive this letter, the convention will have already progressed and you will probably have a clear idea if the split is unavoidable. In this case the Abern question would lose its interest. But in the case that the Minority makes a retreat, I permit myself to insist upon my previous propositions. The necessity of preserving the secrets of the discussions and decisions in the National Committee is a very important interest but not the only one and in the present situation not the most important. About 40 per cent of Party members believe Abern is the best organiser. If they remain inside the Party, you cannot help but give Abern the chance to show his superiority in organisational matters or to compromise himself. In the first session of the new National Committee, the first decision should proclaim that nobody has the right to divulge the internal happenings in the National Committee except the committee as a whole or its official institutions (Political Committee or Secretariat). The Secretariat could in its turn concretise the rules of secrecy. If, in spite of all, a leak occurs, an official investigation should be made and if Abern should be guilty, he should receive a public warning; in case of another offence, he should be eliminated from the Secretariat. Such a procedure, in spite of its temporary disadvantages is, in the long run, incomparably more favourable than to leave Abern, the New York Organiser, outside the Secretariat, i.e., outside the real control of the Secretariat.

I understand very well that you are satisfied with the present Secretariat. In case of a split it is possibly the best Secretariat one could wish. But if the unity is preserved, you can't have a Secretariat composed only of Majority representatives. You should possibly have a Secretariat even of five members—three Majorityites and two Minorityites.

If the Opposition is wavering, it would be best to let them know in an informal way: We are ready to retain Shachtman as a member not only of the Political Committee but also of our editorial staff; we are even ready to include Abern in the Secretariat; we are willing to consider other combinations of the same kind; the only thing we cannot accept is the transformation of the Minority into an independent political factor.

*   *   *

I received a letter from Lebrun on the IEC. A peculiar people! They believe that now in the period of the death agony of capitalism, under the conditions of war and coming illegality, Bolshevik centralism should be abandoned in favour of unlimited democracy. Everything is topsy-turvy! But their democracy has a purely individual meaning: Let me do as I please. Lebrun and Johnson were elected to the IEC on the basis of certain principles and as representatives of certain organisations. Both abandoned the principles and ignored completely their own organisations. These 'democrats' acted completely as Bohemian free-lancers. Should we have the possibility of convoking an international congress, they would surely be dismissed with the severest blame. They themselves don't doubt it. At the same time, they consider themselves as unremovable senators—in the name of democracy!

As the French say, we must take war-time measures during a war. This means that we must adapt the leading body of the Fourth International to the real relationship of forces in our sections. There is more democracy in this than in the pretensions of the unremovable senators.

If this question comes up for discussion, you can quote these lines as my answer to Lebrun's document.

W. RORK [*Leon Trotsky*]

Coyoacan, D. F.

Dear Comrade Dobbs,   April 16, 1940
    *   *   *

We received also your and Joe's communications on the convention. As far as we can judge from here, you did everything you
could in order to preserve the unity of the Party. If under these
conditions the Minority nevertheless commits a split, it will only
show to every worker how far they are from the principles of
Bolshevism and how hostile to the proletarian majority of the
Party. About the details of your decisions, we will judge more
concretely when we have more information.
    *   *   *   *   *   *

I permit myself to call to your attention another article, namely
that of Gerland against Burnham concerning symbolic logic, the
logic of Bertrand Russell and the others. The article is very sharp
and in the case of the opposition's remaining in the Party and
Burnham on the editorial board of the NEW INTERNATIONAL
the article should possibly be rewritten from the point of view of
'friendliness' of expressions. But the presentation of symbolic
logic is very serious and good and seems to me very useful
especially for the American readers.

Comrade Weber devoted also an important part of his last
article to the same item. My opinion is that he should elaborate
this part in the form of an independent article for the NEW
INTERNATIONAL. We should now continue systematically and
seriously our theoretical campaign in favour of dialectical
materialism.
              *   *   *

Jim's pamphlet* is excellent. It is the writing of a genuine
workers' leader. If the discussion had not produced more than
this document, it would be justified.

                         With friendliest greetings for you all,
Coyoacan, D. F.   W. RORK [*Leon Trotsky*]

---

* This refers to *The Struggle for a Proletarian Party*, by James P.
Cannon.—Ed.

Petty-Bourgeois Moralists and the Proletarian Party*

The discussion in the Socialist Workers Party of the United States was thorough and democratic. The preparations for the convention were carried out with absolute loyalty. The minority participated in the convention, recognising thereby its legality and authoritativeness. The majority offered the minority all the necessary guarantees permitting it to conduct a struggle for its own views after the convention. The minority demanded a licence to appeal to the masses over the head of the party. The majority naturally rejected this monstrous pretension. Meanwhile, behind the back of the party the minority indulged in shady machinations and appropriated the *New International* which had been published through the efforts of the entire party and of the Fourth International. I should add that the majority had agreed to assign the minority two posts out of the five on the editorial board of this theoretical organ. But how can an intellectual 'aristocracy' remain the minority in a workers' party? To place a professor on equal plane with a worker—after all, that's 'bureaucratic conservatism'!

In his recent polemical article aganst me, Burnham explained that socialism is a 'moral ideal'. To be sure, this is not so very new. At the opening of the last century, morality served as the basis for the 'True German Socialism' which Marx and Engels criticised at the very beginning of their activity. At the beginning of our century, the Russian Social Revolutionaries counterposed the 'moral ideal' to materialistic socialism. Sad to say, these bearers of morality turned out to be common swindlers in the

---

* This article was first printed in the *Socialist Appeal* of May 4, 1940. The minority split from the SWP after the party convention in April 1940. Burnham, Shachtman and Abern, who held posts by party appointment on the party's theoretical organ, *The New International*, and who were trustees for the party in the New International Publishing Company, usurped the name of the magazine and appropriated its mailing rights as their personal property.—Ed.

field of politics. In 1917 they betrayed the workers completely
into the hands of the bourgeoisie and foreign imperialism.

Long political experience has taught me that whenever a petty-
bourgeois professor or journalist begins talking about high moral
standards it is necessary to keep a firm hand on one's pocketbook.
It happened this time, too. In the name of a 'moral ideal' a
petty-bourgeois intellectual has picked the proletarian party's
pocket of its theoretical organ. Here you have a tiny living
example of the organisational methods of these innovators, moralists and champions of democracy.

What is party democracy in the eyes of an 'educated' petty
bourgeois? A regime which permits him to say and write whatever he pleases. What is 'bureaucratism' in the eyes of an
'educated' petty bourgeois? A regime in which the proletarian
majority enforces by democratic methods its decisions and
discipline. Workers, bear this firmly in mind!

The petty-bourgeois minority of the SWP split from the proletarian majority on the basis of a struggle against revolutionary
Marxism. Burnham proclaimed dialectic materialism to be incompatible with his moth-eaten 'science'. Shachtman proclaimed revolutionary Marxism to be of no moment from the standpoint of
'practical tasks'. Abern hastened to hook up his little booth with
the anti-Marxist bloc. And now these gentlemen label the magazine they filched from the party an 'organ of revolutionary
Marxism'. What is this, if not ideological charlatanism? Let the
readers demand of these editors that they publish the sole programmatic work of the minority, namely, Burnham's article,
'Science and Style'. If the editors were not preparing to emulate a
peddler who markets rotten merchandise under fancy labels, they
would themselves have felt obliged to publish this article. Everybody could then see for himself just what kind of 'revolutionary
Marxism' is involved here. But they *will not dare* do so. They are
ashamed to show their true faces. Burnham is skilled at hiding his
all too revealing articles and resolutions in his briefcase, while

Shachtman has made a profession of serving as an attorney for
other people's views through lack of any views of his own.

The very first 'programmatic' articles of the purloined organ
already reveal completely the light-mindedness and hollowness of
this new anti-Marxist grouping which appears under the label of
the 'Third Camp'. What is this animal? There is the camp of
capitalism; there is the camp of the proletariat. But is there
perhaps a 'third camp'—a petty-bourgeois sanctuary? In the
nature of things, it is nothing else. But, as always, the petty
bourgeois camouflages his 'camp' with the paper flowers of
rhetoric. Let us lend our ears! Here is one camp: France and
England. There's another camp: Hitler and Stalin. And a third
camp: Burnham, with Shachtman. The Fourth International turns
out for them to be in Hitler's camp (Stalin made this discovery
long ago). And so, a new great slogan: Muddlers and pacifists of
the world, all ye suffering from the pin-pricks of fate, rally to the
'third' camp!

But the whole trouble is that two warring camps do not at all
exhaust the bourgeois world. What about all the neutral and
semi-neutral countries? What about the United States? Where
should Italy and Japan be assigned? The Scandinavian countries?
India? China? We have in mind not the revolutionary Indian or
Chinese workers but rather India and China as oppressed countries. The schoolboy schema of the three camps leaves out a
trifling detail: the colonial world, the greater portion of mankind!

India is participating in the imperialist war on the side of Great
Britain. Does this mean that our attitude toward India—not the
Indian Bolsheviks but *India*—is the same as toward Great Britain?
If there exist in this world, in addition to Shachtman and Burnham, only two imperialist camps, then where, permit me to ask,
shall we put India? A Marxist will say that despite India's being
an integral part of the British Empire and India's participating in
the imperialist war; despite the perfidious policy of Gandhi and
other nationalist leaders, our attitude toward India is altogether
different from our attitude toward England. We defend India

against England. Why then cannot our attitude toward the Soviet Union be different from our attitude toward Germany despite the fact that Stalin is allied with Hitler? Why can't we defend the more progressive social forms which are capable of development against reactionary forms which are capable only of decomposition? We not only can but we must! The theoreticians of the stolen magazine replace class analysis with a mechanistic construction very captivating to petty-bourgeois intellectuals because of its pseudo-symmetry. Just as the Stalinists camouflage their subservience to national socialism (the Nazis) with harsh epithets addressed to the imperialist democracies, so Shachtman and Co. cover up their capitulation to American pettybourgeois public opinion with the pompous phraseology of the 'third camp'. As if this 'third camp' (what is it? a party? a club? a League of Abandoned Hopes? a People's Front'?) is free from the obligation of having a correct policy toward the petty bourgeoisie, the trade unions, India and the USSR!

Only the other day Shachtman referred to himself in the press as a 'Trotskyist'. If *this* be Trotskyism then I at least am no Trotskyist. With the present ideas of Shachtman, not to mention Burnham, I have nothing in common. I used to collaborate actively with the *New International,* protesting in letters against Shachtman's frivolous attitude toward theory and his unprincipled concessions to Burnham, the strutting petty-bourgeois pedant. But at the time both Burnham and Shachtman were kept in check by the party and the International. Today the pressure of petty-bourgeois democracy has unbridled them. Toward their new magazine my attitude can only be the same as toward all other petty-bourgeois counterfeits of Marxism. As for their 'organisational methods' and political 'morality', these evoke in me nothing but contempt.

Had conscious agents of the class enemy operated through Shachtman, they could not have advised him to do anything different from what he himself has perpetrated. He united with anti-Marxists to wage a struggle against Marxism. He helped fuse together a petty-bourgeois faction against the workers. He refrained from utilising internal party democracy and from making an honest effort to convince the proletarian majority. He engineered a split under the conditions of a world war. To crown it all, he threw over the split the veil of a petty and dirty scandal, which seems especially designed to provide our enemies with ammunition. Such are these 'democrats', such are their 'morals'!

But all this will prove of no avail. They are bankrupt. Despite the betrayals of unstable intellectuals and the cheap gibes of all their democratic cousins, the Fourth International will march forward on its road, creating and educating a genuine selection of proletarian revolutionists capable of understanding what the party is, what loyalty to the banner means, and what revolutionary discipline signifies.

Advanced workers! Not one cent's worth of confidence in the 'third front' of the petty bourgeoisie!

April 23, 1940.

Balance Sheet of the Finnish Events*
They Couldn't Foresee

'We' foresaw the alliance with Hitler—write Shachtman and Burnham—but the seizure of eastern Poland? the invasion of Finland?—no, 'we' couldn't foresee these events. Such completely improbable and utterly unexpected events necessitate, they insist, a complete upheaval in our politics. These politicians laboured under the impression apparently that Stalin needed an alliance with Hitler in order to roll Easter eggs with him. They 'foresaw' the alliance (when? where?) but couldn't foresee what it was for and why.

They recognise the right of the workers' state to manoeuvre between the imperialist camps and to conclude agreements with one against another. These agreements should, obviously, have as their goal the defence of the workers' state, the acquisition of economic, strategical and other advantages and, if circumstances permit, the extension of the base of the workers' state. The degenerated workers' state attempts to gain these ends with its own bureaucratic methods, which at every step come into conflict with the interests of the world proletariat. But exactly what is so unexpected and so unpredictable about the Kremlin's attempt to get as much as it could from its alliance with Hitler?

If our ill-starred politicians failed to foresee 'this' it is only because they fail to think a single question seriously through to the end. During the protracted negotiations with the Anglo-French delegation in the summer of 1939, the Kremlin openly demanded military control over the Baltic states. Because England and France refused to grant him this control, Stalin broke off negotiations. This alone clearly indicated that an agreement with Hitler would secure Stalin at least control over the Baltic states. Politically mature people the world over approached the matter

---

* This article was first published in the *Fourth International* of June 1940.—Ed.

from precisely this standpoint, asking themselves: Just how will Stalin accomplish this task? Will he resort to military force? And so on. The course of events depended, however, a great deal more on Hitler than on Stalin. Generally speaking, concrete events cannot be predicted. But the main direction of the events as they actually unfolded contained nothing essentially new.

Because of the degeneration of the workers' state, the Soviet Union turned out at the threshold of the second imperialist war to be far weaker than it need have been. Stalin's agreement with Hitler had as its objective the securing of the USSR from a German assault and, generally, securing the USSR from being drawn into a major war. While seizing Poland, Hitler had to protect himself on the east. Stalin was compelled, with Hitler's permission, to invade eastern Poland in order to avail himself of some supplementary guarantees against Hitler on the western boundary of the USSR. As a result of these events, however, the USSR acquired a common frontier with Germany, and by virtue of this very fact the danger from a victorious Germany became much more direct, while Stalin's dependence on Hitler was greatly increased.

The episode of the partitioning of Poland had its development and sequel in the Scandinavian arena. Hitler could not have failed to give some intimation to his 'friend' Stalin that he planned to seize the Scandinavian countries. Stalin could not have failed to break into a cold sweat. After all, this signified complete German domination of the Baltic Sea, of Finland, and hence constituted a direct threat to Leningrad. Once again Stalin had to seek supplementary gurantees against his ally, this time in Finland. However, he met with serious resistance there. The 'military excursion' dragged on. Meanwhile Scandinavia threatened to become the arena of major warfare. Hitler, who had completed his preparations for the blow against Denmark and Norway, demanded that Stalin conclude an early peace. Stalin had to cut his plans short, and renounce sovietizing Finland. These are the salient features of the course of events in the European Northwest.

Small Nations in the Imperialist War
Under the conditions of world war, to approach the question
of the fate of small states from the standpoint of 'national independence', 'neutrality', etc., is to remain in the sphere of imperialist mythology. The struggle involves world domination. The question of the existence of the USSR will be solved in passing. This
problem which today remains in the background, will at a certain
moment come to the forefront. So far as the small and second
rate states are concerned, they are already today pawns in the
hands of the great powers. The sole freedom they still retain, and
this only to a limited extent, is the freedom of choosing between
masters.

Two governments struggle for a while in Norway: the government of the Norwegian Nazis, covered by the German troops in
the south, and the old social-democratic government with their
king in the north. Should the Norwegian workers have supported
the 'democratic' camp against the fascist? Following the analogy
with Spain, it might at first glance appear as if this question
should be answered in the affirmative. In reality this would be the
crudest kind of blunder. In Spain there was an isolated civil war;
the intervention of foreign imperialist powers, however important
in itself, nevertheless remained of secondary character. What is
involved in Norway is the direct and immediate clash between
two imperialist camps in whose hands the warring Norwegian
governments are only auxiliary tools. On the world arena we
support neither the camp of the Allies nor the camp of Germany.
Consequently we have not the slightest reason or justification
for supporting either one of their temporary tools within Norway
itself.

The very same approach must be applied to Finland. From the
standpoint of the strategy of the world proletariat, Finnish resistance was no more an act of independent national defence than is
the resistance of Norway. This was best demonstrated by the
Finnish government itself which preferred to cease all resistance
rather than have Finland completely transformed into a military

base of England, France and the United States. Secondary factors like the national independence of Finland or Norway, the defence of democracy, etc., however important in themselves, are now intertwined in the struggle of infinitely more powerful world forces and are completely subordinate to them. We must discount these secondary factors and determine our policy in accordance with the basic factors.

The programmatic theses of the Fourth International on war gave an exhaustive answer to this question six years ago. The theses state: 'The idea of national defence, especially if it coincides with the idea of the defence of democracy, can most readily be utilised to dupe the workers of small and neutral countries (Switzerland, in particular Belgium, the Scandinavian countries . . .).' And further on: 'Only petty-bourgeois blockheads (like Robert Grimm) from a God-forsaken Swiss village could seriously believe that the World War into which he will be drawn is a means for defending the independence of Switzerland.' Other petty bourgeois equally stupid imagined that world war is a means for defending Finland, that it is possible to determine proletarian *strategy* on the basis of a *tactical* episode such as the invasion of Finland by the Red Army.

Georgia and Finland

Just as during strikes directed against big capitalists, the workers often bankrupt in passing highly respectable petty-bourgeois concerns, so in a military struggle against imperialism, or in seeking military guarantees against imperialism, the workers' state—even completely healthy and revolutionary—may find itself compelled to violate the independence of this or that small state. Tears over the ruthlessness of the class struggle on either the domestic or the international arena may properly be shed by democratic Philistines but not by proletarian revolutionists.

The Soviet Republic in 1921 forcefully sovietised Georgia which constituted an open gateway for imperialist assault in the Caucasus. From the standpoint of the principles of national self-

determination, a good deal might have been said in objection
to such sovietisation. From the standpoint of extending the arena
of the socialist revolution, military intervention in a peasant
country was more than a dubious act. From the standpoint of the
self-defence of the workers' state surrounded by enemies, forceful
sovietisation was justified: the safeguarding of the socialist
revolution comes before formal democratic principles.

World imperialism for a long time utilised the question of
violence in Georgia as the rallying cry in mobilising world public
opinion against the Soviets. The Second International took the
lead in this campaign. The Entente aimed at the preparation of a
possible new military intervention against the Soviets.

In exactly the same way as in the case of Georgia, the world
bourgeoisie utilised the invasion of Finland in mobilising public
opinion against the USSR. The social-democracy in this case too
came out as the vanguard of democratic imperialism. The unhappy
'third camp' of the stampeding petty bourgeois brings up the rear.

Along with the striking similarity between these two instances
of military intervention there is, however, a profound difference—
the present USSR is far from being the Soviet Republic of 1921.
The 1934 theses of the Fourth International on war declare: 'The
monstrous development of Soviet bureaucratism and the wretched living conditions of the toilers have extremely reduced the
attractive power of the USSR for the world working class.' The
Soviet-Finnish War revealed graphically and completely that
within gunshot of Leningrad, the cradle of the October Revolution, the present regime of the USSR is incapable of exercising an
attractive force. Yet it does not follow from this that the USSR
must be surrendered to the imperialists but only that the USSR
must be torn out of the hands of the bureaucracy.

'Where Is the Civil War'?

'But where is the civil war in Finland which you promised?'
demand the leaders of the former opposition, who have now become the leaders of the 'third camp'. I promised nothing. I only

analysed one of the possible variants of the further development of the Soviet-Finnish conflict. The seizure of isolated bases in Finland was as probable as the complete occupation of Finland. The seizure of bases presupposed maintaining the bourgeois regime throughout the rest of the country. Occupation presupposed a social overturn which would be impossible without involving the workers and poorer farmers in civil war. The initial diplomatic negotiations between Moscow and Helsinki indicated an attempt to solve the question in the way it was solved with the other Baltic states. Finland's resistance compelled the Kremlin to seek its ends through military measures. Stalin could justify the war before the broadest masses only by sovietising Finland. The appointment of the Kuusinen government indicated that the fate awaiting Finland was not that of the Baltic states but that of Poland, where Stalin—no matter what the amateur columnists of the 'third camp' scribble—found himself compelled to provoke civil war and to overthrow property relations.

I specified several times that *if* the war in Finland was not submerged in a general war, and *if* Stalin was not compelled to retreat before a threat from the outside, then he would be forced to carry through the sovietising of Finland. This task by itself was much more difficult than the sovietising of eastern Poland. More difficult from a *military* standpoint, for Finland happened to be better prepared. More difficult from a *national* standpoint, for Finland possesses a long tradition of struggle for national independence from Russia, whereas the Ukrainians and the White Russians were fighting against Poland. More difficult from a *social* standpoint, for the Finnish bourgeoisie had in its own way solved the pre-capitalist agrarian problem through the creation of an agricultural petty bourgeoisie. Nevertheless the military victory of Stalin over Finland would unquestionably have made fully possible an overthrow of property relations with more or less assistance from the Finnish workers and small farmers.

Why then didn't Stalin carry out this plan? Because a colossal mobilisation of bourgeois public opinion began against the USSR.

Because England and France seriously posed the question of military intervention. Finally—last but not least in importance—because Hitler could wait no longer. The appearance of English and French troops in Finland would have meant a direct threat to Hitler's Scandinavian plans which were based on conspiracy and surprise. Caught in the vice of a twofold danger—on one side from the Allies and from the other, Hitler—Stalin renounced sovietising Finland, limiting himself to the seizure of isolated strategical positions.

The partisans of the 'third camp' (the camp of the stampeding petty bourgeois) now piece together the following construction: Trotsky deduced the civil war in Finland from the class nature of the USSR; inasmuch as no civil war occurred, that signifies the USSR is not a workers' state. In reality there was no necessity whatever for logically 'deducing' a possible civil war in Finland from a sociological definition of the USSR—it was sufficient to base oneself on the experience in eastern Poland. The overturn in property relations which was accomplished there could have been achieved only by the state that issued from the October Revolution. This overturn was forced upon the Kremlin oligarchy through its struggle for self-preservation under specific conditions. There was not the slightest ground for doubting that *under analogous conditions* it would find itself compelled to repeat the very same operation in Finland. That was all I pointed out. But conditions changed during the course of the struggle. War, like revolution, often develops abrupt turns. With the cessation of military operations on the part of the Red Army, naturally there could be no talk of the unfolding of civil war in Finland.

Every historical prognosis is always conditional, and the more concrete the prognosis, the more conditional it is. A prognosis is not a promissory note which can be cashed on a given date. Prognosis outlines only the definite trends of the development. But along with these trends a different order of forces and tendencies operate, which at a certain moment begin to predominate. All those who seek exact predictions of concrete events should consult the astrologists. Marxist prognosis aids only in orientation. I made reservations several times as to the conditionality of my prognosis as *one* of several possible variants. To clutch now, as the rock of salvation, at the tenth rate historical fact that the fate of Finland was temporarily determined on the pattern of Lithuania, Latvia and Esthonia rather than the pattern of eastern Poland can occur only to sterile scholastics or—the leaders of the 'third camp'.

The Defence of the Soviet Union

Stalin's assault upon Finland was not of course *solely* an act in defence of the USSR. The politics of the Soviet Union is guided by the Bonapartist bureaucracy. This bureaucracy is first and foremost concerned with its power, its prestige, its revenues. It defends itself much better than it defends the USSR. It defends itself at the expense of the USSR and at the expense of the world proletariat. This was revealed only too clearly throughout the entire development of the Soviet-Finnish conflict. We cannot therefore either directly or indirectly take upon ourselves even a shadow of responsibility for the invasion of Finland which represents only a single link in the chain of the politics of the Bonapartist bureaucracy.

It is one thing to solidarise with Stalin, defend his policy, assume responsibility for it—as does the triply infamous Comintern—it is another thing to explain to the world working class that no matter what crimes Stalin may be guilty of we cannot permit world imperialism to crush the Soviet Union, re-establish capitalism and convert the land of the October Revolution into a colony. This explanation likewise furnishes the basis for our defence of the USSR.

The attempt of the conjunctural defeatists, i.e., the adventurers in defeatism, to extricate themselves from their difficulty by promising that in the event the Allies intervene they will change their defeatist policy to a defencist one is a contemptible evasion. It is in general not easy to determine one's policies according to a stop watch, especially under wartime conditions. In the critical

days of the Soviet-Finnish War, as has now become known—
the Allied general staffs reached the conclusion that serious
and quick aid to Finland could come only through destroying the
Murmansk railway by bombing it from the air. From the point
of view or strategy this was quite correct. The question of
intervention or non-intervention by the Allied air forces hung
by a hair. From the same hair, apparently, the principled position
of the 'third camp' also dangled. But from the very beginning
we considered that it was necessary to determine one's position
in accordance with the basic class camps in the war. This is
much more reliable.

No Surrender to the Enemy of Positions Already Won

The policy of defeatism is not punishment of a given government for this or that crime it has committed but a conclusion
from the class relationships. The Marxist line of conduct in war
is not based on abstract moral and sentimental considerations
but on the social appraisal of a regime in its reciprocal relations
with other regimes. We supported Abysinnia not because the
Negus was politically or 'morally' superior to Mussolini but
because the defence of a backward country against colonial
oppression deals a blow to imperialism, which is the main
enemy of the world working class. We defend the USSR
independently of the policy of the Moscow Negus for two
fundamental reasons. First, the defeat of the USSR would
supply imperialism with new colossal resources and could prolong
for many years the death agony of capitalist society. Secondly,
the social foundations of the USSR, cleansed of the parasitic
bureaucracy are capable of assuring unbounded economic and
cultural progess, while the capitalist foundations disclose no
possibilities except further decay.

What unmasks the noisy critics most of all is that they continued to consider the USSR a workers' state at a time when
Stalin was destroying the Bolshevik party; when he was strangling
the proletarian revolution in Spain; when he was betraying the

world revolution in the name of 'People's Fronts' and 'collective security'. Under all these conditions they recognised the necessity of defending the USSR as a workers' state! But no sooner did this same Stalin invade 'democratic' Finland, no sooner did bourgeois public opinion of the imperialist democracies— which covered up and approved all Stalin's crimes against the communists, the workers and the peasants—raise a howl to the skies, than our innovators immediately declared: 'Yes, this is intolerable!' And following Roosevelt they declared a moral embargo against the Soviet Union.

Educated witch-doctor Burnham's reasoning on the theme that by defending the USSR we *thereby* defend Hitler, is a neat little specimen of petty-bourgeois fatheadedness which seeks to force contradictory reality into the framework of a two-dimensional syllogism. By defending the Soviet Republic after the Brest-Litovsk peace did the workers support Hohenzollern? Yes or no? The programmatic theses of the Fourth International on war, which deal in general with this question, establish categorically that agreements between a soviet state and this or that imperialist state do not place any restrictions upon the revolutionary party of that state. The interests of the world revolution stand above an isolated diplomatic combination, however justifiable the latter may be in and of itself. By defending the USSR we struggle far more seriously against Stalin, as well as Hitler, than do Burnham and Co.

It is true, Burnham and Shachtman do not stand alone. Léon Jouhaux, the notorious agent of French capitalism, also waxes indignant over the fact that the 'Trotskyists defend the USSR'. Who should be indignant if not he! But our attitude toward the USSR is the same as our attitude toward the CGT (General Confederation of Labour): we defend it against the bourgeoisie despite the fact that the Confederation is headed by scoundrels like Léon Jouhaux who deceive and betray the workers at every step. The Russian Mensheviks likewise are howling: 'The Fourth International is in a blind alley!' because the Fourth International still continues to recognise the USSR as a workers' state. These gentlemen themselves are members of the Second International, which is led by such eminent traitors as the typical bourgeois mayor Huysmans and Léon Blum, who betrayed an exceptionally favourable revolutionary situation in June 1936 and thereby made possible the present war. The Mensheviks recognise the parties of the Second International as *workers'* parties but refuse to recognise the Soviet Union as a *workers'* state on the ground that at its head stand bureaucratic traitors. This falsehood reeks with brazenness and cynicism. Stalin, Molotov and the rest, as a social layer, are no better and no worse than the Blums, Jouhaux, Citrines, Thomases, etc. The difference between them is only this, that Stalin and Co. exploit and cripple the viable economic foundation of socialist development, while the Blums cling to the thoroughly rotted foundation of capitalist society.

The workers' state must be taken as it has emerged from the merciless laboratory of history and not as it is imagined by a 'socialist' professor, reflectively exploring his nose with his finger. It is the duty of revolutionists to defend every conquest of the working class even though it may be distorted by the pressure of hostile forces. Those who cannot defend old positions will never conquer new ones.

April 25, 1940.

A letter to James P. Cannon†

May 28, 1940

Dear Comrades,

*   *   *

The resignation of Burnham* is an excellent confirmation of our analysis and prognosis concerning the ex-Minority. We don't believe that it is the last separation.

W. R. [*Leon Trotsky*]

---

* Burnham's letter proclaiming his open repudiation of socialism and at the same time announcing his resignation from the self-styled 'Workers Party' set up by the minority after their split in April 1940, is dated May 21, 1940. The text of this letter, never made public by Burnham's collaborators, was printed in the August 1940 issue of the *Fourth International* and is reprinted in the appendix to this book.—Ed.

A letter to Albert Goldman†

June 5, 1940

Dear Friend,

* * *

Burnham doesn't recognise dialectics but dialectics does not permit him to escape from its net. He is caught as a fly in a web. The blow he gave to Shachtman is irreparable. What a lesson on principled and unprincipled blocs! And poor Abern. Four years ago, he found the protector for him family clique in the person of Holy Father Muste and his altar boy Spector; now he repeated the same experiment with the secularised Catholic, Burnham and his attorney, Shachtman. . . . In the good old days we waited, often for years and decades for a verification of a prognosis. Now the tempo of events is so feverish that the verification comes unexpectedly the next day. Poor Shachtman!

With best wishes,
LEON TROTSKY

Coyoacan, D. F.

On the 'Workers' Party†*

QUESTION: *In your opinion were there enough political differences between the majority and the minority to warrant a split?*

TROTSKY: Here it is also necessary to consider the question dialectically, not mechanically. What does this terrible word 'dialectics' mean? It means to consider things in their development, not in their static situation. If we take the political differences as they are, we can say they were not sufficient for a split, but if they developed a tendency to turn away from the proletariat in the direction of petty-bourgeois circles, then the same differences can have an absolutely different value; a different weight; if they are connected with a different social group. This is a very important point.

We have the fact that the minority split away from us, in spite of all the measures taken by the majority not to split. This signifies that their inner social feeling was such that it is impossible for them to go together with us. It is a petty-bourgeois tendency, not a proletarian. If you wish a new confirmation of this, we have an excellent example in the article of Dwight Macdonald.

First of all, what characterises a proletarian revolutionary? No one is obliged to participate in a revolutionary party, but if he does participate, he considers the party seriously. If we dare to call the people for a revolutionary change of society, we carry a tremendous responsibility, which we must consider very seriously. And what is our theory, but merely the tools of our action? These tools are our Marxist theory because up to today we have not found better tools. A worker is not fantastic about tools—if they are the best tools he can get he is careful with them; he does not abandon them or demand fantastic non-existent tools.

Burnham is an intellectual snob. He picks up one party, abandons it, takes up another. A worker cannot do this. If he enters a

---

* This article is reprinted from the October 1940 *Fourth International*. —Ed.

revolutionary party, addresses the people, calls them for action, it is the same as a general during a war—he must know where he is leading them. What would you think of a general who said he thought the guns were bad—that it would be better to wait for ten years until they had invented better guns, so everybody had better go home. That is the way Burnham reasons. So he abandoned the party. But the unemployed remain, and the war remains. These things cannot be postponed. Therefore it is only Burnham who has postponed his action.

Dwight Macdonald is not a snob, but a bit stupid. I quote: 'The intellectual, if he is to serve any useful function in society, must not deceive either himself or others, must not accept as good coin what he knows is counterfeit, must not forget in a moment of crisis what he has learned over a period of years and decades.' Good. Absolutely correct. I quote again: 'Only if we meet the stormy and terrible years ahead with both *scepticism* and devotion—scepticism towards *all* theories, governments and social systems; devotion to the revolutionary fight of the masses—only then can we justify ourselves as intellectuals.'

Here is one of the leaders of the so-called 'Workers' Party, who considers himself not a proletarian but an 'intellectual'. He speaks of scepticism toward all theories.

We have prepared ourselves for this crisis by studying, by building a scientific method, and our method is Marxism. Then the crisis comes and Mr. Macdonald says 'be sceptical of all theories', and then talks about devotion to the revolution without replacing it with any new theory. Unless it is this sceptical theory of his own. How can we work without a theory? What is the fight of the masses and what is a revolutionary? The whole article is scandalous and a party which can tolerate such a man as one of its leaders is not serious.

I quote again: 'What is the nature of the beast (fascism), then? Trotsky insists it is no more nor less than the familiar phenomenon of Bonapartism, in which a clique maintains itself in power by playing one class off against another, thus giving the

State power a temporary autonomous character. But these modern totalitarian regimes are not temporary affairs; they have already changed the underlying economic and social structure, not only manipulating the old forms but also destroying their inner vitality. Is the Nazi bureaucracy a new ruling class, then, and fascism a new form of society, comparable to capitalism? That doesn't seem to be true either.'

Here he creates a new theory, a new definition of fascism, but he wishes, nevertheless, that we should be sceptical toward all theories. So also to the workers he would say that the instruments and tools they work with are not important but they must have devotion to their work! I think the workers would find a very sharp expression for such a statement.

It is very characteristic of the disappointed intellectual. He sees the war, the terrible epoch ahead, with losses, with sacrifices, and he is afraid. He begins to propagate scepticism and still he believes it is possible to unify scepticism with revolutionary devotion. We can only develop a revolutionary devotion if we are sure it is rational and possible, and we cannot have such assurances without a working theory. He who propagates theoretical scepticism is a traitor.

We analysed in fascism different elements:

1. The element which fascism has in common with the old Bonapartism is that it used the antagonisms of classes in order to give to the state power the greatest independence. But we have always underlined that the old Bonapartism was in a time of an ascending bourgeois society, while fascism is a state power of the declining bourgeois society.

2. That fascism is an attempt of the bourgeois class to overcome, to overstep, the contradiction between the new technique and private property without eliminating the private property. It is the 'planned economy' of fascism. It is an attempt to save private property and at the same time to check private property.

3. To overstep the contradiction between the new, modern technique of productive forces within the limited borders of the national state. This new technique cannot be limited by the borders of the old national state and fascism attempts to overcome this contradiction. The result is the war. We have already analysed all these elements.

Dwight Macdonald will abandon the party just as Burnham did, but possibly because he is a little lazier, it will come later.

Burnham was considered 'good stuff' at one time? Yes, the proletarian party in our epoch must make use of every intellectual who can contribute to the party. I spent many months on Diego Rivera, to save him for our movement, but did not succeed. But every International has had an experience of this kind. The First International had troubles with the poet, Freiligrath, who was also very capricious. The Second and Third Internationals had trouble with Maxim Gorki. The Fourth International with Rivera. In every case they separated from us.

Burnham was, of course, closer to the movement, but Cannon had his doubts about him. He can write, and has some formal skill in thinking, not deep, but adroit. He can accept your idea, develop it, write a fine article about it—and then forget it. The author can forget—but the worker cannot. However, so long as we can use such people, well and good. Mussolini at one time was also 'good stuff'!

Coyoacan, D. F.
August 7, 1940.

A letter to Albert Goldman†

August 9, 1940

Mr. Albert Goldman.

Dear Friend:

I don't know whether you have seen Dwight Macdonald's article in the August issue of his *Partisan Review*.

This man was a disciple of Burnham, the intellectual snob. After Burnham deserted, Dwight Macdonald was left in Shachtman's party as the lone representative of 'Science'.

On the question of fascism, Macdonald serves up a poor compilation of plagiarisms from our arsenal which he represents as his own discoveries and to which he opposes some banalities that he characterises as our ideas. The whole—without perspective, without proportion and without elementary intellectual honesty.

However, this is not the worst. Burnham's orphan proclaims: 'We must examine again with a cold and sceptical eye, the most basic premises of Marxism.' Page 266. And what must the poor 'Workers Party' do during this period of 'examination'? What must the proletariat do? They should wait, of course, for the result of Dwight Macdonald's study. This result will probably be Macdonald's desertion himself into the camp of Burnham.

The last four lines of the article can be nothing but preparation for personal desertion. 'Only if we meet the stormy and terrible years ahead with both scepticism and devotion—scepticism towards all theories, governments and social systems; devotion to the revolutionary fight of the masses—only then can we justify ourselves as intellectuals.'

Revolutionary activity based upon theoretical scepticism is the most awkward of inner contradictions. 'Devotion to the revolutionary fight of the masses' is impossible without theoretical understanding of the laws of this revolutionary fight. Revolutionary devotion is possible only if one gains the assurance that his devotion is reasonable, adequate; that it corresponds to its aim. Such assurance can be created only by theoretical insight into the class struggle. 'Scepticism towards all theories' is nothing but preparation for personal desertion.

Shachtman remains silent; as 'General Secretary' he is too busy to defend the 'most basic premises of Marxism' from petty-bourgeois philistines and snobs. . . .

Fraternally yours,
L. TROTSKY.

A letter to Chris Andrews†

August 17, 1940

Dear Chris:

*   *   *

I very much enjoyed your appreciation of the anti-pacifist position accepted by the party. There are two great advantages to this position: first, it is revolutionary in its essence and based upon the whole character of our epoch, when all questions will be decided not only by arms of critics, but by critiques of arms; second, it is completely free of sectarianism. We do not oppose to events and to the feelings of the masses an abstract affirmation of our sanctity.

The poor 'Labour Action' of August 12th writes: 'In this fight against conscription we are with Lewis 100 per cent.' *We* are not with Lewis for even a single per cent, because Lewis tries to defend the Capitalist Fatherland with completely outdated means. The great majority of the workers understand or feel that these means (professional voluntary armament) are outdated from a military point of view and extremely dangerous from a class point of view. That is why the workers are for conscription. It is a very confused and contradictory form of adhering to the 'arming of the proletariat'. We do not flatly reject this great historical change, as do the sectarians of all kinds. We say 'Conscription? Yes. But made by ourselves.' It is an excellent point of departure.

With best greetings, I am

Fraternally,
YOUR OLD MAN [*Leon Trotsky*]

Appendix

SCIENCE AND STYLE

A Reply to Comrade Trotsky

Dear Comrade Trotsky:

I find the Open Letter which you have addressed nominally to me more than a little disarming. It is not easy, I confess, for me to undertake an answer.

In reading it I was reminded of a conversation I had some while ago with one of our good comrades from Central Europe. We were discussing, in that idle and profligate way we intellectuals have, the possible conflicts between the aesthetic sense, the feeling for beauty, and the demands of political action. He told me a story.

A number of years ago, the country in which he lived was going through a period of social crisis. The masses were surging forward, heading, it seemed, toward revolt. One morning, near the height of the movement, a crowd of many thousand workers gathered on one side of the wonderful great square of the capital city of that country. Our comrade was assigned as captain to direct one wing of the workers' detachments.

The sky was dark blue, with the white morning sun throwing across the square the shadows of the buildings that lined its sides. From the side of the square opposite the workers, the troops of the police filed out and took formation: in straight rows, mounted on their tense horses, equipment gleaming. At the shout of command, in a single swift gesture their sabres were drawn, and flashed in the rays of that white sun. The second command came: forward against the workers.

The instant had come for reply: for our comrade, to launch his wing of the workers into a driving counter-attack. But for a long moment he found his will paralysed and his voice stopped by the sensuous beauty of the unfolded scene. And all that day, while the bitter struggle lasted—more than fifty were killed that day, hundreds wounded, our comrade among them—he could not forget that sun, those shadows, that blue sky, those whirling horses and flashing sabres.

So, too, on this verbal battleground, pale reflex—and indispensable spark—of the battles in the streets, I, when all my will should be concentrated in launching my ranked arguments into counter-attack against your letter (so wrong, so false, so very false), find I must stop awhile in wonder: at the technical perfection of the verbal structure you have created, the dynamic sweep of your rhetoric, the burning expression of your unconquerable devotion to the socialist ideal, the sudden, witty, flashing metaphors that sparkle through your pages.

How unpleasant and thankless a duty to submit that splendid structure to the dissolving acids from those two so pedestrian, so unromantic flasks: logic and science!

Comrade Trotsky, while reading and thinking about this Letter, I recalled also the first time that I had ever given really serious attention to your work: in a lengthy review of the first volume of your *History*, publishd in the July, 1932, issue of *The Symposium*. I re-read that review, which I had not done for many years. There, too, I found that I had been compelled to discuss first of all your *style*, your wonderful style, which in fact I analysed at considerable length. And I saw more clearly than ever before what is, in my eyes, an important truth: that you have a too *literary* conception of proof, of evidence; that you deceive yourself into treating persuasive rhetoric as logical demonstration, a brilliant *metaphor* as argument. Here, I believe, is the heart of the mystery of the dialectic, as it appears in your books and articles: the dialectic, for you, is a *device of style*—the contrasting epithets, the flowing rhythms, the verbal paradoxes which characterise your way of writing.

Comrade Trotsky, I will not match metaphors with you. In such a verbal tournament, I concede you the ribbon in advance. Evidence, argument, proof: these only are my weapons.

The Skeleton Undraped

I will now summarise your argument:

With reference to your own position, you assert the following:

(a) The philosophy of dialectical materialism is true.

(b) Marxian sociology, in particular the Marxian theory of the state, is true.

(c) Russia is a workers' state.

(d) A tactic of defence of the Russian state in the present war is correct.

With reference to the position of the opposition—or, more exactly, of Burnham who you claim expresses the 'essence' of the opposition

—you assert the following:

(1) Burnham is a bourgeois democrat.

(2) Burnham rejects dialectics.

(3) Burnham rejects Marxian sociology, in particular the Marxian theory of the state.

(4) Burnham denies that Russia is a workers' state.

(5) Burnham's practical politics are 'abstentionist'.

(6) Burnham rejects Bolshevik organisation theories and methods.

But you not merely assert these individual propositions. You are even more concerned to assert certain *connections* which you allege hold among these propositions.

With reference to your own position, you thus assert the following additional propositions:

(A) From dialectical materialism, *it follows that* Marxian sociology, in particular the Marxian theory of the state, is true.

(B) From the Marxian theory of the state, *it follows that* Russia is a workers' state.

(C) From Russia's being a workers' state, *it follows that* a tactic of defence of the Russian state in the present war is correct.

With reference to Burnham's position, you assert the following connections:

(I) From Burnham's being a bourgeois democrat, *it follows that* he rejects dialectics.

(II) From his rejection of dialectics, *it follows that* he rejects Marxian sociology, in particular the Marxian theory of the state.

(III) From his rejection of the Marxian theory of the state, *it follows that* he denies that Russia is a workers' state.

(IV) From his denial that Russia is a workers' state (and from 1 and 2), *it follows that* his practical politics are 'abstentionist'.

(V) From his being a bourgeois democrat and his rejection of dialectics, *it follows that* he rejects Bolshevik organisation theories and methods.

So far as I have been able, I have been scrupulously fair in presenting here your central *argument*. These 18 propositions constitute that 'unified conception' whose absence you so deplore in the point of view of the opposition. But as soon as these propositions are made *explicit*, as soon as they are brought to the surface from beneath the shrouds of metaphor and rhetoric, it is clear that *each* of them stands on its own feet, that each would have to be proved independently of the others. Moreover, the structure of your argument, of your 'unified conception' and 'explanation', stands or falls on the truth of *all* of these propositions. And who, even of your most ardent supporters, would be so brash as to claim that you have *proved all* of them to be true?

Examination shows, more specifically, that these 18 propositions are either trivial or irrelevant or obviously false or at the least unproved. It would be wearisome, and unnecessary, to demonstrate this with reference to each of these propositions; every comrade has, indeed, material at his disposal to carry out the analysis for himself. I shall confine my attention to only a few of those which raise special problems.

Dialectics as a Red Herring

'Since in the course of the factional struggle,' you write, 'the question (of dialectics) has been posed point blank. . . .' How innocent, objective and impersonal, Comrade Trotsky! Dialectics, suddenly, like Banquo's ghost, thrust its wild face into our political midst, to dismay all sceptics. But, alas, as in the case of all ghosts, it was a very human hand that manipulated the apparatus producing our supernatural phenomenon; and that hand was yours, Comrade Trotsky. Like all good mediums, you attribute the visitation to the working of another and a higher realm—to 'the logic of events', the 'historical course of the struggle'—but like all good observers, we will admire the artistry, and smile at the explanation.

I can understand, and even sympathise with, your recourse to dialectics in the current dispute. There is little else for you to write about, with every appeal you make to actual events refuted the day after you make it, with each week's development in the war smashing another pillar of your political position. An argument about dialectics is 100 per cent safe, a century ago or a century hence. Among those lofty generalities, no humble and inconvenient *fact* intrudes; no earthyest or observation or experiment mar their Olympian calm; those serene words remain forever free from the gross touch of everyday events.

I have participated in a number of previous faction fights, some very bitter, some in which you also were concerned, Comrade Trotsky. Where was dialectics then? How did it happen that no word came from you in those times about the dangers of my rejection of dialectics? Can it be (the suggestion is so banal as to be unseemly in these philosophical days) that the difference has some connection with the fact that in those previous disputes I happened to be on the same side as you? Is the speculation altogether absurd that if, by a chance that cannot be completely excluded, I happened today to be with you and Cannon, dialectics might not have appeared so, shall we say, prominently on the scene?

Comrade Trotsky, I regard you as one of the most competent historians and political scientists in the world. I did so yesterday, when I agreed with you on most points, today when I disagree on a number of very important questions, and will doubtless tomorrow. My beliefs, tolerant scientist that I am, are not at the service of my immediate factional interests. But your qualifications in these fields do not automatically assure your competence also in the fields of philosophy, logic, natural science and scientific method.

I find about 75 per cent of what Engels wrote in these latter fields to be confused or outmoded by subsequent scientific investigation—in either case of little value. It seems to me (and as a Marxist I do not find it astonishing) that in them Engels was a true son of his generation, the generation of Herbert Spencer and Thomas Huxley, of the popularisers of Darwin who thought that by a metaphorical extension of the hypothesis of biological evolution they had discovered the ultimate key to the mysteries of the universe. Nevertheless, Engels made a real effort to acquaint himself with the philosophy, logic and science of his day, and wrote with this acquaintance in mind.

You, however, serve up to us only a stale re-hash of Engels. The latest scientist admitted to your pages is—Darwin; apart from Aristotle, the only 'logic worthy of attention' is that of—Hegel, the century-dead arch-muddler of human thought. Comrade Trotsky, as we Americans ask: where have you been all these years? During the 125 years since Hegel wrote, science has progressed more than during the entire preceding history of mankind. During that same period, after 2300 years of stability, logic has undergone a revolutionary transformation: a transformation in which Hegel and his ideas have had an influence of exactly zero.

You ask me: 'Do you hold that the progress of the sciences, including Darwinism, Marxism, modern physics, chemistry, etc., have not influenced in any way the forms of our thought?' But it is to yourself that you should address this question, not to me. *Of course* I hold that they have (and one way that they have influenced it is to show that Hegelian dialectics has nothing whatever to do with science). *How* the sciences have influenced the forms of thought no one will ever discover by spending even a lifetime on the tortuous syntax of the reactionary absolutist, Hegel, but only by studying modern science and mathematics, and the careful analysts of modern science and mathematics.

In a most sarcastic vein, you keep asking me to 'take the trouble to inform us just who following Aristotle analysed and systematised the subsequent progress of logic', 'perhaps you will call my attention to those works which should supplant the system of dialectic materialism for the proletariat . . .' as if this demand were so obviously impossible of fulfillment that I must collapse like a pricked balloon before it. The sarcasm is misplaced, for the demand is the easiest in the world to fulfil. Do you wish me to prepare a reading list, Comrade Trotsky? It would be long, ranging from the work of the brilliant mathematicians and logicians of the middle of the last century to one climax in the monumental *Principia Mathematica* of Russell and Whitehead (the historic turning point in modern logic), and then spreading out in many directions—one of the most fruitful represented by the scientists, mathematicians and logicians now co-operating in the new *Encyclopedia of Unified Science*. For logic in its narrower sense, C. I. Lewis' *Survey of Symbolic Logic* is an excellent, though not easy, introduction. I am afraid, however, that in all of these works you will find scarcely a single reference to Hegelian (or Marxian) dialectics; nor will you in those of a single reputable con-temporary scientist—except the Soviet scientists, whose necks depend upon such references, or one or two Kremlin hangers-on, like J. B. S. Haldane, in other nations. The study of these works would be not uninteresting; but I am afraid that when we finished we would be not much nearer the solution of the question of the role of Russia in the war.

You have an altogether incorrect idea of logic, Comrade Trotsky. You draw an analogy between a machine or instrument and logic: 'Just as a machine shop in a plant supplies instruments for all departments, so logic is indispensable for all spheres of human knowledge.' This analogy is false. For our politics, the analogy to a machine or instrument or tool is not logic or 'method', but the *party*; the party, the actual party, is the instrument we use to achieve our political goals. Logic is indispensable to human knowledge only in this respect: that logic states the conditions of intelligible discourse, so that we 'violate' logic only at the risk of talking nonsense. But no one has to know the science of logic in order to make sense or even to be a great empirical scientist—in fact very few people know logic, which is a highly specialised and, when divorced from empirical knowledge, rather useless subject. *Perhaps* a clear knowledge of logic ('method') will aid someone to make sense, to be a better scientist (especially in highly theoretical science does this seem possible); but experience does not indicate that this happens as often or as importantly as logicians would like to think it does. Otherwise we may be sure that there would be much less unemployment among logicians.

Nor is there any such thing as an 'unconscious logician'. I read your passage on 'unconscious dialecticians'—your peasant woman and fox—with amazement, hoping to discover that the entire section was meant only humorously. But I was forced to the conclusion that you intended it seriously also. By your reasoning, a toad—or for that matter a stone—must be a scientist, because, forsooth, they both act in accordance with the law of gravity! What makes a scientist (differentiating him from a savage or a stone) is not that he behaves in accordance with scientific law—which all things do equally; and if they don't, the scientific laws are altered to explain better how they do act—but the fact that the scientist *knows* the laws, and knows them not 'unconsciously' (whatever that could mean) but quite consciously, deliberately.

You tell us that workers, proletarians, are 'naturally inclined to dialectical thinking'. Where are these workers, Comrade Trotsky? It seems to me that you are presenting a very damaging advertisement for dialectics. The only workers I, or anyone else, know anything about are these human beings found in the mines of Kennecott Copper, the mills of U.S. Steel, the ships of the merchant marine. ... These workers, in spite of what has been happening in the world, continue to trust John L. Lewis and Citrine and Jouhaux and Stalin, continue to vote Democratic or Republican, continue to believe in capitalism. I think they will change their thinking, perhaps one day very quickly. But I find their thought, for the most part, false or where not false, confused. If this is what you mean by 'dialectical thinking', I can agree with you.

In all the elaborated confusion of your new remarks on dialectics, you make only one attempt at an *argument* in favour of dialectics; and this argument, upon examination, turns out to be both irrelevant and *reactionary*. 'All the great and outstanding revolutionists,' you write, '—first and foremost, Marx, Engels, Lenin, Luxemburg, Franz Mehring—stood on the ground of dialectic materialism'; whereas many deserters from the revolution began with an attack on dialectics. Is this weapon not identical in form with the weapon *in extremis* of all reaction: do you dare to disbelieve when our fathers believed, and their fathers and fore-fathers before them? Has not virtually every single one of us had to break through this very argument in taking our place on the side of socialism? The argument is not an iota more valid when a socialist employs it.

Even if it were true—as it is not—that *every* revolutionist believed in dialectics and *everyone* who was against the revolution disbelieved, this fact (interesting as it would be from a psychological and historical point of view) would not have the slightest relevance to the question of the truth, falsity, or scientific meaninglessness of dialectics. These are two entirely different *types* of question.

You yourself are well able to recognise this difference when you are not subordinating truth to factional rhetoric; indeed, you have often most tellingly insisted upon it. For example: In analysing the Moscow Trials, you (and all of us) showed that the confessions of the defendants could be proved false by the available evidence, by their internal contradictions, and by an understanding of the historical process which culminated in the Trials. The Stalinists replied —and very effectively from the point of view of many persons—by pointing to the undoubted fact that they all did confess. We said: this is a different question altogether, independent of the question of the truth or falsity of the confessions themselves; we also have our hypotheses about why they confessed, but even if these latter are incorrect, it has nothing to do with the truth of what is said in the confessions.

Why Marx, Engels and Lenin believed in dialectics is a problem for psychological and historical examination, and stands on its own feet.

But your account of 'who believed what?' is, shall I say, a little incomplete. You turn a couple of pages of somersaults explaining away the awkward fact that Liebknecht did not accept dialectics while Plekhanov did. But how about the Mensheviks pretty much as a whole, Comrade Trotsky? I have always read that they devoted as much or more attention to writing about and defending dialectics as even the ultra-dialectical Bolsheviks. And, much more pertinently: what of the Stalinist theoreticians, Comrade Trotsky? The bibliography of Stalinist writings on dialectics would fill a shelf or two, I assure you. And, very conspicuously, the sectarians. Did you know, Comrade Trsotky, that of those who have been in our ranks during the past decade, the one by far most concerned of all over dialectics was Hugo Oehler? (It was Oehler, come to think of it, who was the only predecessor of yours in attacking me for anti-dialectics during

a political dispute. That was over the problem of S.P. entry; somehow, at that time, you, Cannon, and even Comrade Wright, failed to
recognise that your bloc with me was unprincipled and that principled politics demanded that you should line up with Oehler until
the 'fundamental question' of dialectics was cleared up. Instead, we
hung together on the 'conjunctural', episodic, merely empirical
tactic of entry. Fortunately, we have learned principles since that
day.) Isn't it remarkable that when our bookstore, under its new
impulse, begins advertising treatises on dialectics, the list is mostly
of Mensheviks, Brandlerites, Stalinists even? . . . And how about
Shachtman and Abern, whose dialectics haven't prevented them
from going astray with me? Now I naturally understand that all
these turncoats—'are not really dialecticians', are just giving lip-
service to dialectics, etc.

Can it be, Comrade Trotsky, that the only really *real* (conscious
and unconscious) dialecticians are: those who agree with you
politically?

*   *   *

You reproach me as derelict in not taking up arms against the
opium of religion-dialectics. Well, Comrade Trotsky, I will match my
writings on dialectics during the past decade with yours against
religion (or for dialectics); we are, I suspect, fellow-sinners with
respect to our anti-narcotic duties.

Nevertheless, *you* have placed dialectics on the agenda. Very well.
I will debate the question with you. But I will do so only when the
two conditions already given in my recent article ('The Politics of
Desperation') are fulfilled: First, that you make clear *what* we are
debating about by formulating significantly the laws and principles
of dialectics. I am not, let me repeat, merely going to juggle words
with you. Second, that we discuss dialectics and not utilise dialectics
as a red herring to throw the party and the International off the
track of the political issues before us.

I do not recognise dialectics, but, as you say, dialectics recognises
me. Evidently, if Cannon has a majority at the Convention, this
recognition will be a blow on the head in the form of a resolution
adding acceptance of dialectics as part of the programmatic basis of
the party—if I interpret your remarks correctly, you have answered
my challenge on this point even before receiving it. I do not know
whether to find this plan more ludicrous or shocking. Let me ask, in
an off-the-record, non-factional aside: Whatever the merits of dialectics, do you imagine, have you so lost your intellectual bearings as to
imagine, that such a question can be settled by the present sort of

factional dispute, followed by a vote at a Convention—a vote, more-over, which would be determined by hard factional lines drawn on quite other issues? But perhaps I can answer my own question, for there *is* a sense in which such questions get settled in such a manner—yes, the history of the past two decades has taught us how to decide even that 2 plus 2 equal 5.

* * *

I return, finally, to the query I raised in my previous article. I will grant you your 'logic of evolution', from quantity to quality to united opposites, from the distant stars all the way to your dialectical peasant-cook and foxes. And now, Comrade Trotsky, please, please, explain to me and all of us: how, just how, does there *follow from* any and all of this the answer to the political dispute we are arguing, a dispute over the *strategical orientation of our movement during the first phase of the second world war*? Your inability to answer this question—and you will not be able to answer it—proves that your introduction of dialectics is an evasion, a perfumed trap for the unwary.

What Are Fundamentals?

It is a popular illusion of ancient lineage that the 'fundamental questions' are those dealing with the grand and often-capitalised nouns like God, Freedom, Immortality, Universe, Reality, Creation, and the like. The churches have always been anxious to sustain this illusion, since these pretended questions, being outside the domain of science, can then be claimed as the peculiar province of the church, and thus the church alone gives answer to man's funda-mental problem. I judge, Comrade Trotsky, from your attack on the opposition for 'neglecting fundamentals', that you remain a victim of this illusion.

Since you and Cannon, following the example of Hardman, Oehler, Muste and Jack Altman, have by now pretty clearly established the fact that I am a teacher, I shall take the liberty of drawing for a moment from my teaching experience. Many students who enter my introductory courses in philosophy have heard vaguely that philo-sophy deals somehow with 'fundamentals'; and they register for the course with the hope of hearing 'answers' to just such questions as I have referred to. To their surprise, and often to their dismay, they discover that their attention is turned to quite another set of topics: they learn to become critical of their beliefs, and how to test them; they learn the difference between significant statement and non-sense; they learn how to clarify problems and how to answer them—

when they can be answered; they learn how science has developed and what the scientific enterprise means, what a hypothesis is, how it is confirmed or refuted; they learn how the vast 'fundamental questions' are not genuine questions at all, but requests for emotional satisfaction—and how the abuse of the intense feelings surrounding these capitalised words has for many ages been used by church and authority, by priest and philosopher and tyrant, to serve obscurantist and reactionary ends. A number of the students resent what they have learned, feel cheated in the expectations they had formed of the course (expectations, in actuality, of verbal balm for their wounded and disoriented feelings), and they do not re-register for the second term. But others, and I believe the best of them, gradually realise that they are reaching daylight from a land of mists, and they find a new confidence like a man whose brain clears after a drunken stupor.

There are no fundamental questions 'in general', Comrade Trotsky. Within each systematised field of knowledge there are certain principles which can be regarded, from the point of view of that field, as fundamental: either in the logical sense of being the basic axioms, postulates, and theorems upon which the logical structure of the field rests; or in the instrumental sense of being the directing aim or purpose which the field serves. But in each field to which we may refer, there are *different* 'fundamentals'.

The only fundamentals relevant to our present dispute are the fundamentals of *politics*—presumably we are not banded together as a society of mathematicians or a school of art. The fundamentals of politics are constituted by: the central *aim*, together with the most important means which are regarded as necessary in achieving that aim. Isn't that obvious? In order to remain members of one political organisation, we of the Fourth International must agree on our central aim: namely, socialism. And we must agree on the most important means which we regard as necessary for achieving that aim: the dictatorship of the proletariat, the revolutionary overthrow of capitalist society, the building of the party, etc. What means are 'important' and how closely must we agree on them? This we cannot answer in advance; only experience can show us, and the limits of required agreement may vary from time to time. Experience has already shown that persons cannot long remain in the same political party if they differ over such a means toward socialism as involved in the dispute over the revolutionary or parliamentary road; it has similarly shown that they can remain in the same organisation when they differ over such a means as a labour party.

Our basic programme (and the same analysis holds for any political party) is properly speaking simply the statement of our central aim and the most important means regarded as necessary to achieve it. It is this, for example, that, in fact, determines the conditions of membership and directs our activities. In addition, of course, in order to meet the requirements of day-to-day or even year-to-year practical activity, the basic programme is supplemented by guiding statements on means regarded as less crucial or more temporary (labour party, New Deal . . . etc.). These, though binding as guides for the party, need not demand agreement from all members, nor constitute conditions of membership.

But what about Marxian sociology (the theory of the state) and dialectics? for it is upon the alleged rejection of the former and Burnham's rejection of the latter that you condemn the opposition's 'disregard of fundamentals'.

In the first place, it is a direct falsehood to say that I, or any other member of the opposition, rejects the Marxian theory of the state. We disagree with your *interpretation* and *application* of the Marxian theory of the state; but all of us proceed in our analysis from the basis, among other factors, of the Marxian theory of the state. Since when have we granted one individual the right of infallible inter- pretation? All of the opposition disagree with your application of the theory to the role of Russia in the present war; some of us (for example, Carter and myself) believe further that the application of the theory to the whole problem of the proletarian dictatorship re- quires clarification. But none of us denies the theory (though naturally, for my own part, I accept it as a hypothesis, not as re- vealed dogma). What else but my insistence on the theory do you suppose would have led me to call my column 'Their Government' —a name I selected some time *before* joining the Fourth Internation- alist movement?

However, the theory of the state is not a 'fundamental' of politics in precisely the same sense that I have explained. If it is funda- mental, it is so from this point of view: that it has been pretty clearly demonstrated that from no other hypothesis can we con- sistently reach such conclusions as are embodied in many of the planks of our basic programme (rejection of parliamentary road, attitude toward imperialist war, dictatorship of the proletariat, etc.), whereas any other theory of the state leads to different (and wrong) conclusions about the necessary means for achieving socialism. Thus it would seem that acceptance of our basic programme logic- ally entails acceptance of the Marxian theory of the state, though this may not be clear at every stage to every person. Nevertheless, so far as *politics* goes, it is the programme and the empirical consequences that follow from it which are fundamental in relation to the theory of the state, rather than the theory fundamental in relation to the programme.

But there is no sense *at all* in which dialectics (even if dialectics were not, as it is, scientifically meaningless) is fundamental in politics, none at all. An opinion on dialectics is no more fundamental for *politics* than an opinion on non-Euclidean geometry or relativity physics. By claiming that it is, you from your side, and Eastman from his, are alike submitting to the same vulgar and damaging illusion to which I referred at the beginning of this section.

You are wrong, Comrade Trotsky. The opposition is very much concerned with fundamentals, but with *political fundamentals*. Our political fundamentals are expressed by and large in the programme of the International and the party. We are proposing to revise one section of that programme, just as we have revised other sections in the past; but we propose to revise it precisely from the point of view of the basic and fundamental planks of the programme: the central aim of world socialism and the crucial means which we jointly regard as necessary for the achievement of that aim.

Comrade Trotsky, you have absorbed too much of Hegel, of his monolithic, his totalitarian, vision of a block universe in which every part is related to every other part, in which everything is relevant to everything else, where the destruction of a single grain of dust means the annihilation of the Whole. I am as opposed to totalitarianism in philosophy as in the state or in the party.

It is false that we reject Marxian sociology; it is false that I reject fundamentals in rejecting dialectics. It is doubly false when you try to bolster up your shaky case on 'fundamentals' with the pretended story that with reference to the events of the present war, the opposition has had a purely episodic position that changed and veered with every change in passing events—that 'the tasks in Finland' were split from 'our position on Poland', and so on. It is not we but you, Comrade Trotsky, and much more grossly Cannon, who, since the war began, have confused the party, those who read our press, and you yourselves, with a succession of bewildering shifts in position which have shown nothing but the helplessness of your doctrine in the face of events. Anyone who has read the *Appeal* knows this to be most blatantly the case. We, on our side, from the time when, shortly after the war began, we saw clearly what kind of a war it was and what Russia's role in it, have consistently analysed events in the light of a single strategical orientation—which we call the strategy of the third camp, it in turn based upon our fundamental objectives. We have made no 'principled' distinctions between Poland and the Baltic countries and Finland; but you and the Cannons and Goldmans have done so, issuing from week to week, self-contradicting analyses and directives. You cannot help doing so, because your central strategical orientation—defence of the Stalinist state and its army—is now in direct conflict with the fundamental objectives of our movement, and you are attempting the impossible—to juggle them both in the same hand.

Your appeal to 'fundamentals' is of exactly the same character as your essays on dialectics: a red herring to divert attention from the political issues at stake.

The Namelessness of Science

You make very merry, Comrade Trotsky, over the anonymity, the namelessness, of the science for which I stand. You find it most droll when our document advocates 'bold, flexible, critical and experimental politics—in a word, scientific politics'. 'With this formula,' you remark, 'one can enter any democratic salon.' I want no misunderstanding, none whatever and no chance of any, on this point.

You find these adjectives 'pretentious and deliberately abstruse'. What is pretentious and abstruse about them, Comrade Trotsky? They are words that every child is acquainted with.

Do they describe science or not, Comrade Trotsky? And if Marxism is part of science, do they describe Marxism or not? Is it the word-magic you find lacking? Where is the dispute clarified by calling for 'Marxist' politics? The dispute is over *what* kind of politics, in the present instance, Marxist politics happens to be. And for me, certainly, 'Marxist politics' means 'scientific politics'; if it did not, then I would reject Marxist politics.

But more may lurk here than we have yet brought to light.

Does science as you understand it, and the truths it demonstrates, have a name? What name? 'Proletarian' science and 'proletarian' truth—*class* science and *class* truth?

If that is right—and I cannot fathom the point of your sneers if it is not—then indeed there is a gulf between us.

Yes, most certainly, the science and the truths I stand for are anonymous, nameless. They are the monopoly of no man or group or class, but a common human possession; for them all men are equal. The truths that science tells are as true for Stalin as for

Trotsky, for Morgan as for Cannon, for Roosevelt as for Browder. Naturally, the psychological and social interests (including, conspicuously, their *class* interests) of men may constitute obstacles, even insurmountable obstacles, to their discovering or admitting these truths; but the truths themselves are based solely on the evidence, and the evidence is available to all men.

You are on treacherous ground, Comrade Trotsky. The doctrine of 'class truth' is the road of Plato's Philosopher-Kings, of prophets and Popes and Stalins. For all of them, also, a man must be among the anointed in order to know truth. It leads in a direction diametrically opposite to that of socialism, of a truly *human* society.

You issue many warnings to the young comrades of our movement. I add an ominous warning to the list: Beware, beware, comrades, of anyone or any doctrine that tells you that any man, or group of men, holds a monopoly on truth, or on the ways of getting truth.

'I Don't Smoke . . .'

'Throughout all the vacillations and convulsions of the opposition, contradictory though they may be, two general features run like a guiding thread from the pinnacles of theory down to the most trifling political episodes . . . the second general feature intimately bound to the first, namely, a tendency to refrain from active participation, a tendency to self-elimination, to abstentionism, naturally, under cover of ultra-radical phrases. . . .' Again the mighty wind of the rhetoric, the sweeping style backed here with the delicious wit of the repeated phrase, 'Thank you, I don't smoke'.

The unsuspicious might gather from the mountainous style in this passage that here at last a real point was being established, and that acres of evidence, of proof, will be spread before us to justify the rhetoric. But the analytic microscope is able to disclose: exactly two, two and no more, items offered for exhibit; two taken singly, and utterly unrelated to the hundreds of other items that constitute the political course of the members of the opposition taken singly or as a group. The opposition is 'abstentionist' in practical politics because: (a) Burnham was opposed to Trotsky's appearing before the Dies committee; and (b) the opposition rejects both sides equally in the Finnish-Russian conflict. Even if both specific charges were justified, when they are compared with the cosmic general conclusion, I can only remark with Prince Hal, as he read over the list of the colossal quantity of wine that Falstaff had ordered as compared with the tiny piece of bread: 'Oh, monstrous! But one poor half-pennyworth of bread to this intolerable deal of sack!'

But let us consider also the two items.

There is not the slightest reason for considering the Dies question as relevant to the general politics of either of the two contending factions. Again you proceed from a *totalitarian* conception, which relates everything to everything, with iron bonds. The NC opposition members divided on this issue; in the ranks, the attitudes expressed crossed the faction lines in both directions. In the eyes of any sensible person, it was certainly a question about which a difference of opinion was natural, and where—assuming that there was a clearly correct opinion—a mistake is to be understood easily as merely a mistake.

But it is surprising to me, Comrade Trotsky, that you are so ill-advised as to bring up this miserable episode in the present context —as an argument against the opposition!

You have a curious way of reasoning. It is in keeping with revolutionary principle to utilise bourgeois parliamentary institutions as a forum. This is not in dispute, and never has been in our ranks. But then you go on to *deduce* from this that it was correct to accept the Dies invitation; and that, *irrespective of results*, the decision was correct, and opposition to it was a proof of violation of revolutionary politics. Your reasoning here is very similar to that which you employ in connection with dialectics and the theory of the state.

But our principle does not hold that it is *always* correct to try to utilise *every* bourgeois parliamentary institution. That would be a completely absurd interpretation. We recognise that principle does not exclude, for example, our going to court against even a working-class opponent; but we are very cautious indeed in applying this principled permission. We will sit in Congresses, but not always or in every Congress: sometimes we *boycott* a Congress, as you, certainly, should very well remember. The principle does little more than to leave the question open; the specific decision always has to be based on an estimate of how the specific situation is related to our political aims, and which tactic under the given circumstances will best serve those aims.

When the invitation to the Dies committee came before the PC, the problem was to estimate what the consequences would be with respect to our aims; there was no problem over principle. Comrade Bern and I made one estimate; the rest of the Committee, and yourself, another.

Who was right? One could not be very sure then—it was in part a guess. *But one can be sure, in my opinion, now,* because now we have the actual consequences to judge by. I was prepared, indeed anxious (as I stated before the New York membership), to be proved *wrong*. But, unfortunately, Bern and I were proved even more correct than we had imagined.

The truth is that Dies won hands down. That is obvious to anyone who looks at events and not at abstract dogmas.

What were the actual consequences:

In the first place, we were compelled to tell a base lie to our members and sympathisers. This lie took the form of an editorial in the *Appeal* in answer to Zack, pretending that we had changed our views on the Dies committee because of this, that and the other consideration, when in truth it was because Trotsky had been asked to testify.

The further consequences were that, through the publicity connected with the invitation and the later withdrawal, we in effect gave a partial white-wash to the Committee and its purposes, to the renegades who had appeared before it; we, you might say, *legitimised* the Committee *in the eyes of the radical workers* (not of the democrats, who were most of them well enough pleased with the committee for some time back). And we also gave what could only seem as a sample of cynical opportunism in our own agitation.

If you had actually appeared before the Committee, this *might* have been counter-balanced by your testimony—though, having watched the Committee's procedure carefully, and the publicity it received, I continue to doubt it. But you did not. Do you think your statement in the *Appeal*, with its few thousand readers, compensated for all the damage?

(Your way of reasoning here is identical with that which you employ in connection with the invitation to Hook, Eastman, *et al.* given at the end of our article, 'Intellectuals in Retreat'. Shachtman and I had sufficient wisdom to understand that none of our opponents would be bold enough to accept the invitation—we discussed the question carefully beforehand. When you read the invitation, you, misjudging the men we were dealing with, flew into a panic, and wrote in horror that we were turning the magazine over to the democrats. Experience proved that we were right and you mistaken. And now you have the temerity to accuse *us* of a lack of political sagacity!)

As for your second exhibit in substantiation of your charge of abstentionism—our policy with respect to the present war. We, you say, 'withdraw from the struggle', 'do not take part in this filthy business'. Here your rhetoric and your content equally betray you,

Comrade Trotsky. Your reasoning on the matter of the Dies Committee is of a type so peculiar that I have seldom heretofore met with it; but your reasoning on this second item comes from a well-known, a very well known variety. It is the eternal charge of reaction when it attacks the supporters of *the third camp*. How many times do we find it in the writings of 1914-18! And today it re-appears from all sides. In this country, *The New Leader* is perhaps the most skilful exponent, and I particularly recommend the column of Charles Yale Harrison for instances of its shrewd manipulation. How Harrison rips into the 'pacifists' and 'Utopian socialists' and all the other 'Idealists' —you could have borrowed your very phrases from him. You've got to take sides now, he shouts; no more standing in your ivory tower! True enough, he takes Mannerheim's side and you Stalin's. But both of you now unite in the attempt to hide from the sight of the workers the only side that can deserve socialist loyalty: the side of the third camp. No, Comrade Trotsky, we do not withdraw from the struggle, or advocate any withdrawal. But we are concerned with whom we struggle, and for what. And we will not fight alongside the GPU for the salvation of the counter-revolution in the Kremlin.

So much, then, for the two items of pretended 'evidence' by which you bolster your grandiose charge of abstentionism.

But to bring such a charge against the present opposition, and myself in particular, is—apart from your two items—to put things at their mildest, absurd. Without any hesitation, I can say with no chance of motivated denial from anyone, that of all leading members of the party, the charge of abstentionism has the remotest application to me. I am, indeed, almost notorious in the party for trying to find ways of participating in almost anything that shows itself on the political horizon: from Ludlow amendments to elections; from Ham and Eggs to labour parties; from conferences to anti-Nazi demonstrations. If any charge were to be seriously brought against me, it would—and with a certain measure of justification—be the exact opposite of abstentionism. Unlike Cannon and Cochran, I am not one of those who are able to boast about how I never make political mistakes. But my mistakes are not *abstentionist* mistakes. Even the most sung of my mistakes of the past year—over policy in auto—was the insistence that we had to head toward one of the conventions (Martin's) as against the initial Cochran-Clarke policy which was that of *boycotting both conventions.*

In this respect, furthermore, I am not at all an exception, but typical of the leading members of the opposition. During the past few years, it is from them that virtually all proposals for active participation in actions of all kinds have come, as against the passive, negative approach of Cannon-Goldman-Lewitt. This difference is for the most part written into the record of the party. The record of the leaders of the YPSL is most illuminating in this connection. This charge of abstentionism, like your other charges, is the product only of the nightmare you are imaginatively creating out of your own false doctrine, and has no relation to reality.

*   *   *

The verdict on the evidence: Proposition (5), like Propositions (3), (C), (II), (III), (IV) . . .—*unproved*; further: false, utterly false.

What Are the Issues?

The dominant issues dividing the ranks of our party and the International are not dialectics or sociology or logic. To pose the question in this manner is an evasion or a fraud. It is with the greatest impatience and reluctance that I have written on them to the extent that I have.

The dominant, the *fundamental* issues, in the present dispute are two, one involving the entire International, the other particularly concerning the Socialist Workers Party.

The first is the central political issue. This has been clarified and simplified by the course of events and the discussion. What it concerns is *the problem of the strategical orientation of the Fourth International in the present phase of the second world war*. It is an issue which every single party member can understand clearly, without any obfuscation from Hegel and dialectical foxes.

The practical politics of every active and serious political organisation is normally governed by what might be called a *strategical focus*, an axis around which the major part of agitation and action revolves. The Popular Front, for example, constituted such a focus, or axis, for the Stalinist movement during a number of years: the agitation, actions, proposals, analyses of the C. I. and its sections revolved around this strategic centre. For our movement, during several years, the orientation toward the Second International was such a focus.

Today there are two tendencies in the Fourth International. They are differentiated by the fact that they propose two sharply different strategical orientations, different axes to govern our practical politics.

Trotsky-Cannon propose *the strategy of defence of the Stalinist bureaucracy as the lesser evil.* It doesn't make any difference what Trotsky-Cannon *say* about their policies; this is what it comes down to in practice. This focus governs their major specific proposals, their agitation, their interpretation of events, their predictions (not always, not consistently, but on the whole—sufficiently to determine the practical direction), their *weighting* of agitation (in the *Appeal,* for example), and so on. Let any party member re-trace in his mind the events of the past months, let him read the party press and internal documents, remember the speeches and committee proposals; and he will see for himself how an understanding of this underlying strategical orientation provides a clear pattern which makes the events intelligible.

The opposition, nationally and internationally (for the dispute has of course already spread beyond the borders of our party, as it should), proposes *the strategy of the third camp.* Any party member who makes a similar review of the actions of the opposition during this period, their proposals and speeches and articles, their interpretations of what is happening in the world, their emphases and stresses, will similarly see for himself how an understanding of this opposed strategical orientation provides an adequate pattern and guide.

This conflict of strategical orientations is the central political issue, and nothing else. When once this key is grasped, a decision should not be hard for the membership of the party and the International. Ninety-five per cent of the polemical output of Trotsky-Cannon can be estimated for what it really is: irrelevance, evasion, smoke-screen. The distinguishing feature of the present factional struggle is not the difficulty of the question at dispute—it is an unusually simple and direct question, but the difficulty of understanding what the question is. This difficulty results from the fact that Trotsky-Cannon, standing on a hopeless position, indefensible on its own merits, are compelled to devote their entire factional energies to the attempt to prevent the membership from seeing what the question is.

The second central issue is the question of the regime in the Socialist Workers Party. This question has been thoroughly treated in the document, 'The War and Bureaucratic Conservatism'. No reply has been made to this document; and it is safe to predict that no serious reply will be forthcoming.

These are the issues. The course of our movement will depend on the answers given to *them.*

Morality and Polemics

Comrade Trotsky, in the course of your intervention in the present dispute, you have struck such heavy blows against the Fourth International that, for my own part, I am not convinced that the International will be able to survive them. I say advisedly that your blows have been directed 'against the Fourth International'; from the narrower factional interests of the opposition they have altogether failed of the effect you have intended; the ranks of the opposition have increased and their determination been strengthened as a result of them, and it is only Cannon's followers who have been disconcerted.

You have done these injuries directly, in your own name; and indirectly, by lending your illustrious name as a cloak for the rotten clique of Cannon.

You have elected to defend a false theory and a wrong policy; and to stand as attorney for a cynical group of small-time bureaucrats. No one can choose such a course and hope to avoid its consequences; as evidenced by your recent articles and letters, these consequences step by step are swamping you.

The truth can only destroy a false doctrine; and therefore you are compelled to evade the truth, and to hide it.

To evade the truth? Witness: Your systematic failure to take up the actual problems posed not only by the opposition but by the realities of the war. Your unscrupulous dragging in of dialectics as a polemical manoeuvre. Your endless discussions of everything under the sun—except the actual issues which the party is facing.

To hide the truth? Yes: Your failure to mention, even, that a belief in dialectics has been professed by Stalinists, Mensheviks, sectarians and others among the enemies of the proletarian revolution. Your never saying a word about property relations in the three Baltic countries which are now Stalin's provinces. Your failure to say a word about the shifts and contradictions in the policy of Cannon toward the war, as shown in committee votes and *Appeal* articles from the days of Poland onward. Your silence, your so very diplomatic silence, on the *specific* charges which the opposition has brought against the Cannon clique.

At the very beginning of the struggle, you made not the slightest effort to discover *what* the position of the opposition was; at every stage you have made no effort to *verify* a single report relayed to you by Cannon and his followers. In your documents you have not once tried to present fairly the position of the opposition, but have invariably given a carefully distorted account of its position—in direct contrast to us, who have always used the most scrupulous care in trying to show exactly what your position is (precisely because only in that way can the membership be genuinely educated). Similarly, on a broader scale, you have distorted what is happening in the war. You attribute to me a position on Russia, on Marxian sociology, in philosophy, which does not have the slightest resemblance to that which I actually hold, and which is well known to you. In your Open Letter you have gravely distorted the history of the relations between Mensheviks and Bolsheviks to accord with your immediate polemical aim.

The distortions breed offspring in their own image. In your article, 'A Petty-Bourgeois Opposition . . .,' you dicovered a non-existent civil war going on in Finland. Then, in later articles, you have tried to get out of the bad hole you had dug for yourself by denying you had said what you said, by giving it another significance than that contained in the clear words of your first statement. You invented an origin in the Communist party for 'the Abern group', and make no effort to abandon the invention now that it has been undeniably disproved. You wrote of the opposition's resolution on Finland, 'As to just how these three "concrete" circumstances (in Finland and Russia) will be "taken into account", the resolution doesn't give the slightest inkling . . .', when the very next lines of the resolution outline the answer to this very problem.

Your defence of a false doctrine drives you away from the truth; your defence of a bureaucratic clique compels you toward the methods of such a clique. When in the history of our movement was a more infamous, and more gratuitous, slander introduced than that footnote to the letter signed 'Rork' (on the 'press'), where the opposition is so clearly linked with 'Stalinist influence'? Where is there a record of a more disloyal sneer than the one you direct against Abern (who has devoted his entire life to the movement) on the basis of a remark *falsely* attributed to him by the gossips of the Cannon clique?

You sin more grievously than you even understand, Comrade Trotsky. In a cheap manner you twice grimace at Shachtman for trying to 'conduct the revolution' from 'the Bronx'. Not merely are you here appealing to a usual reactionary provincialism, directed against the metropolis. Do you know what *further* meaning 'the Bronx' has in this country, Comrade Trotsky? Do you know that to nearly every American it means not only a New Yorker, but a

Jew? And are you so naive as to think that our party—yes, even our party—is altogether immune to influence from such an association? The weapons you are now using have a fearful habit of back-firing.

You attribute to the opposition a practice of gossip and scandal-mongering. This is simply another of your 'deductions' from your airy theory: the opposition is petty-bourgeois; petty-bourgeois individuals go in for gossip; therefore the opposition gossips. Now I will not pretend that in a long faction fight either side can avoid completely a certain amount of personal gossip; to gossip seems to be a fairly general human trait. However, to state that the opposition uses gossip as a *method* is simply *false,* like so much else of what you say with no evidence whatever. It is not the opposition, but the Cannon clique which employs gossip as a tool, an instrument in the struggle, and, furthermore, its chief instrument. For some while, even before the present faction struggle began, it has been systematically corrupting the minds of its followers by the circulation of the vilest personal gossip. This is today its main stock in trade.

I find it revealing in the extreme that the structure of your Open Letter is draped around three tit-bits of gossip—all naturally unverified—in which remarks are assigned to myself, to Abern, and to Shachtman. This is symptomatic. The truth is that your Open Letter, in spite of its pretentious theorising and its grandiose rhetoric, is in reality only a kind of apotheosis, a super-sophisticated rendering, of the gutter-gossip of the Cannon clique. Stripped of its irrelevancies, this is what your Open Letter comes down to: Shachtman is a clownish and superficial Bronx intellectual; Abern a sly and treacherous *intriguant;* Burnham a professor. You deal with the 'dialectical' variations on these themes. The Cannon hangers-on provide the juicy filling that makes them so tasty a side-dish for evening coffee.

From what source springs this unending reiteration of 'academic', 'school bench', 'professor', 'pedant', 'democratic salon' . . .? I have met this often before, Comrade Trotsky, in political struggle; and without any exception it has been a mark of reaction.

Please don't try to tell me that even the gossip of the Cannon clique represents, in a somewhat distorted form, a 'healthy' and 'progressive' response of the 'proletarian rank-and-file'. We know too well the originators of this gossip, and how close they are to being 'healthy proletarians'. The proletariat does well, I grant you, to distrust petty bourgeois, very much including intellectuals and professors. This is in particular true where it is a question of personnel, of organisational leadership. But this does not in the least alter the reactionary character of making, as you do, the sly introduction of appeals to this feeling the central focus of your attack on our *position,* our *arguments,* our policy. In the actual context of the actual struggle, these appeals to anti-metropolitan, anti-intellectual prejudices have exclusively reactionary effects; they pander to backward provincialism, to anti-theoretical, anti-political even, bias. And these effects will be felt beyond the close of the present fight. Yes, they will plague you in months and even years to come when the political disintegration already well on its way among the Cannon forces reaches maturity. Perhaps even you will be discovered to be an intellectual and a big-city man, Comrade Trotsky.

A large section of the Cannon clique—especially its articulate spokesmen—are already deeply sunk in cynicism. They have no perspective beyond their votes. This mood expresses itself in the acceptance of the principle: 'Anything goes!' They act in accordance with this principle. Lies, slanders, gossip, denunciation, contradictions, brutality, fake indignation, rhetoric turned on and off with an actor's spigot. . . . Anything goes! I watched these manifestations with dismay at, for example, the New York City convention. And they do more than corrupt the members of the Cannon clique itself. Many comrades came to me during the course of the New York City convention and remarked that they 'were certainly learning a lot about politics through the faction fight'; alas, the lesson that Cannon and Cochran and Lewitt and Gordon were teaching them was the lesson of 'anything goes'. You have done nothing to counter-act that lesson.

You attempt to turn aside all criticism of your 'methods' by two devices: You say that all who mention methods do so because they are losing on the field of political principles. You say that anyone who objects is doing so from the point of view of God or the Kantian categorical imperative or 'the eternal norms of petty-bourgeois morality'. This is sometimes, even often, the case. But I have no intention of remaining silent about the methods you are now using out of any fear of being called a petty-bourgeois. My moral norms are not drawn from either religion or Kant, and we have refuted your present political policy with arguments and evidence, with a finality that I do not expect you even to try to challenge on its merits.

Yes, I judge a political struggle *morally* as well as politically. Socialism is a moral ideal, which reflective men choose deliberately, by a moral act. Cold and sober scientific analysis convinces me that this ideal dictates an appropriate morality which must govern the struggle for it. Just as we say that the white man cannot be free while the black man is enslaved, so a social order based upon truth and freedom and loyal cooperation cannot be won by those who in their relations with each other base their methods of action on lies and disloyalty and slander. It is dangerous to have a false political policy. But it need not be fatal: for the policy can be changed, if a critical, democratic and loyal *morale* prevails, when experience makes clearer the need for change. But it is disastrous if the very springs of action are poisoned.

You conclude your letter on a strange note, Comrade Trotsky. 'If,' you say to me, 'we can arrive at an agreement with you on the basis of these principles, then without difficulty we shall find a correct policy in relation to Poland, Finland, and even India. At the same time, I pledge myself to help you conduct a struggle against any manifestation whatsoever of bureaucratism and conservatism. . . .' In the face of the events of these past months, you will understand why such a pledge can carry little weight for me. As to agreement on principles: There is only one way in which such agreement is possible for me—when I am convinced that my principles are wrong, and others are right. And I am afraid that the metaphors, even of a Shakespeare, would not be enough to convince me.

February 1, 1940.   JAMES BURNHAM.

LETTER OF RESIGNATION OF JAMES BURNHAM
FROM THE WORKERS PARTY

New York, May 21, 1940

To the National Committee of the Workers Party:

I am compelled to place before the committee the question of my status in relation to the newly formed Workers Party.

The faction fight in the Socialist Workers Party, its conclusion and the recent formation of the Workers Party have been in my own case, the unavoidable occasion for the review of my own theoretical and political beliefs. This review has shown me that by no stretching of terminology can I any longer regard myself, or permit others to regard me, as a Marxist.

Of the most important beliefs, which have been associated with the Marxist movement, whether in its reformist, Leninist, Stalinist or Trotskyist variants, there is virtually none which I accept in its traditional form. I regard these beliefs as either false or obsolete or meaningless; or in a few cases, as at best true only in a form so restricted and modified as no longer properly to be called Marxist.

This communication is not meant to be an elaborate analysis or a lengthy personal credo. Nevertheless, I wish to illustrate my opinion with a few specific examples:

I reject, as you know, the 'philosophy of Marxism', dialectical materialism. I have never, it is true, accepted this philosophy. In the past I excused this discrepancy and compromised this belief with the idea that the philosophy was 'unimportant' and 'did not matter' so far as practice and politics were concerned. Experience, and further study and reflection, have convinced me that I have been wrong and Trotsky—with so many others—right on this score; that dialectical materialism though scientifically meaningless, is psychologically and historically an integral part of Marxism, and does have its many and adverse effects upon practice and politics.

The general Marxian theory of 'universal history', to the extent that it has any empirical content, seems to me disproved by modern historical and anthropological investigation.

Marxian economics seems to me for the most part either false or obsolete or meaningless in application to contemporary economic phenomena. Those aspects of Marxian economics which retain validity do not seem to me to justify the theoretical structure of the economics.

Not only do I believe it meaningless to say that 'socialism is inevitable' and false that socialism is 'the only alternative to capitalism'; I consider that on the basis of the evidence now available to us a new form of exploitive society (what I call 'managerial society') is not only possible as an alternative to capitalism but is a more probable outcome of the present period than socialism.

As you know, I do not believe that Russia can be considered a 'workers state' in any intelligible sense of the term. This opinion, however, is related to far more basic conclusions: for example, that Stalinism must be understood as one manifestation of the same general historical forces of which fascism is another manifestation. There is still doubt in my mind as to whether this conclusion applies also to Leninism and Trotskyism.

I disagree flatly and entirely, as Cannon has understood for a long while, with the Leninist conception of a party—not merely with Stalin's or Cannon's modifications of that conception, but with Lenin's and Trotsky's. I disagree with the theory of the party, but even more, and more important, with the established pattern of behaviour which displays the character of the party as a living reality. The Leninist type of party seems to me incompatible with genuine scientific method and genuine democracy.

In the light of such beliefs, and others similar to them, it goes without saying that I must reject a considerable part of the programmatic documents of the Fourth Internationalist movement (accepted by the Workers Party). The 'transition programme' document seems to me—as it pretty much did when first presented —more or less arrant nonsense, and a key example of the inability of Marxism, even in the hands of its most brilliant intellectual representative, to handle contemporary history.

These beliefs, especially in their negative aspect—that is, insofar as they involve disagreement with Marxism—are not at all 'sudden' or episodic, nor are they products merely of the recent faction struggle. Several I have always held. Many others I have held for some years. Others have, during the past year or two, changed from doubt and uncertainty into conviction. The faction fight has only served to compel me to make them explicit and to consider them more or less in their entirety. I understand, naturally, that many of them are not 'new' or 'original', and that in holding some of them I find myself in very bad company. However, I have never been able to judge the truth of beliefs by the moral character of those who hold them.

* * *

The newly formed Workers Party is a Marxist party, and more particularly a Bolshevik, a Leninist party. This is not a mere matter of definition. It is guaranteed alike by its programmatic documents (especially the key document on 'The Aims, the Tasks, and the Structure of the Workers Party'), by the statements and convictions of the overwhelming majority of its leadership and of a substantial majority of its membership, and by the habits of action of this majority. It is strikingly symbolised by the statement on the masthead of Labour Action that the party is a section of the Fourth International, by the definition of its theoretical magazine as 'an organ of revolutionary Marxism', by the reiterated appeal in the key document above mentioned to 'the revolutionary traditions of Marx, Engels, Lenin and Trotsky' and to the 'principles of Marxism', and by the convention episode of the cable to Trotsky. Nothing whatever in the faction fight indicated a decisive tendency away from this orientation; on the contrary, every sharp suggestion in such a direction was at once blocked. In reality, the split from the Socialist Workers Party was not based upon anything fundamental, and the Workers Party exists now as a faction of the Trotskyist movement. This was the actual cause of the extreme difficulty which the faction found in drawing up its position on 'the nature of the party', and in differentiating that position from Cannon's. This was hard to do, was in fact not done, because the two positions, except in details and emphases, did not really differ.

I do not, of course, wish to mitigate my own share of responsibility of what happened in the immediate and the more distant past. I wish here to record the facts as I see them, among which is the fact that I have not been a full-time political worker and have not accepted a full share of organisational responsibility.

* * *

From the facts about my own present beliefs and the character of the Workers Party, the following conclusion inescapably follows: I cannot be a loyal member of the Workers Party; I cannot accept its programme or discipline; I cannot speak or act for it. Naturally I do not disagree with everything for which the Workers Party stands. I believe that socialism would be a good thing if it can be achieved (though 'socialism as a moral ideal' is

in bad repute among Marxists, we learn). I agree with the Workers
Party attitude toward the war, at least insofar as this was involved
in the just concluded faction dispute. But I share agreement on
those points with many other organisations and tens of thousands
of individuals wholly apart from the Workers Party. To the
extent that I function politically, I cannot confine what I say
and do to rhapsodies on the desirability of socialism and denun-
ciations of both camps in the war. This was brought home to me
with particular keenness by the first public mass meeting of the
Workers Party. For I tried to figure out what I could say, and I
could not find any way of saying what I felt I ought to say
and still appear on the platform as a loyal spokesman of the
group. I finally compromised once more, spoke 'safely' on the
third camp, and felt like a liar when I had finished.

Two alternatives only, therefore, present themselves to me:

Continuing as a member of the party, I can immediately launch
a faction struggle along the lines suggested by this document. This
struggle would, of course, be, from a political and theoretical
standpoint, far broader and more fundamental than the struggle
just concluded with Cannon and would have as its general aim,
from my standpoint, to break the group altogether away from
Marxism.

Or I can simply separate from the Workers Party.

From the usual conception of 'principled' and 'responsible' politics, the first course is incumbent upon me. However, I do not
believe that it makes sense under the actual circumstances. On
the one hand, a sharp faction struggle now in the Workers Party
(in which my point of view would be supported by a very small
minority) would mean the breakup of the group, at the very least
its reduction to impotence—and it begins with foundations none
too firm. What could be gained would not be worth while, would
simply not mean anything politically. On the other hand, I
personally am not willing to undertake leadership in such a
struggle. I am not, have not been, and cannot be a 'practical
politician' and 'organisation man', above all not a leader.

Thus the second course alone remains.

It will be thought and said by many that my present beliefs
and the decision which follows from them are a 'rationalisation'
of, on the one side, the pressure of a soft and bourgeois personal
environment, and, on the other, the influence of the terrible

defeats of labour, and mankind during the past twenty years, and of the war crisis.

I should be the last to pretend that any man should be so brash as to imagine that he knows clearly the motives and springs of his own actions. This whole letter may be an over-elaborate way of saying the single sentence: 'I feel like quitting politics'. It is certainly the case that I am influenced by the defeats and betrayals of the past twenty and more years. These form part of the evidence for my belief that Marxism must be rejected: at every single one of the many tests provided by history, Marxist movements have either failed socialism or betrayed it. And they influence also my feelings and attitudes, I know that.

As for my 'personal life', how is one ever to know which is chicken and which egg, whether unwillingness fully to enter Marxist politics confuses beliefs, or whether clear beliefs keep one from entering Marxist politics fully? I am a little tired, I confess, of the habit of settling accounts with opponents and critics, of deciding scientific disputes, by smug references to 'rationalisation' and the 'pressure of alien classes and influences'. Because this habit is a well established part of the tradition of Marxism is not the least of my objections to Marxism.

My beliefs are facts; and the defeats and betrayals, and the mode of my life and my tastes are also facts. There they are, whatever the truth about sources and origins and motives.

*   *   *

On no ideological, theoretic or political ground, then, can I recognise, or do I feel, any bond or allegiance to the Workers Party (or to any other Marxist party). That is simply the case, and I can no longer pretend about it, either to myself or to others.

Unfortunately, one factor still remains. This factor is a sense of moral obligation and responsibility to my past self—seven years dominated, however, inadequately but on the whole, by Marxism or any comparable structure, cannot be wiped out by a few minutes at the typewriter—and more especially to other persons, to those with whom I have joined in loyal collaboration on both sides, and to others who have been influenced in their ideas and acts by me. Trotsky and Cannon will exploit my decision as a confirmation of their views—Burnham's quitting will be, by their remarkable but humanly understandable logic, evidence for the truth of their opinions on the character of the war, the nature of the Russian state, and the role of Russia in the war. To many members of the Workers Party, my separation will appear as a desertion. From a moral and personal point of view, I cannot but agree that there will be a good deal of truth in this latter judgment.

But this factor, weighed against the others, is no longer sufficient to decide my actions. Indeed, it now seems clear to me that if it had not been for these moral and personal considerations, I should properly have left the party some while ago. On the grounds of beliefs and interests (which are also a fact) I have for several years had no real place in a Marxist party.

This communication constitutes my definitive resignation from the group. However, because of the obligations which I recognise, I am, within strict limitations, prepared to discuss with the committee, if the committee so wishes, the manner of my separation. There are four alternatives:

1. The committee can expel me. There would be no difficulty in finding grounds for expulsion: I have already written an article, which, if published in the non-party press (and there is the opportunity for such publication), would be adequate grounds.

2. I can simply withdraw, without any special notice being taken on either side, from the group and its activities.

3. I can be, nominally, granted a 'leave of absence' for six months. If this alternative were chosen, there should be no misunderstanding. The future is never certain, but the probability of such a leave's coming to an end would be very slight indeed.

4. I am, finally, prepared, if the committee feels that it would make any serious difference in this first period of the group's independent existence, to carry out a form of partial collaboration during the next two months. This would consist primarily of writing signed and unsigned articles for the party press, consistent with the party's position; and during that time refraining from public acts contrary to the party and its programme. At the conclusion of these two months, any of the three other alternatives could be put into effect. I would not like this fourth solution, to be quite honest, but, as I have stated, I am prepared to accept it.

*   *   *

Writing this letter has been a painful and difficult task for me. It is in no way an impulsive act, but has been preceded by the most careful and lengthy deliberation. I am above all anxious that I avoid giving any impression that I seek to excuse or extenuate myself, my own weaknesses or deficiencies or failures. I do not propose to blame others or history for my faults. When I say that I reject Marxism, I do not at all mean that I am scornful of or consider myself 'superior to' Marxists. Not at all. I am humble, believe me, before the loyalty, sacrifice and heroism of so many Marxists—qualities found so widely within the ranks of the Workers Party. But I cannot act otherwise than I do.

Believing as I do, I cannot wish success to the Workers Party: but I can and do wish its members well. To the extent that each of us, in his own way and arena, preserves the values and truth and freedom, I hope that we shall continue to regard ourselves as comrades, whatever names we use and whatever labels may be tied around our necks.

Fraternally yours,
JAMES BURNHAM.